Dressays

Dressays

An Anthology of Writing about Clothing

Edited by Rosie Findlay

BLOOMSBURY VISUAL ARTS
LONDON · NEW YORK · OXFORD · NEW DELHI · SYDNEY

BLOOMSBURY VISUAL ARTS
Bloomsbury Publishing Plc, 50 Bedford Square, London, WC1B 3DP, UK
Bloomsbury Publishing Inc, 1359 Broadway, New York, NY 10018, USA
Bloomsbury Publishing Ireland, 29 Earlsfort Terrace, Dublin 2, D02 AY28, Ireland

BLOOMSBURY, BLOOMSBURY VISUAL ARTS and the Diana logo are trademarks of
Bloomsbury Publishing Plc

First published in Great Britain 2026

Cover design by Charlotte Daniels
Cover image © Oliver Marr

'Dressays' on cover and pp. i and iii by Mirren Kessling, 2025

A catalogue record for this book is available from the British Library.

A catalog record for this book is available from the Library of Congress.

ISBN:　HB:　　978-1-3504-7325-6
　　　　PB:　　978-1-3504-7324-9
　　　　ePDF:　978-1-3504-7327-0
　　　　eBook:　978-1-3504-7326-3

Typeset by RefineCatch Limited, Bungay, Suffolk
Printed and bound in India

For product safety related questions contact productsafety@bloomsbury.com.

To find out more about our authors and books visit www.bloomsbury.com
and sign up for our newsletters.

For my mother Sarah, with love

Contents

Acknowledgements

Working on this book has been a sustaining joy and a labour of love, one immeasurably supported by a vast number of people. I am indebted to my editor, Frances Arnold, who believed in this book from the first and whose thoughtful guidance and immense expertise were a welcome and necessary anchor throughout. Frances, I don't know what I would have done without your patience and humour. I'm so thankful to have worked together on this. Thanks also to Martin Thompson and the rest of the team at Bloomsbury Visual Arts, who have been a pleasure to work with.

Many people lent their expertise to assist my efforts to contact authors. Thanks especially to Aea Varfis-van Warmelo at *Granta*; Jane Conway-Gordon; Emily Perkins at St Anne's College, University of Oxford; the librarians supporting the Listening and Viewing Service in the British Library; Anne Marcus at the Jewish Genealogical Society of Great Britain; and Dr Lucie Whitmore, whose suggestions, introductions, and friendship were utterly indispensable. Special thanks to Haley Mlotek for your editorial support at the proposal stage, and Lily Sheehan for your considered and invaluable critique on the book's shape and direction.

Dressays was realised thanks to the support of the School of Communication and Creativity at City St George's, University of London; the Association for Art History, and Duncan Lockard and Eddie and Hannah Gandevia, whose generosity made possible the inclusion of several essays. My dear friends, I can't thank you enough. I treasure our friendship so much.

To everyone who supported my fundraiser by buying a tee: thank you! I hope you love reading the book now it's in your hands.

The cover image was photographed by Ollie Marr, who beautifully captured the book's spirit and feeling. Ollie, what a joy to collaborate with you on this. Many thanks to Dipa Patel for playing dress-up with us on a sunny afternoon and to Mirren Kessling for immediately embracing this book and dreaming with me to help it find its readers. I adore the illustrated title you created and am so proud to feature it on the cover.

My deepest thanks to each of the contributors for allowing me to include your essays. It really is an honour. I hope you enjoy seeing the throughlines and resonances between your piece and others in the collection.

Finally, my heartfelt thanks to my parents for bestowing on me your celebration of clothes and colour, of reading and language, and for the always of your steadfast love.

Introduction

Rosie Findlay

This is a book of essays that explores how dress weaves with our lives, revealing the complex, deeply felt bonds we have with our body, our loved ones, our communities, and the worlds through which we move. Clothes are the material equivalent of words: inanimate articles that, when used, seem to assume a life of their own. Both are laden with memories and layered with the trace of people who have made, worn, loved, and discarded them. Like language, dress is replete with meanings that are ambiguous and shifting, changed over time, employed to address everyday life. Our dress is also in conversation with us. If my fingers circle the watch on my left wrist, my grandmother's watch, I could tell you about when I put it on for the first time. How, looking down, I realized with shock that I have her hands. How in that moment, I was a child again, glimpsing the watch at her cuff, asking for the story of how she came to own it. If I say that I think of my grandmother each time I wear it, you will understand what I mean: that to wear her watch and think of her is to feel my love for her intensify and be reminded of how I felt in her presence – to feel again her love for me. It is also to see in a rushing carousel all the things that call her to me – the books inscribed in her looping handwriting, her heavy CDs of opera recordings – and the time we spent together, the tone of her voice, her impatience, her generosity.

We hit the limits of language because it's not a thought at all but an experience, conjured by the touch of her object on my body. Her watch continues to collect stories and patinate with associations, but of me now. And it is so common – we, all of us, possess garments that tie us to people we love, people we have lost or pushed away, communities we were or are still part of, and perhaps most strangely, those that remember who we once were.

Not all the memories clothes conjure are fond: they have the power to betray, subvert, obstruct, disappoint, humiliate, and grieve us, too. This is perhaps why we are eager to discard, donate or burn the ones that return us somewhere we'd rather forget, or those that did nothing for us, either aesthetically or in terms of feeling. By examining how dress prompts such immediate and deeply felt responses, these essays show that clothes don't just rest on the body's surface – they interact with us, producing knowledge, eliciting feelings and memories that seem to wend with the garments themselves, yet extending beyond them to bind other people to us or push them away.

In this way, *Dressays* deepens beyond the truisms that often arise in writing on dress – that it is a form of self-expression, that it is a way of speaking – to consider how it helps us navigate ourselves and the worlds to which we belong. Each essay is grounded in personal narrative, yet all reach beyond the individual to advance our understanding of how what we wear bears and shapes meaning: saturated with emotion, politically charged, and inextricable from shared cultures and histories. Together, they present a record of how dress becomes part of our experience of the world and ourselves as interconnected beings in it. Clothes are not just *there*, inert, but are inextricably woven with our lives, enfolded in our relationships with others and becoming part of us.

The suspicion that to be interested in dress is to be morally shallow or stupid has haunted fashion in Western Europe for centuries, certainly since the satirists had a field day with women's ever-widening crinolines in the 19th century. The connotation persisted wherever Anglo-European fashion spread, through imperialism, colonization, and the internet: that to think about clothes is to be deeply superficial, as if one cannot think *with* them but rather, that they are antithetical to thought. As if attending to clothes leaves nothing between the ears but rolls of ribbon. This is a particularly binaristic way of considering dress, where insight is separated from the experiential self and its apparently cluttering accoutrements – and it is a silly one. We carry knowledge about dress in our bodies, and perhaps this is why it is difficult to articulate how it is meaningful – as fashion theorist Lucia Ruggerone writes, 'at least part of [our experience of being dressed] is extra-cognitive, *in the flesh*'.[1] Yet whether you get to choose what you put on or not, whether you take pleasure in outfits or think dressing in the same look each day is a sign of your intelligence, whether your favourite garment is a pair of Margiela Tabis found on super-sale, the last pair and your size, or a pair of worn trousers that feel like a hug each time the waistband meets your hips, you experience yourself and the world through what you wear.

The truisms I mentioned resonate for a reason – they skim the surface of what we're talking about when we're talking about dress. It's curious that clothing is often described as a visual medium when it's as tactile and material as it is visual. Focusing on the look of dress is certainly pleasurable, but what do we lose sight of when we exclusively attend to this aspect at the cost of its other sensory and perceptual properties? This book deliberately does not include many images, neutralizing the cultural dominance of seeing dress as primarily visual to allow these other, often overlooked, dimensions to materialize. By drawing them out in the fullest expression of language, these essays help us to better recognize what dress does to and for us. It refuses neat dualisms even as it seems to enforce them. Where do we stop, and clothes begin? That we can take them off seems an obvious answer. And yet: prescription glasses make our vision work differently. The act of weaving a basket can serve as a reminder that we are enmeshed with the rest of the living world, and that we bear responsibility to the plants that give of themselves for this work. Our feet are deformed forever by shoes that rub, protruding bones and hob-nailed toes silently reproaching us even once the awful things have been gotten rid of. And how do we explain the rush of lavish grief when our hands find a jumper, lovingly darned, that returns to us the person who loved it most? The essays in this collection question whether we are readily extricable from what we wear by reminding us that we have never been separate from the material world; we are part and parcel of it.

Dress also forms a site at which our entanglements with other living beings play out in ways sometimes loving, sometimes violent. Who gets to say what our clothes mean, and what they make of us? The everyday politics of dressing shows itself in the ways that social relations play out through appearances. Forcing people to wear these clothes and not those is one of the most basic forms of control that can be exerted over a person: a visceral reminder of where authority and power lie. So much is evident in the exhaustive list of clothing-related restrictions Meena Kandasamy details in her essay about garment manufacture and caste discrimination in India. As she writes, 'Long before capitalism enters this scene of crime, caste had other rules. About wearing clothes, about not wearing clothes, about how to wear clothes and about washing clothes. There is nothing that is beyond the pale of regimentation by the caste system.' To be told that your body represents inherent sinfulness or danger, that your gender is a fiction, or that your body is in its very being wrong or unlovely is to be subjected to violence. And for clothes to be framed as the means of redress, supposedly remedying the problem that is you, exacerbates the injury. (Perhaps it is no coincidence that one of the earliest meanings of 'dress' was to put straight, to set right – dress as a means of correction.)

Yet even dressing according to socially accepted conventions doesn't necessarily protect the wearer. In her memoir of growing up in 1960s London's Orthodox Jewish community, Ruth Gershon details the care with which teenagers had to navigate the codes of acceptable dress: 'Don't be common, flash, spivvy or cheap. (This applied to my brothers, too. They were forbidden suede shoes.) Not too much jewellery. Don't wear loads of makeup. Don't wear high heels with trousers.' She describes the delicate, confusing line that had to be held: to not look non-Jewish but not look 'too Jewish', while also not appearing rough or unrefined. The flimsiness of clothes' ability to protect was laid bare when Ruth's older brother attended a school interview after his Common Entrance exams. Sitting before the headmaster in his bar mitzvah suit, David was told, '"you're too neat and tidy; you'll never get your hands dirty; your sort don't know how to work". In bewilderment and anguish my mother threatened to mess up his hair and put mud on his face the next time.' The frequency with which people whose very being leaves them vulnerable to being fetishized, hated or feared are singled out because of what they are wearing reminds us that appearances are a battleground for human dignity and social recognition.

Several essayists in this collection grapple with the feelings that arise from being objectified: how it feels to be looked at and not seen, as Anne Anlin Cheng vividly describes, transforming your body into a thing and rendering you a stranger to yourself. Others, like Esmé Weijun Wang, show how clothes offer a means of reclaiming yourself and of rewriting your relationship to the world. She refuses the stigma and assumptions her interlocutors may associate with her schizophrenia by dressing in brilliant, fashionable clothes: 'see my ordinary, even superlative appearance! [. . .] what kind of lunatic has a fashionable pixie cut, wears red lipstick, dresses in pencil skirts and tucked-in silk blouses? What sort of psychotic wears Loeffler Randall heels without tottering?' Wearing an ankle-length white sari, or vibrant, tailor-made bùbá and sokoto, trawling charity shops for approximations of designer looks or adopting a signature red lip all become everyday acts of refusal and self-definition.

As they map how clothes render us socially legible in complex and contested ways, these essays also reveal that dress is not separate to our experience of being in the world but is inherent to it. One volume could never capture all of the multitudinous ways of dressing and being dressed, but the essays collected here thoughtfully consider how dress extends and threads through many different experiences – of chronic illness, disability, being a child, caring for a loved one, feeling like a failure, being racialized, grieving, being self-alienated, coming to terms with gender, and custodianship of nature. Collectively, they articulate that which sits beyond language: the knowledge we accrue at the site of ourselves, through feeling, experience, through touch – and through clothes.

I started to collect these essays before I knew that was what I was doing. At the time, I was running a master's degree in fashion studies and always included a class devoted to considering how clothes tell our personal histories. Instead of assigning academic literature theorizing the relationship between clothing and identity, I preferred to assign some of these pieces. I found they invited my students, and me, to think with the authors' stories (and their clothes) and, by extension, reflect on our own. Cheng's essay on her struggle between loving the beauty of dress and the discomfort it induces due to how other people racialize her never left the reading list. Karena de Perthuis's reflection on darning her late partner Mark's jumper as he received treatment for terminal cancer was one that frequently left my students speechless. Both essays are included in this volume. I am proud that this collection also includes work by two writers who studied with me: Isabel Mundigo-Moore's devastating essay on anticipatory grief responds to Karena's work, exploring the abjection of her father Arturo's clothes, testament to the many lives he lived, as he received palliative care at home. Honor Wilson deftly and humorously catalogues the sartorial lodestars who showed him a way to dress into his masculinity: Steve Buscemi's turtle-necked Carl Showalter in *Fargo*; dapper rebel Johnny Cash and his dad, an expert in the intricate codes of menswear.

I am always struck by how eager people with an interest in fashion are to talk about clothes and how little opportunity they have to do it. The relief and enthusiasm I saw in students when they read writing that surfaced this implicit knowledge was palpable and sparked my desire to create more space for more people to think deeply about dress. I began to search for other essays that illuminated the invisible weave of garments, feeling and experience. Where I found thematic gaps, I commissioned new essays by poets, academics and writers on topics such as how fatherhood and masculinity entwine with style, how self-adornment can become a resuscitation apparatus, helping a wearer navigate chronic illness or being in the diaspora, and how dress entangles with friendship. I hope that bringing these essays together will show not only how many common throughlines invigorate our very disparate experiences of dress but how many ways there are to consider it.

Some of the essays were written within an academic style, so their writers engage closely with intellectual debates and draw on prior literature to situate their experience. Others were initially published in literary magazines or on arts and culture websites, so make limited reference to other works. Rather than amend any of the previously published essays in an attempt to create some kind of formal unity, I preferred to leave their differences and resonances to sing as they will to you. The humour, the citations, the wordless clashes between parent and child, the reaching through clothes for someone loved and lost, the memories and search for selfhood collectively discard binaries between analysis and lyricism, mind and body, material and spiritual, self and other. Instead, these essays richly and variously advance the theory that we are, all of us, caught in a living weave with one another and the garments that carry and clothe us.

In the spirit of throwing the door wide open, my definition of 'dress' encompasses adornment and body modification along with everyday practices vital to thinking about clothes, such as sewing, having garments tailored, and mending and shopping for them. Perhaps surprisingly to some, I have included in my categorization of dress other material objects that we wear, such as jewellery, wigs, prosthetic limbs, and baskets. This stance is influenced by anthropologists Joanne Eicher and Mary-Ellen Roach-Higgins, who defined dress as 'an assemblage of modifications of the body and/or supplements to the body' that includes 'a long list of possible direct modifications' – such as tattoos, scarification, piercings, hairstyles and perfume – 'as well as an equally long list of garments, jewellery, accessories and other categories of items added to the body as supplements'.[2] This is a useful definition because of how encompassing it is: as the authors note, it spans cultural and national differences in adornment and bodily modification, and is 'free of personal bias or social valuing [and] bias [. . .,] inclusive of all phenomena that can accurately be designated as dress'.[3] The things we wear are not always clothes but also form part of the material culture with which we adorn ourselves. They collectively transform the body into a dressed self. In fact, perhaps it is the marginal objects that most reveal the permeability between us and dress: instead of either/or, these objects are both. We could see a prosthetic leg, a wedding ring or a wig as an extension of the organic body – vital to it psychically, emotionally and somatically, but not part of the body itself; modifying the wearer's appearance and rendering them socially legible in a desired way; not clothes but still dress.

Here, I also follow Carol Tulloch, who defines 'style' in the African diaspora as a kind of 'agency – in the construction of self through the assemblage of garments, accessories, and beauty regimes that may, or may not, be "in fashion" at the time of use'.[4] By extension, dressing is a 'process of self-telling', a narrative of self through style.[5] This self-narration does not just occur when wearing clothing, but in the practices and processes of adornment, which collectively materialize our look and help us make sense of ourselves. Desiree Cooper writes that even as Alzheimer's Disease encroached on her mother's personality, it never stole her vanity: 'there were many days when we would be late for an appointment because I couldn't stop her from primping'. Dressing as herself and enacting the rhythms of daily preparation that have characterized her life is not ancillary to Cooper's mother's sense of self but essential to it, stored as body memory even in the terrifying face of forgetting. Sewing clothes for her daughter is part of how Thao Thai cares for her and connects to the material lineage of her Vietnamese family, master sewists who 'can look at a Macy's mannequin through narrowed eyes, then go home to draft the same blouse—for a fraction of the price—from bits of leftover fabric'. And Amy Key's lyrical essay reveals how clothes wend us with our friends, as she maps a shifting mosaic of lending garments, being given them, stealing a belt, having a loaned pair of shoes destroyed, a satin cheongsam lost, and dreaming of a couture dress made of rustling razor clam shells. Woven through Amy's essay are threads of covetousness, carelessness, tenderness, affinity and joy that invigorate dressing alongside friends, locating yourself through them – in distinction from them – both at the same time. The richness inherent in these everyday experiences is also why *Dressays* is not overly concerned with fashion. While some of the essays touch on the desire to look fashionable or mention the names of certain storied designers, this book is more concerned with the ordinary: that which we put on to make ourselves up.

Intriguingly, not only does our dress reverberate with cultural meanings that other people participate in and recognize, it connects us to others, through feeling. At times these feelings may have clarity and force (like the driving need to find and wear clothes that no-one else has); at other times, they may be pre-cognitive, indistinct and imprecise – the dawning dread that what you're wearing is somehow not right, the rising nausea when you catch a stranger looking at you a little too intently for a little too long. But feelings are not just ours: while experienced individually, they also circulate collectively, moving through us as a current in water. As Roberto Filippello and Ilya Parkins have observed, both feeling and fashion in their common use seem to 'adequately mediate between the psychic and the social, the individual and the collective'.[6] The feelings produced and held by clothes are subtle, powerful. They permeate us and other people, too. These essays demonstrate how difficult it is to extricate our sense of self from material things and reveal what a myth it is to consider dress as something that separates us from other people. They call us to attend to not only what is often unspoken, but what is hidden or deliberately obscured. The things we wear are mostly made by human hands, yet how easy it is to focus on the pleasures of dressing without a thought for the life of the garment before it came to you. Fiona Wright details the alchemy by which, '[a] single filament, a fibre of flax or wool or polymer, is spun into a thread', explaining that '[a]ll fabric work is transformation.' She narrates the months it took to sew a ruffled blouse, only to see, in the final stages of hemming it, an ad for a mass-produced, fast fashion equivalent for fifteen dollars. How to reconcile the creative, slow and pragmatic work of homemade clothes with the exploited, often-invisibilized labour of sewists whose skills are compressed against impossibly tight margins of time and quantity, and often undertaken in dehumanizing conditions? The alienation inherent in industrialized, hierarchical systems that divide us from each other and our world in the name of progress and capital also surfaces in Kandasamy's essay on the ways caste discrimination iterates through garment manufacturing, and is reflected in Jane Tynan's piece on the emergence of synthetic rainwear in the mid-twentieth century. She argues that these plastic garments reflect an attitude towards our world that sees it as a storehouse of resources to be appropriated, controlled or feared. Her inert plastic raincoat literally separated her from her familiar 'weather world', its supposed necessity supported by discourses that framed the weather as an Other to be feared and mastered. Witness instead Robin Wall Kimmerer's call to recognize the lives that are given to make the objects that sustain our lives. 'Just think of the tree and all its hard work before you start', her teacher John Pigeon instructs as she prepares to weave a black ash basket. 'It gave its life for this basket, so you know your responsibility. Make something beautiful in return.'

Read together, I hope the resonances and insights that call to one another across these essays illuminate the similarities as well as the particularities of how we relate to clothes and how they relate to us. The foundation of personhood here is the perceiving, feeling self, simultaneously distinct from others and enmeshed with them. To read these essays is to witness the ways we influence and shape one another, even when pulling away to choose a different definition of self. Even this takes place against the horizon of a shared lifeworld, within the context of a culture that offers certain possibilities for conceiving of identity, with which we are all compelled to interact in some way. As writer Gavin Van Horn reminds us, attending to the ways we are kin with other living beings – human, animal, plant and planet – is a form of '(re)connect[ing] our bodies, minds, and spirits within a world that is not merely a collection of objects but "a communion of subjects".'[7] By foregrounding the sensory, the feelingful and the somatic, these essays return us to the world as they show us how entwined we are.

The Look

Anne Anlin Cheng

1.

I was fourteen and lost in front of a particularly alluring pair of shoes in a shop window in the mall. I felt my mom's hand at my elbow urging me away. I thought it was her way of saying no to the shoes until I looked up and followed her line of gaze: an adult white man was staring at me from outside the other corner of the store, his neck strained forward through two panes of glass. He did not see my mother watching him watching me. It was the kind of look that was at once concentrated and abstract; the thrust of it seemed to bore right through me to a point behind me, making me at once obdurate and transparent.

A few years later, I would remember that look, when on the Métro in Paris I found another white man looking at me with the same kind of intense, blank stare that made me wish I was thousands of miles away. Back then, an older Parisian friend had cautioned care, explaining that there were French men who still thought Asian women were prostitutes. I remember being shocked by the bizarre assumption. Since then, I have come to learn the deep histories of French colonial rule in "Indochina" and, in my own adopted country, the prevailing nineteenth-century American notion, at times even written into laws, about pestilential Chinese prostitutes. In the twentieth century, U.S. masculine and militarized presence in Asia spawned its own expansive racial-erotic imagination, stoking for more than two centuries this sexual notion about Asiatic femininity. Now, this association between Asian femininity and crass availability in Western, masculine imagination seems to me far from eccentric.

At fourteen, I was too naive to suspect that such a gaze might have been sexual. I had thought such looks must be filled with scorn or hate. Now, knowing that sexual desire does not preclude racial disdain, I recognize that those looks could have been, and mostly likely were, combinations of both.

I hate how that mix of derision and desire still instills fear in me. Anger would be preferable. I grew up in the United States with most of the freedoms that my immigrant parents wished for me, but my American Dream would be punctuated at the edges by fleeting encounters that no longer surprised me but have never ceased to reach the pit of my stomach. Strange white men who cooed, "Me love you long time"; unsolicited reminiscences of men who were "once stationed in Vietnam or Korea"; the unwanted ni hao ma or konichiwa when I walked down the street; coffee dates with myself interrupted by slips of notes that announced "I adore Asian women"; being told I was beautiful when I knew that was not what was meant.

Years later, as a professor on my first day of teaching at a prestigious East Coast university, I was heading to my first lecture, armed with my syllabus and my game face, when a young blond man, clearly an undergraduate, bumped hard into my shoulder with a breezy "Ni hao ma" tossed in his wake. My brain froze. Was this another one of those creepy men, or simply a student who had been taking a Mandarin class?

2.

I have never been able to reconcile my deep discomfort with being seen by strangers with my love for clothes. How is it that someone who has been trained by the world that it is better not to be noticed can also be someone who enjoys sartorial play? Can I be a feminist and still love fashion? Can a woman of color participate in acts of beauty without self-harm? What is beauty for the "unbeautiful"?

People always assume that women dress for others, as a gambit for attention, either for the admiring male gaze or the envious gaze of other women. And if a woman were to dress "just for herself," it must be a form of narcissism. A woman with sartorial preoccupation must be either a hapless victim (prey to commodity culture and patriarchal expectations) or a cunning performer (someone who refashions herself at will). And when it comes to a woman of color, whose relationship to commodified sexuality is so fraught and historically compromised, it is especially difficult to talk about beauty and style without making her either self-objectifying or plain uppity. We can probably all safely debate the beauty of a thing – a flower or a painting – without too much heat, but when it comes to the beauty of a person, especially a woman of color, we are suddenly in a minefield of objectification, fetishization, and appropriation, at risk from others and from ourselves.

A friend once noted that he thought *the* question that every woman must face is the question of beauty. Even if a woman ultimately decides to reject beauty, he said, it remains the question that every girl-becoming-woman must negotiate. I was not so sure a woman could reject beauty even if she wanted to, because the issue is not her response but the injunction implicit in the question. But I took his point and asked what he thought *the* question would be for men. He thought about it and said, "Probably the question of jobs, career, his moneymaking potential." This all sounds old-fashioned, yet probably not far from what is still true.

In ancient Greece, the word for adornment, *kosmos*, means both "decoration" and "world order." This is why the words *cosmetics* and *cosmology* share an etymological root. Presumably there was a time when the act of self-adornment was not seen as shallow or superficial but as originating from a desire to have the human body echo and be in tune with the invisible forces of the universe: the body as world and the world as body. In this view, the decorated human body itself serves as a carrier, a micrograph, of the visible world. (In modern Greek, a gossip is someone who will tell your business to the whole *kosmos*, reminding us that "makeup" – putting a face on – is connected to a kind of citizenship, a signing up to participate in the glamor of sociality.) The ornament of clothing, far from being inert or fake, promised to expand the body's periphery, extending its connection to the world. We humans, especially women, have long lost that sense of undividedness from the world.

Maybe that kind of connection was always no more than a human wish, but surely there was a time during human development when such at-oneness with the world existed. Psychoanalysts postulate what they call the oceanic or, rather aptly, pre-mirror stage, when you do not yet see your own reflection as an Other. For a woman, that moment could only be pre-womanhood, before a girl has to think about *having a relationship* with her body. There's this story that my mother loves to tell about the time I went to my elementary school in Taipei not only out of uniform but also wearing the most garish outfit. That year my grandparents had returned from their annual trip to America and brought back for me the surprising gift, not of more dresses, but of a pantsuit. The top was bright canary yellow, made from some synthetic, textured fabric that was in truth a little itchy but reminded me of a sea of bubbles. The shirt sported sharp button-down collars and a long, wide, bright orange tie. The sleeves ballooned out extravagantly, like bells, only to cinch back in tightly at the wrist by a row of five small, covered buttons. Then there was the bottom: a pair of front-seamed, bell-bottom pants, in orange, of course.

I had never seen anything so cool in all my life. I insisted on wearing this glowing yellow-orange mirage to school, even though it was school picture day. My mother warned me that she would not come get me at school or make excuses for me should I be sent home. I told her not to worry. To this day, my mother does not know, nor do I recall, what tale I spun to get the teachers to allow it. Somewhere out there in photo graveyards there is a photograph of two neat rows of Taiwanese kids in black and white uniforms . . . and then me, in my bright yellow and orange bell-bottom suit and tie.

3.

I miss that girl, not because she enjoyed being seen but because she didn't care that she was. Her pleasure in that outfit was more felt than remembered. Imagine that: to be so at home in the world, so undivided from your own body, that what you wear is but an extension of *being in the world*.

Maybe it is in nostalgia, or simply in compensation for that memory of lost plenitude that, as an adult, I am particularly drawn to clothes that are world-making: sartorial constructions that seem to generate milieus of their own, clothes so meticulously constructed that they seem capable of standing alone, sometimes even *standing in* for the human body. I am thinking of those creations that are so saturated with narrative possibilities that the human wearer becomes their embellishment rather than the other way around: Kim Novak's auratic grey suit in *Vertigo*, Maggie Cheung's architectural chipaos, Emma Peel's unpeelable body suits, Iris Van Herpen's stark bone dress.

These creations, though different in context and time, share one quality for me: an object-expressiveness, a thingliness so ontologically suggestive that it survives in the imagination, acquiring an inner life beyond the women or characters accompanying them.

What seduces the eye and the mind here is not the fleshly female body per se but the allure of the supplemental becoming primary, of the inanimate that has grown sensorial and gorgeous. It's not a coincidence that these sartorial revenants veer towards *costume*: not because they are fantastical or artificial but because they amplify and celebrate that unnerving gap between body and dress, person and persona, human and thing.

Wearing these creations, one can be both more and less oneself.

A woman can hide in that gap, a pocket of becoming.

Fashion has always teetered between the need for uniqueness and the demand for mass production, between art and market. In the early twentieth century, the

German philosopher Walter Benjamin used the term *aura* to refer to the unique originality of a work of art, highlighting art's onetime presence in a specific time and space. Benjamin thought that we, in the twentieth century, had lost the magic of aura because in an age of accelerated mechanical reproduction, art can be reproduced, bought, and exist anywhere, anytime, as a copy. But I wonder if a concept like glamor, a conscious engagement of artifice and itself often a citation of other recognizable figures (like Lady Gaga citing Madonna citing Marilyn Monroe), might hold out for us some possibilities for aura today? Unlike beauty, which is often idealized, naturalized, and thought to be God-given (in spite of it being heavily socially, culturally, and racially determined), glamor is not apologetic about its artifice. Instead of deadening reproducibility or natural authenticity, glamor is all about the enchantment of *synthetic malleability . . .* and its potential for surviving in repetition.

This is why the outfits above are both glamorous and potentially "auratic." While all of them can and have invited copies and imitations, each subsequent replica (and each subsequent wearer) can only fulfill these outfits' most intense fantasies by harking back to the idea of some possible, originary presence: a reproduction that allows you to inhabit, just a little, the auratic space of the imagined original. Without such promise, a grey suit is just a grey suit. (In *Vertigo*, Novak's Madeleine will herself turn out to be a spellbinding counterfeit, a copy of a charismatic but lost, or simply nonexistent, original.) These sartorial creations are thus imbued, not so much with beauty as with a specific and slightly decentering flirtation with the dream of *presence:* an act of adornment/covering that renders selfhood visible to the self.

I like to think of this kind of aesthetic pleasure not as something that only invites consumption but also as an experience that triggers a psychical transaction, one in which our sense of being a person transitions, deliciously and precariously, into our sense of being a thing, and vice versa. The British cultural theorist Rachel Bowlby, who writes smartly about the experience and history of shopping, once described the checkout counter as a moment of anxiety, of de-transcendence, when you fall from shopping's pleasures of hunting and gathering into the reality of having to pay. I think of the moment of getting dressed, of the "checkout" moment in the dressing room, as a similar though much more potential-filled moment: a psychical exchange when you have given up a little of yourself in order to be a little of the thing you love, and in being that thing, you become a little more yourself.

Of course that room for play – that slippery moment between *who* and *what* you are – is tricky. There is both freedom and danger in sliding between being a person and being a thing, especially for a woman of color, who is always already made into an object (of desire, of use, of denigration). It is politically dicey to talk about a woman finding escape in being thinglike. But, sometimes, for those bodies made heavy by mainstream cultural fantasies, disappearing into synthetic self-extensions – that is, fashion – can provide a temporary relief from the burdens of having bodies and their inevitable weighty visibility. Sometimes you cover yourself up in order to reveal more of yourself, and sometimes the covering relieves you of being you.

Those who have been deemed unusual- or odd-looking tend to turn to the resources of glamor, because glamor, as a particular form of extravagant cloaking, has the potential to liberate women – not by providing a shield of desirability (because desirability also makes women vulnerable), but, rather, by extending them a temporary guise that saves them from the burdens of "authentic personhood." I suspect women from Bette Davis to Josephine Baker to Stefani Germanotta know this well.

4.

All of this may explain why I had such a moment of consternation – something between recognition and recoil – one day in the Metropolitan Museum of Art when I was confronted by this sculpture (or is it a garment?) made by contemporary Chinese artist Li Xiaofeng (Figure 1).

This is Beauty, and this is Ugliness. This is femininity elevated to the status of (not-to-be-used) Art and (to-be-used) debased Things. Composed wholly of shattered ceramics, this dress, according to the placard, was made to be actually "wearable." But to wear this is to put on the weight and shape of *another, already existing body:* one body dreamed up by history, a body that is the residue of centuries of ideas about Asia, femininity, porcelain-imaginary, domesticity, the burdens and privileges of person-as-art/thing.

Is this Chinese femininity or its arrested development? Armor or exposure? Winged victory or grounded flight? Devastation or recuperation? Antiquing or dumpster diving?

Maybe this woman-thing is bearing a form of witness, testifying to the continuities belied by these dyads. Maybe this *is* Chinese femininity on display for and in the West, a stranded but still-standing shell that bears the fractures of its making.

Maybe this is what survival looks like.

Figure 1 "Beijing Memory No. 5," Li Xiaofeng, 2009. Qing period shards. Red Gate Gallery, Beijing. Display from *China: Through the Looking Glass*, 2015, Metropolitan Museum of Art.

Photograph by the author: Anne Anlin Cheng.

5.

When my daughter turned eighteen, I started to make mental notes of things I want to tell her but can't. I have not told her, for instance, that in the hospital when she was born, holding such love in my arms, I thought that if I were to die in her arms one day, I would be content. I have not told her this because it is terribly morbid and selfish. For similar reasons, I have also not been able to bring myself to tell her about the kind of gaze and encounters that I confessed here. It's not only that I think certain life experiences cannot be passed on; it's also that I am always struggling between preparing my kids for the real world and protecting them from its toxicities.

My daughter's childhood was spent in a small but cosmopolitan town. Her preschool class of twelve had only one monoracial child, and he was a Swedish national. Whereas my middle school history book in Georgia devoted its chapter on the Civil War primarily to the invention of the cotton gin, my daughter at age six was already explaining the word *segregation* to her younger brother. When both marveled together at what seemed to them an unimaginable universe where such inequality could exist, I realized how better educated they are about American racial history than I was, but also how, by being habituated to the virtues of diversity, they remain innocent about the still-brutal realities of racism.

My daughter grew up with love, privilege, and an ease with the world that has allowed her to be an affectionate, demonstrative child who has also been able to walk into new daycares and schools alone without a backward glance.

Do I want to puncture that ease? Didn't I in fact work hard to give her this refuge? Do I want to contaminate or prescript her world prematurely by telling her that there are people who would despise her just because of who her parents are, or because of the way she looks? Do I want to tell her the queasy fact that derision can wear the face of desire? Am I being irresponsible or cowardly by not telling her? Or are such warnings pointless because no amount of being told something like this can approximate the unexpected violence of such an experience?

Did I not dream of a world where she is not divided from her own body?

6.

My daughter was born on Mischief Night, the night before Halloween. So October is always a big month for us. When they were small, every August in anticipation of Halloween and before my school semester starts, my kids and I would gather to discuss and plan their Halloween costumes. I treasured these planning sessions because it was *our* project and because I got glimpses into how they saw themselves. I think children love dress-up, not for disguise or escape, the way it often is for adults, but because it is an exercise in possibility, a rehearsal for what they could be or imagine they already are. As they got older, my daughter started helping out and then taking over the sewing: a fine-boned Victorian gown after she read *Pride and Prejudice*; a demon slayer from some anime who carried a life-size boomerang that she crafted out of papier-mâché; a mythic warrior wielding a mask of Medusa.

Unlike me, my daughter the seamstress is not limited by ready-made patterns or even by materials. She thinks anything is possible. When she was seventeen, she wanted to make a costume despite the pandemic and the quarantine. She had been reading the Arthurian legend and decided to reimagine what Uther Pendragon would have been like had he been a woman. I found her at the kitchen table making a list of her own: bevor, cuirass, rerebrace, plackart, pauldron, gauntlet, cuisse, greaves, and sabatons . . . a litany of armorial bearings. She bound her body with rolls of duct tape, making a mummy of herself, on top of which she drew the segmented suit. She then cut herself out of that second skin, pieces of which became the base patterns for the armor that she fashioned out of foam boards, cloth, and pieces of plastic she found in her dad's workshop that she heated up and molded.

Weeks after that Halloween, I found in the corner of her room the discarded duct tape husks, hollow but still holding the shape of her slim torso, arms, and legs. I thought about her going off to college next year, which means leaving behind the shelter of love that so far has been hers for the taking. I thought about the beauty of new shells and the emergence of new vulnerabilities. She will soon have to see – or might already be seeing – her body as a thing-in-the-world. Has she been crafting armors or extensions?

The word *blazon* comes from the French for "coat of arms" or "shield" and describes a lineage of heraldry. But in literature it alludes to a type of poem, a poetic device in which the (usually female) body is dissected and cataloged. For men, a blazon is a legacy; for women, a condition of fragmentation. I hope fervently, against all that I know, that my daughter will continue to fashion for herself all that is possible in a broken world.

Darning Mark's Jumper: Wearing Love and Sorrow

Karena de Perthuis

Comfort

In the winter of 2010, I darned a jumper belonging to my partner. It was a nice jumper – an upmarket streetwear label – but had been stored in a plastic bin bag, attacked by moths and was now scattered with bullet-sized holes and fraying at the cuffs. In an attempt to make the mending seamless and return this neglected, ten-year-old garment to a state of relative newness, I used three different wools. When the darning was too tight, the ply too thick or the colour wrong, I undid my handiwork and started over again. Despite these efforts, the end result was not quite the feat of invisible mending I had imagined, and his jumper looked somewhat imperfect and scarred. Around this time, I was due to present a conference paper on fashion, clothes and memory. And because it had been his idea to write the paper, and because he was a man who considered himself resolutely outside of fashion, and because he was in hospital and could not attend, I ended the paper by describing Mark's reaction to my not entirely successful darning. Running his hand over the valleys of uneven wool, he said: 'I love that you can see where it's been darned.'

Two years later, I returned to that original paper with the intention of using its ideas as a starting point for a longer essay. I wanted to write about the nature of our attachment to old clothes. I had in mind my favourite t-shirt which, after more than a decade of wearing, was dissolving at the seams. Still, I kept wearing it. I wanted to write about Roland Barthes's paradigm of fashion that included a definition of 'pauperisation' as being when 'a garment is worn beyond its natural replacement time'.[1] I wanted to write about how fashion, despite a reputation for being obsessed with novelty and change, had – in the concept of chic – also honoured wear and ageing. I was less interested in (but could not ignore) the popularity of vintage, distressed and recycled clothing; the 'aesthetics of poverty';[2] and what Barbara Vinken calls the aesthetic manoeuvre that shows 'old as old'.[3] I wanted to take a resonant phrase from Georg Simmel about fashion's 'psychological shimmer of permanency' and argue that old clothes represented the essence of longevity, the desire for permanence that is the other half of fashion's perpetual quest for novelty.[4] Most of all, I wanted to write about Mark's jumper. But no matter how hard I tried, it refused to fit, its presence ambushed every attempt to insert it into a theoretical discussion. Mark's jumper could not be thought of in the abstract; it demanded a narrative of its own.

When I included the darning of his jumper as a personal anecdote, a snapshot biography tagged onto the end of an academic paper, Mark was already gravely ill. A few months earlier, he had been diagnosed with stage four cancer and given six months to live. In writing him into my paper, I was materialising his presence, a presence denied only by his illness. If in doing this I was putting faith in something vaguely occult, the act of darning owed even more to the supernatural. Taking a ragged, moth-eaten and dusty garment, washing and drying it in the sun, painstakingly removing the pilled balls of wool and then repairing the multiple holes and damaged edges was more than care for a material object. Every step in the process of darning – from buying the wool to blending the yarns, anchoring the thread and weaving over-and-under to create the grain of the patch – was an act of love. Each passage of the needle, each stitch, was restoring something that had been eaten away and I didn't pretend to ignore the symbolism. This was more than the resurrection of a woollen jumper.

Like the meals I cooked, where every ingredient was supposed to fight the disease that his many doctors proclaimed was a lost cause, this was an act of reconstitution. Of course, just as I did not always believe that the incorporation of certain foods would cure him, I did not always believe that the love and care I put into mending his jumper would have any actual effect on his body. I knew I could do nothing about the virulent cancer that attacked his lungs, his liver, his bones; nothing about the brain tumours that whittled away his sense of self, deleting files of memory. I could do nothing about the side effects of the drugs, the radiotherapy, the chemotherapy; nothing about the even more debilitating and humiliating effects of the disastrous experiments of a quack doctor he had turned to in desperation. But I could give back life to his favourite jumper, the jumper that he would wear close to his skin, that would keep him warm, that would protect and give him comfort. And this was no small thing.

After Mark's death, this jumper became the thing of his that most recalled him to me. I slept in it, wrapped in arms that once wrapped him. At first I wore it layered with a t-shirt of his I had taken to sleeping in after picking it up off the floor one day and immersing myself in his smell. It was a t-shirt he wore often and at the time it annoyed him that my "theft" had taken it out of circulation, as if I did not have the decency to wait until he died before appropriating his things. Eventually, I wore the jumper on its own, the prickly wool – nothing like the smooth caress of his skin – embracing my neck, my arms, my back, my belly, my breasts, consoling me deeply. Wearing this jumper I would dream of him, vivid, potent dreams. From these dreams – dreams that mimicked the act of love where garments are discarded so urgently, so unconsciously, that it is only later, when you find them in discarded huddles on the floor, that you realise that at some point they must have been removed – I would awake naked, sure of his presence and overwhelmed with desire. Long after the smell of him had faded to something more imagined than real, memories of his body remained in the shape of his jumper, in its past, but most of all in the uneven patches of darning that could conjure up the touch of his hands as he had fingered the wool, his voice coming to me in the soft wonder of the remembered words: I love that you can see where it's been darned.

Darning

What did Mark mean? I love that you can see where it's been darned. There is nothing significant about darning which, by definition, is a small, domestic act. Unlike its more popular, more visible cousin knitting, it is not an act of creation. On the contrary, it has been described as a 'mind-boggling tedious and time-consuming' chore from bygone times, 'right up there with mangling the laundry'.[5] In our advanced capitalist economy, where the possibility of discarding and replacement is the default option, things to be darned, like things to be mended or ironed, sit in a basket waiting their turn. Darning is an in-between act of low priority, something to be done while watching TV – or not done at all. If we do get around to darning a garment, it is to extend its life, or because it matters enough *not* to be replaced. Either way, once darned, the garment becomes unique, singular – literally, irreplaceable.

There is one famous anecdote about darning. It comes to us from John Locke who used it to illustrate a philosophical question regarding the essential nature of physical objects. In some accounts, the anecdote involves the worsted stockings of Sir John Cutler, which are darned by his maid with silk thread over and over until nothing is left of the original. But the more common account involves John Locke's own woollen socks: if he were to darn a hole in a favourite sock, would it still be the same sock? What about if he added another darned patch, and then another, and another until the sock was entirely a patchwork of darned holes? Would the sock be fundamentally changed? Would it still be "his" sock? These are metaphysical questions that divide philosophers. Some say yes, some say no. One way to solve the paradox is to consider the frame of reference, some criterion that is specific to Locke's sock. For example, if it is possession that counts, then what the sock is made of – its constituent materials – becomes irrelevant. On the other hand, caution Giselle Walker and Elizabeth Leedham-Green: 'If possession is insufficient to the enquiry at hand, they cease to be the same socks once they've been darned, and [at this point they] stop being metaphysically interesting.'[6] This is not good news. Or rather, this is only bad news if what I want is a darned jumper that is metaphysically interesting. I could get caught up thinking about relevant frames of reference, or whether altering the material constitution of Mark's jumper changed its essential nature. But perhaps this is all too abstract. I am not dealing here with a jumper that has been completely reconstituted through darning – and even if I were, I'm not sure that I would agree that Mark's darned jumper (or Locke's darned sock) is the same jumper (or sock) as its undarned original.

In this, I am not alone. I make this discovery by way of doing a topic search for darning online, something I soon realise I should have done long ago. First, I scroll through information about how to darn correctly. After all this time, I am only slightly surprised to find that my technique is wrong; it is no wonder that Mark could see where his jumper had been darned. The best link is illustrated with a pamphlet, issued by the UK Board of Trade during World War II, called 'How to Darn Holes and Tears'. From readers' comments and tutorials, I learn that there are special tools and materials – such as darning mushrooms and darning wool – and that the correct darning technique involves working from the back of the garment and ensuring that the tension is always even. Tips and advice are passed down from mothers, grandmothers and even a 'Grandpa' or two; photographs illustrate garments "before" and "after" – the latter sometimes accompanied by a trumpeting 'Tadaa!' Everyone is after the same thing: a sock or jumper that is seamlessly, invisibly mended. The philosophy of 'Make Do and Mend' permeates readers' comments. A burned-out light bulb, a doorknob, a lemon or rolled-up magazine can be used in place of a wooden mushroom or egg; a single strand of embroidery thread or crochet wool also does the job; a third sock can serve as a ready-made patch for the pair. All small fragments of advice, stitched together by an individual sense of achievement and pride that the abstract musings of philosophers and their thought experiments cannot begin to embrace.

I find these stories of personal achievement, frugality and extending the lifetime of a knitted item uplifting, but I am not part of this world. There is nothing here that gets to the essence of my relationship with Mark's jumper. Nothing that gets to the depth of what I feel, what I experience with this one thing. When I leave the internet and come back to books, Leslie Chamberlain's exploration of Martin Heidegger's engagement with materiality strikes a chord. Heidegger's 'great idea', writes Chamberlain is that 'the this-ness of a thing is what differentiates it from all other things in existence'.[7] For Heidegger, philosophy was mistaken about the nature of materiality. Distinctions of subject/object, truth/appearance and the elevation of reason above all imposed a conceptualisation on objects that closed down multiple possibilities. 'Things', wrote Heidegger, 'are infinitely more, and other, than what they represent in the homogenous medium of strict concepts.'[8] Chamberlain makes the point that this reinvention or renegotiation of what materiality actually was is perhaps not so new now, but in the late nineteenth and early twentieth centuries the rescuing of this-ness that Heidegger traced produced a key distinction: "*that* things are", not "*what* they are".[9]

Writing about things, about stuff, I know is certainly not so new now; within the field of anthropology, for example, the study of material culture is a unique discipline, one that has stretched our understanding of the material beyond the world of artefacts and objects to embrace a larger conceptualisation of culture and, even, immateriality.[10] Closer to the topic at hand, the literary and cultural theorist Peter Stallybrass, for one, has written brilliantly on the materiality of clothes, in particular, interrogating our post-Cartesian embarrassment about things, wondering why 'the life of matter is relegated to the trash can of the "merely", simply because they are "mere things"'.[11] I'm familiar with this tradition; still, it is comforting to know that somewhere in philosophy there is a place for "mere things" like darned jumpers as 'infinitely more, and other'.

Haunting

That an old and ragged jumper figured so largely in my grief, bringing me closest to Mark, *becoming* him, has much to do with the role that clothes have played in my life. For years, my work revolved around designing, making and buying clothes for other people; added to this is a decade or more of writing, thinking and teaching about clothes, costume and fashion. Perhaps more than most, I am deeply involved with the things I wear; I buy vintage and second-hand, I recycle and remodel styles, I design and get things made. What I do buy I generally keep forever. I have three wardrobes and hardly ever throw anything out. Mark, too, for all his professions to be unaffected by fashion, was not unaffected by clothes. For him they were not anonymous items, but things with history, memory and meaning. Upon being diagnosed, one of the first things he wanted to do was go shopping – not for anything "new", but for things from his past. We tracked down a pair of sunglasses like ones he used to have, and hunted for an elusive pair of jeans, as if attempting to recreate the younger, healthier self he once had been.

Like me, he hung onto things – an over-sized, thick cabled cardigan, patterned with snowflakes and reindeer that had belonged to his father, an incomplete collection of surf club t-shirts and faded western shirts all shared the crowded space of his wardrobe with rarely worn suits and handmade English shoes that gave him a sense of confidence and authority at important meetings. He kept in his memory for years details of what I was wearing when we first met, could recall whole outfits I had once worn and was never immune to the power of clothes. After a fight one morning, acted out on the newly public stage his illness imposed upon us, he emerged dressed in a vintage hand-knitted vest I had given him. Throughout the summer it had hung in his wardrobe unworn; wearing it now for the first time was an olive branch, his way of wordlessly apologising in front of the audience of his friends, "speaking" through clothes in an intimate dialogue that had nothing to do with them communicating as "signs". So, to be consoled by his jumper, to imagine that its sleeves are his arms, its body is his body, and that in wearing his jumper I am wearing *him*, is not out of the ordinary; for me, it is second nature.

Often portrayed in films and books, such dependence by the heartbroken and bereaved on the clothes of lovers who have died is not uncommon. Tilda Swinton, as Eva in *We Need to Talk About Kevin*, sits in her rented living room on a shabby couch clutching in her hands the Led Zeppelin t-shirt of her dead husband, twisting it like rosary beads, sobbing into it, burying her face in the garment that is impregnated by his smell. In *Brokeback Mountain* Jack (Jake Gyllenhaal) keeps for years the shirt of Ennis (Heath Ledger) hanging beneath his own shirt in his small closet, the two garments wrapped around each other in eternal embrace. But alongside these stories of remembrance, there are also stories of the clothes of the dead being discarded or banished. In his essay, 'Worn Worlds: Clothes, Mourning and the Life of Things', Stallybrass refers to a scene from Philip Roth's autobiography, *Patrimony*, that describes the author finding his father on the day of his mother's funeral in their bedroom, chucking her clothes into a plastic garbage bag to be taken to Jewish relief while, in another part of the house, mourners gather. He is completely without sentiment and cannot get rid of them too soon – these empty material traces, these 'symbolic relics' that, writes Roth, 'were no substitute for the real companion of fifty-five years'.[12]

The question, 'What are we to do with the clothes of the dead?' is at the centre of Stallybrass's essay. It is also the question confronted by Henry James after the suicide in Venice of his friend Constance Fenimore Woolson. Her relatives had seen to the packing of her papers, paintings and mementoes to take back with them to America but had left the contents of her wardrobe and dressing tables untouched. In his novel *The Master*, Colm Tóibín describes Henry's dilemma. Anxious to safeguard Constance's privacy from snooping friends, he confides only in her trusted gondolier, Tito, who dismisses the suggestion that maybe a convent would be interested in them: 'Not the clothes of the dead . . . no one will want the clothes of the dead.'[13] Nor can her clothing, like the letters he has so methodically sorted, be burned. And so in the pink glow of dusk, the two men ferry her dresses, her coats and skirts, her stockings, her undergarments and shoes along the Grand Canal and beyond the Lido to bury them in the inky water of the lagoon. In the fading light of day, the presence of the dead woman is palpable – in the clothes redolent of her smell, in the 'strange contentment' felt by Henry and in the calmness of the place where she is their only witness. When it comes to carrying out the 'grim task', Henry finds he cannot do it; it would be as if he was lifting and dropping her body overboard. In the end, after blessing himself, it is Tito who reaches for the first dress, then another and another, tenderly placing them on the calm bed of water, murmuring prayers as they float away and sink beneath the surface. It is only when all her garments have been buried in their watery grave and the writer and the gondolier are set to return to shore, that Tito becomes aware of the dark shapes, 'like black balloons', surrounding them – the dresses, pregnant and billowing, returned to the surface. Henry is prepared to leave it to the grey mist and dark blanket of the approaching night to enfold the guilty evidence. But, again, it is Tito who acts; again, blessing himself as he pushes the dresses back down with his pole, working with a furious determination until the last one is finally, and eternally, buried.

Not the clothes of the dead . . . no one will want the clothes of the dead. Like clothes without bodies, the clothes of the dead can make us uneasy. They are inanimate, ghostly, empty things with arms and legs, that hang inert in closets or congregate with other discarded clothes on the racks of op shops or dealers in second-hand clothes, imitating but never able to be the bodies they once dressed. In a well-known passage from the opening pages of her pioneering book, *Adorned in Dreams,* Elizabeth Wilson writes of how clothes in museums 'hint at something only half understood, sinister, threatening; the atrophy of the body, and the evanescence of life'.[14] A parallel point is made by Jean Cocteau when writing about the freshly washed dresses he comes across in a farmyard at

Rochecorbon, 'hanging in the sun, side by side, like Bluebeard's wives, only lifeless. They lacked their souls, and the soul of a dress is a body'.[15] This way of thinking – that the soul of a dress is a body – is almost orthodox in certain branches of fashion and dress studies, but it's a proposition of which I have never been entirely convinced. Do clothes really need the animating presence of a body to be considered complete? Or is there another way to think about what we are speaking of here? What about the memory of a body? Or the life of cloth itself? Wilson is right about the inherent spookiness of clothes in museums. These clothes, imbued with memories of previous lives, recall a sense of human frailty, their presence a melancholy boast of survival, as if it is not their owners who have discarded them but they who have discarded their owners. To the visitor, wearing unexceptional, everyday clothes, the intricacies of a period costume or a piece of couture have a way of announcing their presence, as if each thread of silk brocade, each hand-stitched pleat or time-worn sleeve is party to something we can never share. And it's not only garments of the highest quality that evince this air of exclusivity. Even an old t-shirt can make us feel a little immaterial, especially if that old t-shirt was designed by Vivienne Westwood, came from a shop in the King's Road, London, called World, witnessed the invention of The Sex Pistols and travelled the too-fast-to-live road with its too-young-to-die owner, Sid Vicious.

Why then not accept the 'ghostly existence' of clothes?[16] Why not value it? As soon as Henry gathers a bundle of Constance's clothes in his arms, he feels her presence, a presence that remains as he and Tito make their way out to the lagoon she loved and continues until the last dress is finally and completely submerged.[17] Wearing the jacket of his dead friend, Allon White, while presenting an academic paper, Stallybrass is so overcome he cannot continue. Later, he realises that, for the first time since his death, his friend has returned to him. As he began to read his paper, Stallybrass writes:

> I was inhabited by his presence, taken over. If I wore the jacket, Allon wore me. He was there in the wrinkles of the elbows, wrinkles that in the technical jargon of sewing are called 'memory'; he was there in the stains at the very bottom of the jacket; he was there in the smell of the armpits. Above all he was there in the smell.[18]

Stallybrass goes on to explain that he has always wanted to be touched by the dead, wanted them to haunt him, had 'even hoped that they would rise up and inhabit me'.[19] It's a sentiment I understand. *This* is the embodiment of grief, of mourning. Unexpected garments – a ragged jumper, an old jacket – are not what you wear to mourn; rather, the wearing is the mourning itself, the materialisation of the absent body. To believe in the possibility of such haunting is to banish the notion that clothes are empty of the person who once wore them. Instead of inanimate, ghostly and empty, they are poetic, vital and alive; the dress, the jacket, the jumper, a body remembered. Maybe, even (why not?), its soul.

Fetish

Upon mentioning to someone – I can't remember who – what I was writing in relation to Mark's jumper they asked if I would consider seeing a medium. So far removed from the realm of possibility is the chance that I would go down this path, or, for that matter, even know anyone who would make this suggestion that, as I write now, I wonder if hadn't dreamt the whole encounter. Certainly, the notion of a medium coming to me in a dream makes more sense; things my rational, everyday self would not contemplate, my unconscious, dreaming self would find perfectly normal. I am not, however, blind as to why the connection – wherever it came from – might be made. Elements of the irrational and the occult run through the narrative I have woven around Mark's jumper. I don't believe in witchcraft, I don't believe in ghosts, I don't believe in a realm occupied by mediums. But I do believe in the medium of clothes. I know that Mark's jumper is "not Mark", and yet, his darned jumper remains only nominally detached from his body and through tears of grief I escape to a place of enchantment, a place of memory, of love, of loss and desire, to a place where he is whole.

Such ideas sit uneasily with who we are meant to be as modern, rational subjects. They are primitive and animistic, harking back to a shadowy, pre-modern, pre-capitalist world. To attach 'ideas of a superstitious, magical and spiritual nature' to clothes, writes Wilson, is to transform them into 'something like secular fetishes'.[20] One of the most provocative thinkers on clothing, dress and fashion, Wilson's exploration of what she calls 'Magic Fashion' draws on the concept of the fetish as a way into understanding 'the enduring mystery of the meaning of clothes'.[21] Part of that mystery can be attributed to the intimate relation that exists between garments and bodies, a relation that sets apart clothing – the things we wear next to our skin – from other treasured objects in our lives, such as photographs, heirlooms or a child's toy. In the branch of fashion scholarship that is informed by cultural studies, this intimate relation and the blurred boundary that exists between body and garment, between the self and the not-self, is central to the study of the 'inner meaning of clothes'.[22] Although there is much overlap, this approach contrasts with that of the dress or costume historian and their tradition of focusing on the garment-as-object. Although Wilson is a foundational member of the cultural studies approach, she notes that neither methodology adequately accounts for the 'quasi-magical properties and meanings' of a garment.[23] It is this terrain of the 'unexplained residue' that she attempts to explore using the idea of the fetish, a concept that, from the beginning sought to leach any intrinsic power from the things we wear closest to our skin.[24]

To fetishise an object is to give it life, to grant a different relationship between people and things from the one mapped out for us in the modern capitalist economy. What interests Wilson in the concept of the fetish is its origins as an object with condensed magical or religious power that has an active relationship with the body of the wearer. Beginning with the etymology of the word 'fetish' itself, as a concept fetishism has a complicated and complex history that is difficult to simplify.[25] First elaborated in the sixteenth and seventeenth centuries with the establishment of trade between Europe and West Africa, the term was originally associated with anthropology and the religious and cultural significance of an object. Late in the eighteenth century, 'fetishism' was invented as a theoretical term that received widespread acceptance.[26] In the following centuries, Marx and, later, Freud would appropriate the concept of fetishism and apply it, respectively, to the commodity form and sexual behaviour. Fetishism, then, has (at least) three distinct meanings, from three different traditions, but in all, elements of clothing, the body and magic play a defining role.

Derived from the pidgin word *fetisso*, the fetish can be traced to the Portuguese word (*feitiço*), meaning 'magical practice' or 'witchcraft', which, in turn, can be traced to the Latin word, *facere*, meaning 'to make'. *Facere* is also the root of the word, 'fashion' (*facio*) and, in its anthropological sense, from the start the fetish was associated with objects worn on or close to the body. Made from materials that, to Western eyes, ranged from the "worthless" (grasses, wood, leather, beads) to the precious (silver and gold), these objects – amulets, pouches and so on – signified to the original owners as both 'dress and ornament, and to something reverenced as a Deity'.[27] By contrast, for the European entrepreneurs who traded in them their value was purely economic. Condemned as pagan worship or witchcraft by, first, the Catholic Portuguese (who differentiated their own 'legitimate' religious accoutrements, such as rosary beads from the 'illegitimate' fetish object), and then the Protestant Dutch, the concept of the fetish was developed to demonise the power of 'alien' objects. This is not to say that objects did not retain interest but that the nature of that interest was economic; to the European entrepreneur, the fetish could be highly sought after, not for its intrinsic power or any meaning it held, but for its exchange value as a desirable commodity to be sold for profit in the marketplace. This shift is important, writes Stallybrass, because it implied:

> a new definition of what it meant to be European: that is, a subject unhampered by fixation upon objects, a subject who, having recognized the true (i.e. market) value of the object-as-commodity, fixated instead upon transcendental values that transformed gold into ships, ships into guns, guns into tobacco, tobacco into sugar, sugar into gold, and all into accountable profit. What was demonized in the concept of the fetish was the possibility that history, memory, and desire might be materialized in objects that are touched and loved and worn.[28]

As described in the book Stallybrass wrote with Ann Rosalind Jones, *Renaissance Clothing and the Materials of Memory*, the demonisation of worn objects reflected a growing uneasiness with unclear divisions of social categories. In the 'cloth economy' of the Renaissance, clothes were interwoven with the self, moulding and shaping the physical and social subject. By contrast, in the Enlightenment, the significance of clothes to the constitution of the self unravelled: as conceived by the modern mind, 'subjects are prior to objects, wearers to what is worn'.[29] Further complicating the modern subject's relationship with things, the period of the sixteenth and seventeenth centuries witnessed the emergence of the commodity form. Clothes-as-objects had, of course, always been detachable from the wearer; they could move from body to body, be pulled apart, remodelled, passed on, sold or pawned. They had value as currency, forming a substantial part of the payment made by the monarch to the aristocratic attendant, the craftsman to the apprentice and so on, in what was, to a certain extent, a non-monetary economy. But they were also materialisations, with animating and constitutive powers, that stitched the subject to the state, the son to the father, the wife to the husband, the servant to the master.

More than surface embroiderings, in the Renaissance clothes-as-objects were 'fashionings' that transformed; social relations of loyalty, paternity and servitude; symbolic meanings of history, love, memory and loss could be deeply embodied in things that were worn, whether they were made of silk, velvet, wool, linen, leather, metal or precious stone. Clothes-as-commodities, on the other hand, were 'fashion', detachable and discardable goods that became 'the commodities upon which international capitalism was founded'.[30] The significance of this is noted by Wilson: in the nineteenth century the commodity form would underpin the rhetorical and theoretical ideas of Marx's theory of commodification. In Marx's writings, however, there was a crucial shift in the meaning of the fetish in relation to the human actor; whereas the anthropological fetish was understood to bestow power on the owner or wearer, the commodity fetish involved human disempowerment and alienation. What was lost with capitalism – 'the most abstract society that has ever existed' – was meaningful relations between people and things, between us and clothes.[31]

Commodity

In his essay 'The Cultural Biography of Things', Igor Kopytoff makes the point that the division between people and things is 'culturally speaking, exceptional' and unique to capitalism.[32] There is, for example, the reality of pre-capitalist exchange as described by Marcel Mauss in his classic study, *The Gift*, where objects exchanged are described as '"personified beings that talk and take part in the contract. They state their desire to be given away". Things-as-gifts are not "indifferent things"; they have "a name, a personality, a past".[33] We have already seen that clothes in the Renaissance could be 'worn deeply'; in the sense that they were 'seen as printing, charactering, haunting', they were things that literally fashioned, described by Jones and Stallybrass as 'material establishers of identity itself'.[34] But when it comes to the subject in modern capitalist economies, writes Kopytoff, physical objects and people are polarised: at one end, 'physical objects . . . represent the natural universe of commodities', while at the other, people 'represent the natural universe of individuation and singularization'.[35]

From his 'commonplace' definition of a commodity as 'an item with use value that also has exchange value', Kopytoff expands our understanding of a commodity from this definition to one that takes into account the notion of commoditisation as a process.[36] In short, things do not remain things; commodities do not remain commodities. Stallybrass illustrates superbly this process of commoditisation in his essay, 'Marx's Coat', where he describes how, as much as Marx was in and out of debt, his coat was in and out of the pawnshop. Over the course of its migrations back and forth from the pawnshop, Marx's coat shifted in and out of its status as commodity and thing. Returned to Marx as something he could wear, that kept him warm and that performed all the functions of a coat, it was 'decommodified', its phantom-like existence replaced by sensuous characteristics, its 'thingliness' returned. But even as his coat held the potential for decommodification, its potential for recommodification remained. Haunted by the possibility of being turned into a liquid asset, Marx's coat was not the only possession in his poverty-stricken household that was in 'a constant state of being-about-to-disappear'.[37] From his aristocratic wife's family silver to the children's clothes, nothing was safe from 'the spectre of dispossession'; everything was potentially up for recommodification by being converted into cash.[38]

Measured by Kopytoff's simple definition of a commodity as an item with use value that also has exchange value, the one thing that would rescue Marx's coat from the spectre of dispossession and establish it permanently in the realm of things would be for it to become so threadbare as to be unwearable. Unwearable it would be unsaleable, and unsaleable it would be stripped of 'the unmistakeable indicator of commodity status'.[39] This is not, it goes without saying, the condition in which Marx anticipated the theoretical coat of *Capital*, much less his own, being returned to its owner.

Non-saleability, however, has its own appeal. If 'to be saleable or widely exchangeable is to be "common"', notes Kopytoff, its opposite is to be 'uncommon, incomparable, unique, singular . . . and not exchangeable for anything else'.[40] Such 'non-commodities' exist on polar planes, ranging from things that are 'uniquely valuable', such as heirlooms, to those that are 'uniquely worthless'.[41] As an instance of the latter, Kopytoff proffers a pair of old slippers which have been with someone for so long that parting from them is 'unthinkable' and, like a grandmother's wedding ring or great-grandfather's war medal, are 'priceless'.[42] But as a casual glance in the window of any pawnshop will testify, when it comes to an object's status as a permanently deactivated non-commodity, heirlooms are not as safe a bet as Kopytoff's categorisation might seem to imply. In our yearning for the truly singular, incomparable and unique, we are left then to contemplate the world of old slippers. This is also to return us to the world of ragged t-shirts, old jackets and darned jumpers – those things that have been touched and loved and worn for so long that, not only have they become a part of us, they have also become unsaleable. This is not to say they have no value; such things are priceless, uniquely worthless and, to use the expression with the full force of its meaning, we literally cannot give them away.

Things

Mark's jumper is not an indifferent thing; it states its desire to be kept; it is imbued with history, memory, love, life, loss and desire; it is infinitely more, and other. When I wear Mark's jumper, I am wearing love and sorrow. But at one point, it was also a consumer object, a mass-produced commodity manufactured by who-knows-whom in who-knows-where in who-knows-what conditions. That is the paradox of our relationship with things in 'a society dominated by capital and consumption', writes Wilson;[43] in many ways, we have no choice but to attach ourselves to material goods. They are what we have. They *are*.

I come back to Mark's words: I love that you can see where it's been darned. When he pulled his jumper out of the plastic bin bag where it had been stored for several winters and asked me if I could do something with it, he of course didn't want it returned as the same dusty, neglected thing. But neither did he want it to be reconstituted entirely – he didn't want it to be new, he didn't want it to be different; he wanted only to be able to wear it again. But in the process of redressing the neglect of years and attempting to return it from its entropic state, something else happened, and the mundane chores of washing and repairing were elevated to an act of nurture, care and love. My darning, imperfect and exposed, failed to erase or efface the signs of time; it betrayed traces of where my hands, my fingers had been. It became singularised, individual, unique. At the same time, it recalled earlier, less grief-stricken times, when the jumper – and Mark – had been whole. In the midst of crisis and rupture and feelings of utter helplessness, it was a materialisation of the small things I could do; it brought comfort, it signalled love, it reminded. This jumper that was touched and loved and worn.

Dedicated in loving memory to Mark Cherry.

The Same Yellow Dress

Amy Key

1. Bryony wore my shirt the other night. Black, button-down and pleated with long, flared sleeves. I loved seeing her in it; she wore it differently to me, giving it a chicer, more contemporary edge. The shirt borrowed her character. Bryony wearing it made me feel that she's at ease in my clothes, as though I could take from that an ease with proximity to me.

2. A third of the way through Sheila Heti's novel *How Should a Person Be?* I reached a section that opened up a strange emotional space within me. It is an email to the protagonist Sheila from her friend Margaux, and it concerns Sheila and Margaux buying the same yellow dress. Margaux writes:

> 'i know i can be intense sometimes. . . but I wanted to say that it really started me in miami when you bought the same yellow dress that I was buying'

> 'i think it's pretty standard that you don't buy the dress your friend is buying'

> 'i really do need some of my own identity, and this is pretty simple and good for the head. i'm going to get rid of the dress now, cause it makes me a little sad to look at it.'[1]

Sheila is 'hurt and shocked' by the email. I understood Sheila's response, but I sympathised with Margaux – it gave me pangs to read how this yellow dress made her feel, and I was disturbed and confused by my strength of feeling about it. I set aside the book for several days before I could return to it.

3. One of the silliest things I've ever done is shoplift the belt from a coat in a high street chain store. In my late teens I borrowed my then-best friend's newish coat to wear on a night out. It was a little black trench coat, in a light

faux leather. When I got home in the early hours I noticed the belt was missing. I was so frightened of my friend, who fiercely guarded her belongings and knew how to be angry, that I convinced myself it wasn't an option to come clean. And I was so broke, I couldn't afford to replace it. So I got up before everyone else and went to the shop as it opened.

I had a plan: I'd "try on" the coat and steal the belt while in the changing rooms, then slide it into the loops of my friend's coat the instant I returned home. It was a great coat that really needed its belt.

4. My friend Emily once wore my favourite cardigan to a nightclub, and she kissed a boy I fancied. It was from Karen Millen but way more ornate than the stuff they usually sold. This was back in 2000, or 2001. It was a wrap style, with gold and blue embroidery over a vaguely paisley print. It looked bohemian and antique. Seeing Emily get what I wanted while in my clothes made me feel as though my clothes had abandoned me. I still have that cardigan somewhere.

5. My grandma Eva loved to say, 'look after your clothes and they'll look after you'.

6. When I was 17, I bought an incredible pair of 1970s, very high platform shoes from a charity shop. They were elaborately made, with woven brown leather and cork soles. My dad asked me if he could loan them to a work colleague to wear to a fancy-dress party. I said that he could. The soles disintegrated when she wore them and to say sorry, I was given a £20 voucher for Next, which really wasn't my scene. I'm pretty sure he was having an affair with the woman who wore the shoes.

7. My body size has changed a lot throughout my life and sometimes I've not been able to wear other people's clothes, or vice versa. It seems elaborate but I like the idea of having pyjamas, new underwear, socks and cosy jumpers in a range of sizes so that there's always something I can offer when it's needed. Who doesn't want to be able to warm up someone who is feeling cold?

8. At university I adopted my flatmate Sarah's coat. It was from Guess: black suede, hip-length, with Mongolian sheepskin collar and cuffs. I felt extremely Anita Pallenberg in it, and I wore it to destruction. I always avoided a conversation about whether Sarah might want the coat back.

9. My sister Rebecca and I have often bought the same clothes, and this has occasionally been a source of tension, a thing to be negotiated and mutually agreed. But now we do it less often. As our tastes have diverged, I think of it nostalgically. My favourite was a satin miniskirt with a skinny belt from Oasis. Mine was hot pink and hers was bright orange. We also both bought the same jacket from Warehouse. It was made of nylon and had a quilted silver lining. Mine was black and hers was red. I'd wear mine with a 1970s Wrangler denim jacket underneath it that I bought from the kids' section of a charity shop for 75p. Sometimes when she was out, I'd borrow something of hers without asking and she would do the same. I didn't want to be told no.

10. Becky and I have the same pair of soft, grey, wide-legged, cropped lounge trousers from Marks & Spencer. We bought them during the pandemic. I like to think of her wearing her pair, working from home, while I wear my pair, working from home. We also each have one of a pair of blue, Art Deco, glass candlestick holders. I like to think of them each holding lit candles, out of sight of each other.

11. I daydream often about a question – *if I could have any garment in the world, what would it be?* The last time I asked my friend Amy this we both said McQueen's dress made from razor clam shells, shown in his Spring/Summer 2001 collection, *Voss*. I'd suspend it like a mobile from the ceiling, opening a window to let a gentle breeze in. The breeze would agitate the shells, so they'd chime.

Speaking with *Women's Wear Daily* (*WWD*) of what inspired the dress, McQueen said he was walking on a beach in Norfolk with a friend and there were thousands of razor clam shells there. He found them so beautiful, he knew he had to do something with them. He told *WWD*, 'the shells had outlived their usefulness on the beach, so we put them to another use on a dress. Then Erin [O'Connor] came out and trashed the dress, so their usefulness was over once again. Kind of like fashion, really'.[2]

I looked up pictures of the runway show, and Erin O'Connor leaves a trail of broken shells in her wake. Apparently the models in the show were instructed to walk as though they were having a nervous breakdown.

12. One time I stayed at Bryony's house, and I wore some new-old pyjamas. They were a putty-pink colour, cotton sateen, loosely fitting. Bryony loved them, so I bought her a pair from eBay.

13. For my birthday one year I went to the Peckham Rye Park for a picnic with some friends. I forgot to bring a coat and in the evening, when we moved to a nearby beer garden, I felt cold. My friend Megan lent me her sweet red cardigan. It was handknitted, she'd bought it at a thrift store. At the end of the night she gave it to me – *I've lots of cardigans like this*, she said, *and it really suits you*.

14. Sometimes I think of a dress my sister had. It was vintage – crushed green velvet, mini-length, long sleeves, with a small rosette at the slashed neckline. I pine for this dress.

15. An acquaintance and I often like the same clothes. *We're from the same factory*, she says.

16. When I donate clothes to charity shops, which I do often, I sometimes imagine they won't be bought, and I feel sad. It's as though I'm fretting over a small child who appears to be alone in the school playground, wondering if they have any friends. This happens most when I give away a garment that has meant something to me (quite often the things I donate are the basic items we are told will transform our look, the blank tees and shirts of a capsule wardrobe. It is only occasionally that I donate something I've actually worn and loved). When I've worn and loved a piece of clothing, I feel I've charged its material particles with something of myself. As though the soul sloughs off like skin does.

17. I love how my friend Anthea dresses. She really knows how to put things together, but there's nothing about her look that I could replicate. She gives the clothes their gestures.

18. A rich friend from school once tried to take me horse-riding, and the boots she loaned me wouldn't go over my calves. Horse riding had denied me first on grounds of class and then on grounds of my unsuitable body. As if the horse knew this, it threw me off immediately.

19. I go through affairs with colours. I loved to wear yellow of all shades and then it was coral pink and then it was grass green and then it was blue and then it was lavender. I don't realise I'm doing it until I'm several garments deep. Now I'm drawn to apricot, but apricot seems harder to come by and besides, I'm trying to keep my colours in motion.

20. I asked my friend Rhik the other day if he'd ever shared clothes with a partner. Not really, he said, but if they liked a t-shirt or hoodie or something of his, he wanted them to have it. I have no items of clothing that once belonged to someone I've slept with, but I do have a pair of my friend Richard's socks, which come almost up to my knees.

21. My friend Camellia works with a palette: baby blue, pink, lilac, palest yellow. Her textures are silk, satin and lace.

22. Why was I so moved by the conflict between Margaux and Sheila over the yellow dresses? It's strange how we want to at once merge ourselves with the people we love best and keep our edges sharply defined. Knowing me is also knowing what I am not.

23. At Becky's civil partnership I did an outfit change for the reception, putting on a sea-green dress covered in a couple of kilos of beaded fringe. When I danced the beads came off, scattered over the dancefloor like demerara sugar, and they were crushed under my gold platform shoes.

24. A man I was sleeping with for a while was fond of telling me, *I want to be wearing only you.* And every time he said this I imagined my body draped across him like a shawl. Now I corrupt the image: instead of a shawl, I'm plastic burger cheese melting under a grill.

25. A friend once lost a lot of weight very quickly and nothing fit her anymore. She told me she longed for a pretty dress. I decided to give her a blue satin cheongsam I'd bought from a vintage store and worn when I was 16. I figured it probably wouldn't fit me again and was so beautiful I thought it needed a new life. A couple of weeks later I asked her if she'd worn it yet and she told me she'd lost it on the way home. She delivered this news to me as though it was nothing. I didn't and still don't believe her.

26. When I was a kid, I wore a lot of hand-me-down clothes. My parents were rarely able to afford to buy me new ones, and especially not expensive ones. One of the reasons I got a Saturday job at 14 was so I'd have money to buy my own clothes. I didn't want the borrowed identity of other people's cast-offs, I wanted a clothing identity all of my own. I didn't want anyone to be able to

replicate what I wore, or how I wore it. At the same time, I wanted to go unnoticed. It was as though I only wanted to be seen by people receptive to how I looked and remain invisible to anyone who might mock it.

27. A loaned dress comes with the expectation of reciprocation.

28. One day at college, I saw a girl dressed in clothes that had an affinity with my own: tiny band t-shirts, flares, vintage sportswear, black polo necks, eyeliner. We noticed each other and within a few weeks became inseparable. But to maintain this mutual fascination, I had to enforce an invisible boundary between us, which meant while our style was in accord, I never ever wanted us to wear the same things. For the first time in my life I felt cool, I felt I had a style, and I couldn't risk corrupting that. So I would always shop alone, out of her view. If she wore skirts, I would wear dresses. If she wore knee-high boots, I'd wear platforms. If she was going out in vintage, I'd wear new. We were like contrasting, complementary bed linens. I wanted people to see us together and think, they both look good, but Amy's outfit, that's the one I really love.

29. *I really do need some of my own identity.*

30. I am trying to interrogate why it was so threatening to see a friend in my clothes when I was younger and all I can come up with is scarcity. There wasn't enough of anything to go round. When I had something I loved to wear, something that was coveted, it was the only power I felt I had, and I could not give that up.

31. My favourite outfit from this time was inspired by Tom Ford's 1996 Autumn/Winter collection for Gucci. Black velvet kick-flare trousers, a rip-off black patent snaffle belt, a black polo neck and patent Mary Janes. I've never felt better in an outfit before or since. I have a memory of walking into a pub on Christmas evening that year wearing this look and I had a feeling, as I felt eyes on me, that I now understand as erotic.

32. I think my clothes do look after me in a way. But only if I choose well. If I can have a conversation with the clothes, if wearing them feels collaborative, then the clothes and I can stick together.

33. When I fantasise about clothes, I think of a line from Brenda Shaughnessy's poem 'McQueen is Dead, Long Live McQueen', 'What is beautiful, what is terrifying, / what is absurd in me?'[3] Because the clothes might reveal it.

34. I think now if I went out wearing the same dress as a friend I would find it really fun, campy almost. It would be like a sign that says, *ask us about what we're wearing.*

35. When I was younger I was so uncertainly myself that what I wore stood in for who I was. Clothes became a material expression of *I'm not like other girls* (how I longed to locate those exquisite points of difference!). But now there's no mistaking me. I'm just like other girls. It's not how I look in the clothes, it's my relationship *to* the clothes that has more texture.

36. If I were to think of a piece of clothing that has been a friend to me, looked after me as my grandma might have said, it would be a very soft, cropped Adidas sweatshirt in bright green. When I wear it, I feel at ease, as though in the company of a friend who is happy to be alone together with me.

37. When I summon my friends in my mind's eye, I dress them too. They look so good.

We Have Lost Too Many Wigs

Desiree Cooper

As a black child born in 1960, I was only a curious spectator during the black consciousness movement. In addition to the dashikis and the upraised fists, what impressed me the most were the prodigious, kinky halos of black hair. I was agog by the be-Afroed activists like Angela Davis and blaxploitation screen queens like Pam Grier.

My mother, on the other hand, was horrified. She wore her thick hair straightened and flowing down her back or finger curled into a prodigious beehive. For her, Afros were a personal offense, and she regularly berated the black entertainers on television for glamorizing what was later commercially called "natural hair." Braids, kinks, and puffs were for poor people or little girls too young to endure the straightening process. Decent Negro women did not leave the house with their nappiness showing.

Despite my admiration for Afro "bushes," there was never a question that I would wear my hair straightened, and that process became a ritual that bound Mom and me to generations of black mothers and daughters. She'd shampoo my hair at the kitchen sink, then wend it into ropy plaits as I sat flinching between her knees. That's where I learned the meaning of a term that every black woman knows: tender headed.

My hair took all night to dry. The next morning, we'd get up early and she'd straighten it with a hot comb heated on the kitchen stove. I trusted her completely as she brought the comb, smoking like a branding iron close to my scalp. Only rarely did she singe the rim of my ear, or the rise of my forehead. The result would be a colored approximation of white beauty. The process was so laborious, that I learned early to shrink in terror from summer splash parties, humidity, exercise, mist, and, God forbid, rain.

To be fair, my mother didn't invent the insidious colorism that put a premium on "light skin and long hair." It has been thousands of years in the making as

European culture divided women of color based upon how closely they approached whiteness. But having landed on the "lighter" end of the color spectrum, my mother never questioned her genetic stroke of luck. Beauty may be only skin deep, but her embrace of the white beauty aesthetic went down to the bone.

My maternal grandmother, Bettie Goode, claimed to be black, but there was little in her appearance to suggest it. I've done some genealogical research, and she appears in 1910 census records as a mulatto living in the railroad junction town of Waverly in rural Virginia. Her mother, a midwife named Mary Parker, was listed as a mulatto as well. Bettie's father was, by all accounts, a white landowner named Logan Birdsong, a scion of an influential family in Sussex County, Virginia. Mary and Logan never married—miscegenation was illegal in Virginia until 1967. Still, it was commonly known throughout town that the white bachelor, Logan, had taken up with Mary, the colored midwife, and fathered seven of her eight children, including Bettie.

Bettie and her siblings continued to enjoy the Birdsong privilege as they thrived in the rural black community. Some of the children eventually moved north, passing for white by day at work, then going home to their black families at night. Others became landowners themselves and relatively wealthy in the town of black sharecroppers and millworkers. Bettie was well loved for her gentle ways and white skin. In fact, she was called "Miss Dolly" most of her life because as a child she'd looked like a porcelain baby doll.

When Bettie married Junius Goode, it was not to pass on her white privilege. His complexion was as rich as a cup of chicory, and all of their five children were praline brown. For my mother, the baby of the family born during the Depression, the only remaining connection to the Birdsong pedigree was her telltale mane of long hair, a racial inheritance that earned her unique status in the black community. Despite her lack of focus on her studies, she was always teacher's pet. Without any special athletic ability, she got to be a cheerleader. All of the girls wanted to be her friend, and the boys stood in line for a date. In everything, all my mother had to do was to pull forward her waist-long braid to prove that she was just a hair better than everyone else.

By the 1990s, the Second Great Natural Hair Movement had begun to take hold in the United States. This time, "natural hair" meant letting black hair do what it wanted and forcing this new measure of beauty upon mainstream America. Cornrows (a system of plaiting close to the scalp that resembled furrows ready for planting) were so popular that even whites couldn't wait for their Mexican vacations to try them. Black models walked down runways nearly bald. African braids sprouted in corporate settings. (And just to demonstrate the cancer of internalized oppression, black women often interwove straight Asian hair into their African braids to create a Rapunzel effect.) Some black women were getting an intricate system of thin, uniform, dreadlocks. Instead of letting the hair lock in thick, natural clumps made famous by Bob Marley, the hair was crocheted into a grove of thin locs that could be styled like loose hair.

I watched this revolution as I approached my mid-thirties. I had long traded the hot comb for a chemical relaxer, but I desperately craved the freedom exuded by women wearing natural hair. They exercised! They walked in the rain! They took extended vacations without a hotplate! I admired the adamant beauty of their ostentatious puffs, braids, and locs. They seemed so evolved.

By then, I was raising a daughter, and spending hours with her between my knees, twisting her ample, wavy hair into long braids, each tipped with a bead. I'd come to love the way her hair curled so fiercely and frizzed into a magnificent mane. I questioned my decision to continue straightening my own hair. What kind of example was I setting for her?

I found out when she was only four, and neighborhood kids had gathered at our backyard pool for a cookout. While her brother and their friends were having a ball, I noticed her sitting on the edge, watching.

"Why don't you get in?" I asked.

"I don't want to get my hair wet," she said.

Where had she gotten the notion that she shouldn't get her hair wet? I went from shocked to furious. I lifted her gently into my arms and threw her into the pool.

As my mother reached her sixties, the demands of detangling, straightening, rolling, and dyeing her hair became too much. Along with her signature gold loop earrings, ruby lipstick, and cross necklace, she added a straight-haired wig to her morning toilette.

At first, she only wore it on special occasions, or when the Virginia humidity kept her from being presentable. But when her own bountiful hair began to thin dramatically, she was never without her wig, even to run to the grocery store or to line dance with the "Jammin' Seniors" at the YWCA. A sienna hairpiece with shoulder-length loose curls and feathery bangs, became her trademark look.

Eventually, Alzheimer's stole many aspects of my mother's personality, but never her vanity. There were many days when we would be late for an appointment because I couldn't stop her from primping. She'd lavish attention on her wig, traumatizing it with damaging oils and brutal brushings until it looked just right. She'd search in vain for the strappy sandals I'd trashed for her safety. She'd try to smear solid deodorant on her cheeks for rouge, take a black Sharpie to her graying eyebrows, or strip off the clothes she'd just put on in order to start all over again.

But as she neared her eighties, she started neglecting her appearance. There were days when she would take off her wig and toss it under the bed, beneath her chair, in the dirty clothes. Some days, she refused to put it on at all. I panicked the way a mother might panic if her teenager tried to go to school in a bikini. Her baby-thin hair still grew down to the middle of her back, but I couldn't bear people staring at the wisps that barely covered her balding crown. I felt the need to protect her from her own humiliation, to preserve her dignity. Who was she without her hair?

The situation was even more complicated because there were days when she would be in a tizzy, doubling back inside to look for her wig, patting the top of her head to explain to me what she wanted. And there were other days when she'd whip the wig off before I could get her into the car. I could never guess when she really didn't want it, when she had simply forgotten it, or when, like an empress without her clothes, she would suddenly realize with horror that I had let her wander out in public, wigless.

Dreadlocks have had global spiritual meaning for many cultures, including ancient Egyptians, Hindus, the Maasai warriors of Kenya, and Jamaican Rastafarians. For me, the hairstyle feels like a reclamation of my soul. I am now in my late fifties, having been locked for more than a decade. Finally, I belong in the sorority I've so desperately wanted to join for much of my adult life.

Unlike so many fashion trends that are ignited by the young, black women who lock their hair are often older and, as a dear friend of mine explained, "Done with the dumb shit." We no longer care about the needs and wants and opinions of others. We are confident enough to challenge people to love us the way we are. We realize that going along to get along will eventually kill us. We greet each other as sisters as we pass on the streets, and often complement each other. Like sharing our stories of overcoming addiction, we ask, "How long have you been locking?" When we see women with straightened hair looking at us curiously, we are tempted to say, "If you had started locking when you first wanted to, you'd be free by now."

But as wonderful as the journey has been, I had to be jarred from my mental colonization in order to embrace it. Right out of law school, I'd married into a well-to-do Detroit family of doctors. My husband was also a lawyer with political ambitions. All the women in our social circle straightened their hair; the only exceptions were artists or oddballs.

As if the constraints of my social life weren't enough, there was my professional life to consider. At work, black hair telegraphed as much about me as would a skull and crossbones tattoo, a diamond watch, or a missing front tooth. If I wore my hair straight, it meant that I was promotable, nonthreatening, and acceptable. Conversely, natural hair would signal that I was combative, angry, anti-white, and radical. Was wearing natural hair worth locking myself out of economic opportunity?

None of these considerations was as stultifying as the thought of breaking my mother's heart. Even as I'd grown older, she'd held fast to her image of me as a straight-haired version of herself. Whenever I had changed my hairstyle, she would mope, personally offended that I had chopped it off, or gotten rid of bangs, or plaited it into braids (which was like a knife in her heart). I had the courage to stand up to my social circle, to my colleagues, even my husband and children. But did I have the guts to denounce the privilege of "good hair" that my mother so deeply cherished?

But when, at forty-five, my marriage fell apart, all pretentions crumbled. Suddenly, my life was my own. I immediately began the process of locking. About three years later, I found a photo of me on a family vacation, my locs still new and curving around the contours of my face. We were standing on the *Maid of the Mist,* cruising the white waters of Niagara Falls. Despite the turmoil in my life at the time, I radiated joy. I had finally become who I was.

The day came when my mother's wig disappeared completely. I turned the house upside down looking for it. I prayed that I hadn't inadvertently thrown it out with the trash, not realizing that Mom might have stuffed it in a grocery bag or rolled it in tissue paper.

When my search proved fruitless, Mom and I embarked upon a search for a new wig. At the wig shop, a white woman with Kool-Aid-colored hair greeted us warmly.

"Have a seat right here, Miz Cooper, and we'll take care of you," she said, gesturing to a plush chair in a mirrored cubby. Mom took her throne, allowing us to go through the store to bring her samples.

Daring to test my mother's resolve, I selected a bobbed black wig full of frizzy ringlets—something more race-appropriate. She frowned immediately, but not wanting to appear impolite in public, bowed her head to try it on.

"Oh, how pretty!" the saleswoman cooed.

But my mother wasn't having it. "No," she said, suddenly able to find her words. "Too thick." By which she meant nappy.

We left the shop with something akin to the wig she'd worn for years—shoulder-length, loose, auburn curls (with bangs, of course). I actually broke the bank and bought two. This time, I would keep one in my room in case she managed to lose the new one.

A week later, I found the first wig. She had put it in the plastic sleeve that protected the morning newspaper and hidden it in her nightstand drawer. That was the same day that the new wig disappeared.

We went months like that, losing and finding wigs, wearing and not wearing them, refusing to leave the house without them, but then tossing them in the backseat of the car on our way out to dinner. Each time, I frantically conducted search and rescue missions, dreading the moment I'd have her all dressed for an appointment only to find that she wouldn't leave the house without her hair.

I never discussed my decision to lock my hair with my mother. I knew that she hated it; for years, she'd suggest that the only way I'd catch a boyfriend was to get a makeover. Once, I found her staring at me. Finally, she asked, "Why did you do that to your hair?" It was as if she believed that I had imported the coarseness or teased up the kinkiness as an intentional act of violence against my light-skinned heritage. Had she repressed, or merely forgotten, all of those years she'd spent in the kitchen, hot-combing my natural hair straight?

One day, long after she had fallen into the abyss of lost memory, I noticed her scowling at my hair. I lost my patience. "This is my natural hair—get used to it!" I shouted. "I'm not going to spend the rest of my life trying to make it look like I'm white."

Insulted, she shot back, "You *are* white."

Nowadays, strangers come and go—nurses, social workers, respite caregivers, physical therapists. Many are white, which is an awkward boundary for my mother, who remains a child of the Jim Crow South. She is wary of the intimate touch of the chipper, white nursing assistants, and the personal questions from the blonde social workers with their judgey notebooks. She cannot make cogent sentences, but she becomes agitated and nervous, her eyes pleading for me to help her give all the right answers. She is hyperaware of the probable assessments that whites must be making about her, her home, and her family.

Inevitably, she finds her way back to that familiar crutch. She is, after all, beautiful, popular, and a Birdsong. As the workers pack up their things to leave, she grabs them by the arm to insist upon a tour of the house. She points and smiles at her framed needlepoint on the wall. She gestures like a game show hostess at the expensive furnishings now cluttered with tchotchkes and vases of artificial flowers. She points out the enormous, framed graduation pictures of my brother and me. My mother especially cherishes that picture of me, where I am posed with my wavy hair lying softly on my breast, a black Mona Lisa.

With each room, she seems to be saying, "We are not ordinary blacks. We are acceptable, cultured. We are as good as you are."

To put a fine point on it, she turns her head to the side, pulls out her long, thin braid, and says, "See?"

High-Functioning

Esmé Weijun Wang

At midday I entered the Chinatown Mental Health Clinic's guarded front doors, wearing a careful expression as I clipped into the waiting room. Inside the tiny space sat an elderly Chinese couple on a bench. The woman was clutching her head, and I considered how it takes so much—too much—energy to act as though our addled minds are all right. Few of the psychiatric facilities I've stayed in house those with the luxury for such performances. I was reluctant to stare, but felt monstrous for turning away from her pain, which was exactly what I did when I approached the partition and stated my purpose through the por-hole to the woman behind the glass: "I'm a member of the local speakers' bureau, and I'm here to tell my story."

To the clinic I wore a brown silk Marc Jacobs dress with long sleeves, carefully folded up to the elbows. Buttons up to the dip between my collarbones, finished with a tied bow. No jewelry, save for a silver bangle and my wedding ring. Black wedge heels. Flat scars crisscrossed my bare ankles like dirt tracks. I wore an organic facial moisturizer that smelled like bananas and almonds, Chanel's Vitalumière Hydra foundation in 20 Beige (discontinued), and a nubby Tom Ford lipstick in Narcotic Rouge (also discontinued, replaced by the inferior Cherry Lush).

My makeup routine is minimal and consistent. I can dress and daub when psychotic and when not psychotic. I do it with zeal when manic. If I'm depressed, I skip everything but the lipstick. If I skip the lipstick, that means I haven't even made it to the bathroom mirror.

In 2017, every morning I take a small and chalky pink pill; every night I take one and a half of the same pill. Haloperidol is, Dr. M reasons, what has kept me functioning without either delusions or hallucinations for the last four years, though for most of 2013 I struggled with what Sylvia Nasar, in *A Beautiful Mind*, calls schizophrenia's "dislocation of every faculty, of time, space, and body."

My official diagnosis didn't change to schizoaffective disorder for years. The disorder had been suspected, but not recorded, because schizoaffective disorder has a gloomier prognosis and more intense stigma than bipolar disorder does, and even psychiatrists can be swayed by the perceived severity of a different *DSM* code. Psychiatry also operates by treating symptoms and not a root cause, and so my psychopharmacological treatment was not impacted by the dramatic change in my chart. In *Blue Nights*, Joan Didion remarks, "I have not yet seen that case in which a 'diagnosis' led to a 'cure,' or in fact to any outcome other than a confirmed, and therefore an enforced, debility." My new diagnosis bore no curative function, but it did imply that to be high-functioning would be difficult, if not impossible, for me.

My talk for the Chinatown clinic was one that I adjusted for a variety of audiences: students, patients, doctors. It began with this line: "It was winter in my sophomore year at a prestigious university." That phrase, "prestigious university," was there to underscore my kempt hair, the silk dress, my makeup, the dignified shoes. It said, *What I am about to disclose to you comes with a disclaimer.* I didn't want my audience to forget that disclaimer when I began to talk about believing, for months at a time, that everyone I love is a robot. "Prestigious university" acts as a signifier of worth.

Other signifiers: my wedding ring, a referent to the sixteen-year relationship I've managed to keep; descriptions of my treatment plan as if it were a stable, infallible Rosetta stone, when in fact the plan constantly changes in response to my ever-changing brain chemistry; the mention of the small online business, based on digital products and freelance work, that I started in early 2014. With these signifiers, I am trying to say that I am a wife, I am a good patient, I am an entrepreneur. I am also schizoaffective, living with schizoaffective disorder, living with mental illness, living with mental health challenges, crazy, insane— but *I am just like you.*

Whom "you" refers to depends on which talk I am giving. One of the clinic's group leaders, Henry, told me that I'd first be speaking to an audience of "high-functioning schizophrenics." Most of them, he told me, had been meeting there every week for ten years. I couldn't tell if this was said with pride as he guided me into the small meeting room.

There were fewer than ten people inside, not including Patricia, the head of the speakers' bureau. Almost all of them were, like I am, Chinese, save for one elderly white woman whose eyes cast about the room like hyperactive Ping-Pong balls. Before the talk began, Henry passed around photographs from a field trip.

No one handed the photographs to me, the outsider. Without seeing the snapshots, I could only guess at the destination of a field trip for "high-functioning schizophrenics": maybe city hall, or perhaps a jaunt to Muir Woods. The group quietly admired the photographs. Some of them spoke with the lilting disorganization that I associate with people who live relatively well with schizophrenia, given that they were spending time at the clinic—but who would immediately be labeled by many as crazy, to be pitied and even avoided.

Before the presentation began, Henry brought out a party-sized bag of Lay's. He searched the corners of the room for napkins and paper plates as a handsome twentysomething pried open the bag with his big hands. Nobody seemed terribly interested in engaging with me, and I was too busy reviewing my papers for this, my first talk in a clinical setting, to initiate contact. Patricia introduced the presentation by briefly speaking about the different kinds of stigma. A few people interrupted her with meandering commentary and needed to be gently rerouted by Patricia or Henry. The quiet ones avoided eye contact and said nothing.

With this group, I deviated from my script. When I told the story of my diagnosis and recovery, I exchanged complex language for simpler terminology. I removed the term "avolition." I leaned into descriptions of experiences that I thought they'd understand—including, in Mandarin, my mother's explanation for why she lied to my first psychiatrist about our family history of mental illness: "We don't talk about these things." In the final moments, I quoted from an email she sent after I resigned from my full-time editing position, having realized that the job was triggering psychotic episodes: "Fly free. I love you." The talk was designed to be inspiring. I was trying to light up the room with hope.

When I finished, two people were crying. Patricia, tear-streaked, showed me her arm: goose bumps. "I thought I had it bad," said the other woman who was crying, and my heart stammered in my chest. I *was* her, but I didn't want to *be* her. I was the one at the head of the table, visiting. She was the one who had come to this clinic every week for the last decade. Not much was changing for her—but everything, I had to believe, was possible for me.

During my first inpatient experience at a psychiatric hospital, I met two patients who were treated as markedly different from the rest of us: Jane and Laura. Jane was middle-aged and chatty; Laura was the only other Asian person on the ward, and spoke to no one. We patients rarely spoke of our diagnoses—at the time, I was diagnosed with bipolar disorder, with traits of borderline personality disorder—but everyone knew that Jane and Laura were the two with schizophrenia.

Jane was friendly, and frequently rolled up in her wheelchair to share disjointed monologues about the psychiatrists' "mind control experiments," ramblings paranoid enough to be considered psychotic, yet realistic enough to be unsettling to my vulnerable mind. In less coherent periods, her stories dissolved into the verbal nonsense known as "word salad," in which one word only tenuously relates to the one that came before it, and the assortment of them means nothing at all. These problems with communication caused her to be excluded, by doctors' decree, from otherwise mandatory group therapy sessions.

I never interacted with Laura, but I remember her yelling as she was pulled out of the hall bathroom, interrupted during an attempt to vomit up her medications. "They're poison!" she screamed as two nurses yanked at her long, skinny arms. "They're trying to poison me! They're trying to kill me!"

A natural hierarchy arose in the hospital, guided by both our own sense of functionality and the level of functionality perceived by the doctors, nurses, and social workers who treated us. Depressives, who constituted most of the ward's population, sat at the top of the chain, even if they were receiving electroconvulsive therapy. Because we were in the Yale Psychiatric Institute (now the Yale New Haven Psychiatric Hospital), many of those hospitalized were Yalies, and therefore considered bright people who'd simply wound up in bad situations. We had already proved ourselves capable of being high-functioning, and thus contained potential if only we could be steered onto the right track. In the middle of the hierarchy were those with anorexia and bipolar disorder. I was in this group, and was perhaps even ranked as highly as the depressives, because I came from Yale. The patients with schizophrenia landed at the bottom—excluded from group therapy, seen as lunatic and raving, and incapable of fitting into the requirements of normalcy.

High-functioning patients had the respect of the nurses, and sometimes even the doctors. A nurse who respected me would use a different cadence; she would speak to me with human understanding. One gave me advice, saying that I needed to "dye my hair back"—it was clownishly red at the time—and "get down to normal living." As condescending as such words seem to me now, they were more than what was offered to those like Jane and Laura, who received only basic care. Forget about life advice—there was no hope for them beyond low-grade stability. Expectations are often low to begin with; in *A Beautiful Mind*, Nasar remarks that "unlike manic-depression, paranoid schizophrenia rarely allows sufferers to return, even for a limited period, to their premorbid level of achievement, so it is believed."

The psychiatric hierarchy decrees who can and cannot be high-functioning and "gifted." A much-liked meme on Facebook once circulated on my feed, in which a chart listed so-called advantages to various mental illnesses. Depression bestows sensitivity and empathy; attention-deficit/hyperactivity disorder allows people to hold large amounts of information at once; anxiety creates useful caution. I knew immediately that schizophrenia wouldn't make an appearance. Creative genius is associated with madness, but such genius, as explored in Kay Redfield Jamison's *Touched with Fire*, is primarily linked to depression or bipolar disorder. An exception is outsider artist Henry Darger, whose influential 15,145-page work *In the Realms of the Unreal* is both brilliant and the work of an obsessive, troubled mind that may or may not have been afflicted with schizophrenia—either way, Darger's inability to function in "normal" life is inextricable from his art.

With such unpleasant associations tied to the schizophrenias, it is no wonder that I cling to the concept of being high-functioning. As in most marginalized groups, there are those who are considered more socially appropriate than others, and who therefore distance themselves from those so-called inappropriate people, in part because being perceived as incapable of success causes a desire to distance oneself from other, similarly marginalized people who are thought to be even less capable of success.

An example of such distancing can be seen in Jenny Lawson's book *Furiously Happy: A Funny Book about Horrible Things*, which is often recommended to me as a hilarious memoir that embraces those with mental illness. Lawson, the beloved blogger behind *The Bloggess*, has been diagnosed with a variety of disorders, including depression and avoidant personality disorder. Yet she explains early in *Furiously Happy* that she is on antipsychotics—not because she is psychotic, she assures us, but because it decreases the length of her depressive episodes. "There is nothing better than hearing that there is a drug that will fix a terrible problem," she writes, "unless you also hear that the drug is for treating schizophrenia (or possibly that it kills fairies every time you take it)." But that line distressed me: for Lawson, my psychiatric condition, and the medications I take for it, put me on par with a fairy-killer; but if I were taking Haldol as a "side dish" for depression, I'd remain on the proper side of the mentally unwell.

Lawson, I'd like to believe, is trying to be honest rather than mean-spirited. Schizophrenia and its ilk are not seen by society as conditions that coexist with the potential for being high-functioning, and are therefore terrifying. No one wants to be crazy, least of all truly crazy—as in psychotic. Schizophrenics are seen as some of the most dysfunctional members of society: we are homeless, we are inscrutable, and we are murderers. The only times I see schizophrenia mentioned in the news are in the context of violence, as in *Newsweek*'s June 2015 opinion piece titled "Charleston Massacre: Mental Illness Common Thread for Mass Shootings." In this article by Matthew Lysiak, psychosis is linked to mass shooters such as Jiverly Wong, Nidal Hasan, Jared Loughner, and James Holmes. In the paragraph on Holmes, his treating psychiatrist is described as having written—and here I imagine a voice dripping with doom—that Holmes "may be shifting insidiously into a frank psychotic disorder such as schizophrenia." Immediately following that line, the piece reads, "On July 20, 2012 Holmes walked into an Aurora, Colorado movie theater and killed 12 people, injuring 70 others."

In a 2008 paper, Elyn R. Saks recalls, "When I was examined for readmission to Yale Law School, the psychiatrist suggested I might spend a year working at a low-level job, perhaps in fast food, which would allow me to consolidate my gains so that I could do better when I was readmitted." While fighting with my insurance company over disability benefits, I tried to explain that I can't work at McDonald's, but I can run a business based on freelance work. Place me in a high-stress environment with no ability to control my surroundings or my schedule, and I will rapidly begin to decompensate. Being able to work for myself, while still challenging, allows for greater flexibility in my schedule, and exerts less pressure on my mind. Like Saks, I am high-functioning, but I'm a high-functioning person with an unpredictable and low-functioning illness. I may not be the "appropriate" type of crazy. Sometimes, my mind does fracture, leaving me frightened of poison in my tea or corpses in the parking lot. But then it reassembles, and I am once again a recognizable self.

A therapist told me in my midtwenties, when my diagnosis was still bipolar disorder, that I was her only client who could hold down a full-time job. Among psychiatric researchers, having a job is considered one of the major characteristics of being a high-functioning person. Most recently, Saks has spearheaded one of the largest extant studies about the nature of high-functioning schizophrenia. In it, employment remains the primary marker of someone who is high-functioning, as having a job is the most reliable sign that you can pass in the world as normal. Most critically, a capitalist society values productivity in its citizens above all else, and those with severe mental illness are much less likely to be productive in ways considered valuable: by adding to the cycle of production and profit. Our society demands what Chinese poet Chuang Tzu (370–287 BCE) describes in his poem "Active Life":

Produce! Get results! Make money! Make friends! Make changes!
Or you will die of despair.

Because I am capable of achievement, I find myself uncomfortable around those who are visibly psychotic and audibly disorganized. I'm uncomfortable because I don't want to be lumped in with the screaming man on the bus, or the woman who claims that she's the reincarnation of God. I'm uncomfortably uncomfortable because I know that these are my people in ways that those who have never experienced psychosis can't understand, and to shun them is to shun a large part of myself. In my mind, there is a line between me and those like Jane and Laura; to others, that line is thin, or so negligible as not to be a line at all.

When asked, "What do people who live successfully with schizophrenia have in common?" for an awareness-raising social media campaign, Dr. Ashish Bhatt answered, "Often those persons who live successfully with schizophrenia are ones who have positive prognostic factors, which include good premorbid functioning, later age of symptom onset, sudden symptom onset, higher education, good support system, early diagnosis and treatment, medication adherence, and longer periods of minimal or absent symptoms between episodes."

Some of these factors and characteristics are determined by fate; others, however, have proved to be susceptible to human intervention, giving many people with schizophrenia—particularly young ones—a better chance to live high-functioning lives. In 2008, the National Institute of Mental Health launched a research initiative called RAISE (Recovery After an Initial Schizophrenia Episode), designed to explore the efficacy of certain kinds of early-intervention treatments. These types of treatments, known as Coordinated Specialty Care (CSC) treatments and supports, comprise a combination of tools, including case management, medication and primary care, cognitive-behavioral therapy, family education and assistance, and supported employment and education. Introducing this holistic approach to treatment takes into account a greater variety of factors that improve the odds for recovery. And, unlike in many other types of first-episode psychosis intervention, clients are encouraged to help guide their own treatment—thus contributing to higher rates of compliance and a greater sense of autonomy. Feeling some degree of control over their lives is particularly important for a population of people who are vulnerable to having none. As Dr. Lisa Dixon, director of OnTrackNY, told the New York Times, "We wanted to reinvent treatment so that it was something people actually want."

After the RAISE initiative determined that CSC treatment improved outcomes for people in the early stages of schizophrenia, early psychosis intervention programs began to appear around the country. As of 2016, such programs existed in thirty-seven states. At Stanford, the Prodrome and Early Psychosis Program Network started in 2014; in San Francisco, where I live, the Prevention and Recovery in Early Psychosis Network also addresses first-episode psychosis. Many provide services free of charge.

"Yet you *look* very put-together," Dr. M told me. I'd told her that, as a part of therapy, I was working on improving my hygiene. Showering became a challenge shortly after I began to hallucinate in college; my first experience with hearing voices occurred when a phantasm in the dorm showers intoned, "I hate you." This might have unnerved me enough to make me anxious about showering forever after. But because I care about my appearance, because I used to be a fashion blogger and writer, because I worked, for a time, at a fashion magazine and then as a fashion editor at a start-up company, I pass for normal more easily than do my comrades in the schizophrenias. When I browse the virtual aisles of La Garçonne, I am considering a uniform for a battle with multiple fronts. If schizophrenia is the domain of the slovenly, I stand outside of its boundaries as a straight-backed ingenue, and there is no telltale smearing beyond the borders of my mouth.

To some degree, the brilliant facade of a good face and a good outfit protects me. My sickness is rarely obvious. I don't have to tell new people in my life about it unless I want to. Although I no longer fret about when to disclose my psychiatric condition, I'm still aware of the shift that occurs when it happens. At a writers' residency, one woman responded to my disclosure with "I'm surprised to hear that. You don't seem to have those . . . tics and things." I reflexively smiled at this backhanded compliment. I suspect that she found comfort in being able to place me in a category separate from my brethren whose limbs and faces jerk from tardive dyskinesia, a horrific side effect of antipsychotic use that remains even if the medication is stopped. At a literary party, a wealthy patron who knew of my diagnosis told me that I should be proud of how coherent I am. In both anecdotes, I thanked the well-meaning women involved.

There are shifts according to any bit of information I dole out. Some are slight. Some tilt the ground we stand on. I can talk about the fact that I went to Yale and Stanford; that my parents are Taiwanese immigrants; that I was born in the Midwest and raised in California; that I am a writer. If the conversation winds its way to my diagnosis, I emphasize my normalcy. See my ordinary, even superlative appearance! Witness the fact that I am articulate. Rewind our interaction and see if you can spot cracks in the facade. See if you can, in sifting through your memory, find hints of insanity to make sense of what I've said about who I am. After all, what kind of lunatic has a fashionable pixie cut, wears red lipstick, dresses in pencil skirts and tucked-in silk blouses? What sort of psychotic wears Loeffler Randall heels without tottering?

My trajectory as a fashion writer began in 2007 with a blog called *Fashion for Writers (FFW)*. At the time, big-name bloggers such as Susie Bubble, a.k.a. Susanna Lau, were developing cachet with the *Devil Wears Prada* old guard—Susie once even included *FFW* in her "blog roll" of links—which seemed to gesture toward the democratization of a historically elite industry. I could not afford the high-end stylings of Jane Aldridge, the wealthy Texan behind *Sea of Shoes*, but I had enough pocket money for 1930s dresses from Etsy and an enormous white faux-fur coat that earned me the nickname "Abominable Snowman" in graduate school. The oldest *FFW* posts, created while I was still a lab manager, mixed inane style commentary (e.g., pontificating on the return of pussy-bow secretary blouses) and clumsy "outfit of the day" photos taken with my digital camera propped up on books and, eventually, locked onto a cheap tripod.

In graduate school I invited a college friend, fellow writer and clotheshorse Jenny Zhang, to join *FFW*. We were both Chinese American, twentysomething women working to get our MFAs in blindingly white Midwestern towns, and Jenny, who had majored in ethnic studies, aimed the blog in a more political, and more interesting, direction. Eventually, Jenny took over *FFW* entirely before ending it in favor of greener pastures. Meanwhile, I moved on to work at a dubiously operated fashion and lifestyle magazine before settling in at a start-up that sold and produced vintage-inspired fashion, where I honed my copywriting chops and editing skills as I finished my debut novel. I sank my discretionary income from the start-up job into vintage, ultrafeminine silk chiffon and georgette and organdy dresses the color of candy floss, adorned with bows and tied up with satin ribbons; for a while, my Twitter profile read, "Taiwanese American. Weaponized glamour," the latter being a reference to Chaédria LaBouvier's work on the concept of "using beauty and style in direct, political ways that subvert dehumanizing expectations." Her thoughts on weaponized glamour are perhaps best known in her writing about Chimamanda Ngozi Adichie; Adichie, as a black woman author who writes about politics, who is dark-skinned and a feminist, is not an expected model of beauty to some, but is defiantly glamorous nonetheless.

I went to the Alexander McQueen exhibit *Savage Beauty* at the Met in 2011 because it was a significant occasion for people in the fashion industry, however peripheral. *Savage Beauty* reflected art as madness, darkness, beauty, death. McQueen's 2010 suicide hung over everything, throwing long shadows on the walls and the dresses. He'd ended his life not long after the death of his mother, and then the death of his friend Isabella Blow.

The piece that most beguiled and frightened me was a blank-faced, pure-white mannequin in a suit of inky feathers. In this ensemble, plumage forms massive shoulders that could be wings; the body displays a nipped, severe waist. There is nothing charming about this aviary costume. Encounter this creature in the shadows, and death has surely come to claim you. McQueen said about his clothing, "I want to empower women. I want people to be afraid of the women I dress," which is another truth about fashioning normalcy: the way I clothe myself is not merely camouflage. It is an intimidation tactic, as with the porcupine who shows its quills, or the owl that puffs its body in a defensive offensive: *dress like everyone should be terrified of you.*

And yet there are things that good costuming can't hide. For one season, I saw shadowy demons darting at me from all angles, and I couldn't control my response, which was to jump to the side or duck or startle at things that no one else could see. If I was with someone, I'd pretend afterward that nothing had happened, and usually my companion or companions who knew of my diagnosis would generously pretend that I hadn't just ducked, rather dramatically, for no reason. But I was mortified. It didn't matter how pulled-together I seemed when I was dodging specters that no one else could see. I knew that I looked crazy, and that no amount of snappy dressing could conceal the dodging. Because such movements were a necessary concession to my craziness, I responded by trying even harder to seem normal when I wasn't being assailed by hallucinations. I went dancing. I drank Jameson on the rocks and ate potato skins in Irish bars and pizza joints. I did all the normal things I could think of.

At the Chinatown clinic, I was led downstairs into a different room to give a second talk. This one was brighter, cleaner, and clearly the clinicians' domain. A water cooler stood burbling in one corner. The tables had been moved to flank the walls, allowing space for an assembly of folding chairs in the middle. The clinicians begin to wander in—men and women in business casual who found seats and stared into the middle distance. There was one man who sat in the back and actively scowled; his face read, *I can't believe I have to come to this goddamn thing*. He made me nervous, but it was also true that all of them, even the friendly-seeming ones, made me nervous.

Being faced with this many clinicians took me back to my first psychiatric hospitalization, when a battalion of psychiatrists, social workers, and psychologists made their daily rounds throughout the unit to interrogate us about how we were doing. The flock of officious questioners stopped by when I was sitting on the threadbare sofa near the television, or listlessly pushing around puzzle pieces at a table. Rarely did I experience such a radical and visceral imbalance of power as I did as a psychiatric inpatient amid clinicians who knew me only as illness in human form. During that first hospitalization, I learned that clinicians control when inpatients are granted privileges, such as being able to go downstairs for meals or outside to smoke for ten minutes twice a day. Most important, it was my team of clinicians who decided when I could go home. I became accustomed to playacting for the benefit of doctors: *Look! I'm happy! I'm fine!* In response to "Are you thinking about hurting yourself or others?" there was only one proper answer, which, regardless of what I said, was always followed by suspicious, persistent questioning. Knowing that it was time for me to talk about being crazy in front of a group of such people, even as a free woman, ratcheted up the rhythm of my already frantic heart.

When it was my turn to speak, I tried to sound eloquent. I slid "avolition" back into the talk. I emphasized, again, my education. I played up the entrepreneurship, mentioning the digital products I'd built and the clients I'd worked with. I added an extra bit of information about my time as a lab manager, when I was the head of a multisite study about bipolar disorder, and made weekly visits to the Stanford Department of Psychology's respected Bipolar Disorders Clinic as a researcher and not as a patient. The Bipolar Disorders Clinic is one of the best of its kind in the country, and I briefly wondered if these clinicians would even be able to find work there, which was a defensive and sour thought. All this posturing reads as paranoia, and even unkindness, toward the professionals who came to the clinic, who were not making as much money as, say, a psychiatrist at the Bipolar Disorders Clinic, and who did this good work because they'd been called to do it.

I finished my talk. No one was crying. the scowling man was still scowling, but less aggressively so.

As I sank back into my folding chair, Patricia asked if there were any comments or questions. A bespectacled woman raised her hand. She said that she was grateful for this reminder that her patients are human too. She starts out with such hope, she said, every time a new patient comes—and then they relapse and return, relapse and return. the clients, or patients, exhibit their illness in ways that prevent them from seeming like people who can dream, or like people who can have others dream for them. When she said this, I was fingering the skirt of my exquisite dress. I'd fooled her, or convinced her. Either way, I knew, was a victory.

The Work of Human Hands

Fiona Wright

It has taken me five months to sew my most recent piece of clothing, not counting the days, at some point last year, that I spent tracing off the pattern onto a huge roll of architect's paper unfurled across my living room floor. Five months, and six and a half metres of fabric. Five full spools of sewing thread and three machine needles, worn through. I didn't hurry, in part because I couldn't: I was working with organza, a delicate and slippery fabric, which is prone to distortion when cutting, and to pulling and sliding under the needle. It also frays at the slightest provocation – it is a nightmare, but a very beautiful one.

I also didn't hurry because I didn't have to.

It has taken me five months to sew a single top. Phrased like this, it sounds ridiculous: I could normally whip out a simple blouse, a shirt over two or three evenings at the most. And all I can offer as qualification is to say that it is *quite* a top. It is a panelled blouse – five self-lined pieces for the front, six at the back – with buttons down the spine, and short puff sleeves, elasticated at their lower hems. Most importantly, it is covered in flounces – four long bodice flounces, crossing over the shoulder seam and spilling out between the panels; one circular flounce sewn into each armscye, and four glorious rows of flounces running around and around the width of each ball-shaped sleeve. The effect of them is wonderful: the slim fit of the bodice seems to burst out at the shoulders, exploding into layers of ruffled curves, all of which bob and bounce with any movement. Business at the front and party at the sides, I exclaimed to my English-born girlfriend, who didn't get the joke.

Every time I tried it on, as a work-in-progress, anyone who was nearby couldn't help but say, *but where are you going to wear it?*

To the corner store, I'd say, or to pick up the step-kids from school. What I was really saying, of course, is *I don't care.*

I had never sewn a flounce before, let alone one from such unforgiving fabric. A flounce is counter intuitive as a pattern piece, as a piece of fabric: it is perfectly round, with a much smaller circular hole in the centre. Doughnut-shaped, essentially. It is slit in one place, from the outside to inside circle, then hemmed along the outside edge (I swear I spent four of the last five months folding, pressing, trimming and stitching hems). And then it is opened out, pulled straight – its wonderful waving curls unfurl when the inside curve is stretched out to lie linearly, and the larger outside volume must fan out to compensate. It's a simple principle, but it still feels remarkable: a transformation.

All fabric work is transformation. A single filament, a fibre of flax or wool or polymer, is spun into a thread. A thread is woven or knotted to become a piece of cloth. And this piece of cloth is sewn into an object, into something protective, decorative, useful, worn. It becomes a tool in its own right. It is an alchemy, of the quietest, most domestic kind.

I am telling you about my five-month top because I have never worked so intricately and for so long on a single piece of clothing, and because I know the time I spent on it is tied up in how ridiculously delighted I am by the result. I didn't keep track of my hours of sewing, a few on most weekday evenings, an afternoon or two each weekend. I didn't try to quantify them in any way – but they are remembered in the garment. Some of them visible – the doubled lines of tiny stitches, the four-step buttonholes – and many of them not: the temporary tacking together of the doubled layers of the bodice, the pinning and pressing, the basting in of the sleeves. When I wear the top, the work of my body upon my body, it sometimes feels like it is this labour, more than anything else, that I'm displaying.

And I am telling about my five-month top because in the final days of its construction, when all that was left was to sew up the hem and on the buttons (both done by hand), some algorithm whirring away within my browser started trying to sell me a many-ruffled shirt, for less than fifteen dollars, with shipping free.

It is one thing, I think, to know about the horror of fast fashion, in an abstract, however well-meaning or -feeling way. To know about its dependence on exploitative work in awful, dehumanising conditions, about the worst of its retailers that notoriously add a full thousand new products to their range each day. It is one thing to have a sense of the human cost of its low prices and high speed, to know that you are unavoidably bound up in its system in whatever small or large way. But to encounter it like this, with those hours of work still unfolding in my fingers, hit me differently and anew.

I am, and have always been, resistant to thinking of my sewing as resistance, largely because it is not political in its motivations. I sew for the pleasure of it, for the satisfaction and pride that comes each time I learn or figure out something new; each time that transformation happens before my eyes, and by my own hands. I sew because it is expressive: this fabric, in these shapes, to dress my body, a display. And I sew because it is a kind of dignity – most of the garments that I make are for myself or for my girlfriend, and both of us inhabit bodies that are wildly deviant, in the mathematic sense of the term. It has felt powerful, to self-determine our clothing's fit.

All of these things, though – pleasure and leisure, expression and even (especially?) dignity – they are always political, in who has access to them, and in the shapes they take.

I don't know how to think about my sewing, which I find meaningful and which I love, within its context in the wider world.

Sewing is still, even at its most massive, industrial scale, necessarily human work. This is because, as Sofi Thanhauser argues, fabric is unusual and difficult material: it is 'fussy and unpredictable', it stretches and shifts, and it comes in a wide range of textures and weights – some flimsy, some stiff, some slippery or stubbled or sticky – all of which require a specific kind of attention and handling.[1] It is, in this regard, unlike any other industrial material, all of which are engineered to behave consistently, mechanically. Even at industrial scale, sewing requires what Thanhauser calls 'the subtle manipulation of tension that can only be done by a real human hand.'[2]

And yet, industrial sewing is an utterly estranged kind of labour. A person sewing in a clothing factory – even of the least exploitative kind – will attend to one isolated process in the chain of production – sewing the same seam, for example, over and over, on thousands of identical garments. (My own mother once worked in this way in a jeans factory, tasked with sewing in the zippers, just zipper after zipper, right across the day. I hate inserting zippers and sometimes suspect this is inherited.) One repeated task, isolated and without the meaning of the whole – without any of the pleasures and reward of seeing and feeling each small task accrue to something more. This is to say nothing, of course, about the crowded, unventilated and fire-prone buildings in which this happens, the industrial poisons workers are exposed to, the long hours, impossible quotas and unliveable pay. It is to say nothing about the fact that most garment workers are women and children of colour, and liable to be fired and blacklisted or detained should they advocate for conditions even a little more humane.

My sewing is as different from this as it is possible to be, and I don't know how to reconcile this. What it can possibly mean that the self-same act that brings me so much joy imprisons and demeans so many others. My sewing is not resistance – it is a luxury. And luxury, too, is always political.

There's a German clothing brand whose machinists all work with their hands dipped in black dye. They sew white fabric into shirts, jeans, jackets, the dye transferring at every place that they touch. Each piece is slightly different in its mottled patterning, some streaky with the imprints of fingers, others blotchy from the press of entire hands. In some, the jackets and jeans especially, very few white patches remain; in all, the dye is darkest on the areas of fiddly detail – lapels and collars, waistbands, armscyes, the reinforced crotch seams of jeans. It's not just the work that is made visible in these garments – every touch, every pinch, every press – but also the strange intimacy of making clothes. It is, after all, against these intimate, touch-sensitive parts of the body – neck, belly, armpit, groin – that the most-handled pieces of fabric will press.

It is, of course, an intervention. A reminder of the invisible human labour that goes into making clothes, all the more evident in the range's knock-offs (for want of a better word) of common touristic garments – white t-shirts, printed with a picture of the Brandenburg Gate and the word *Berlin* in huge banner-like font beneath it. Blackened with fingerprints, especially around the neck, it is impossible to think of these objects as benign.

I realised recently that the very first factories – still novel enough a phenomenon to be called *manufactories* – were all designed in the service of textile production. So, too, some of the first industrial machines – the spinning jenny and flying shuttle, which mechanised spinning and weaving, respectively, then the water frame and spinning mule, which harnessed hydraulic power for these processes. (I have a friend who, whenever we are bemoaning the forces and impact of capitalism on our lives, always proclaims, *it's all the fault of the spinning jenny!*)

It was in these factories, too, that labour first came to be quantified by time – where a spinner or weaver was paid according to the hours spent at their task, rather than their output, and where a working day was thereby untethered from the work at hand, no longer finishing whenever the task was complete. And where our idea of time became so closely tied to monetary value to the point where we now find it difficult to envision a kind of time that isn't 'spent' or 'saved' or 'wasted' or 'invested', or where using five months of it to make a single top is anything other than ludicrous.

In a contemporary sewing factory, a worker is expected to sew around 100 of their individual seams each hour. It is expected that a T-shirt will be made, complete, in three minutes and 43 seconds.[3] It is an intensity of time, and of labour, that I find difficult to fathom.

What I love most about sewing does not and cannot happen under these conditions. It is not the individual tasks themselves, the cutting of fabric, stitching of seams, the folding and tacking, that bring me so much pleasure, but the way that these tasks accrue, the way they build upon each other to transform a flat piece of cloth into something three-dimensional and architectural. The construction of clothing is constantly surprising: one piece, layered then flipped, is suddenly an in-panel pocket; a series of long panels turned sideways and joined are suddenly a batwing sleeve. It often seems illogical until the fabric is twisted or turned out, and then it suddenly makes sense. It often feels like a strange magic, this metamorphosis happening beneath my hands.

I have felt this most on the few garments I have made for which I drafted the pattern myself – a skill I'm still in the early stages of learning. With these the transformation feels total: you begin with nothing more than a set of numbers – your body's measurements, a few equations – and a pencil and piece of paper. You start with next to nothing, and finish with a shirt, a skirt, a pair of pants, zipped or buttoned up against your body (and specifically fitted to it). We have so few opportunities to work like this anymore, to start with the most basic of materials and build something intricate and beautiful – and practical – through every step, from there. So few opportunities for unalienated work, body and mind engaged together, the whole process ours and ours alone. This too is a luxury.

When all that is valued is speed, and with it, productivity, we lose the possibilities of making other meanings. We lose the alchemy, the magic – and we lose any sense of mastery, which is one of the greatest satisfactions I have found in learning to properly sew. It takes time to develop new skills and new dexterities, to think and to learn. And even more importantly, it takes time to play. Perhaps, instead, it is this that I am displaying when I wear my five-month top: my playfulness, what I have learned, and the pleasure I have found while doing so.

Wisgaak Gokpenagen: A Black Ash Basket

Robin Wall Kimmerer

Doonk, doonk, doonk. Silence. *Doonk, doonk, doonk.*

The back of the ax meets the log to make a hollow music. It drops three times on one spot and then John's eyes shift a fraction down the log, where he strikes again. *Doonk, doonk, doonk.* As he raises the ax above his head, his hands slide apart on the upstroke, then together on the down, shoulders pulling tight under his chambray shirt, his thin braid jumping with every impact. All the way down the log he pounds triplets of crushing blows.

Straddling the end of the log, he works his fingers under a split in the cut end and gives it a tug. Slow and steady, he peels off a strip of wood the width of the ax head in a thick ribbon. He takes up the ax and pounds another few feet. *Doonk, doonk, doonk.* Again he grasps the base of the strip and peels it back along the pounded line, taking the log apart strip by strip. By the time he pounds the last few feet, he has worked off an eight-foot splint of gleaming white wood. He holds it to his nose to breathe in the goodness of new wood and passes it around for us all to see. John coils it into a neat hoop, ties it fast, and hangs it on a nearby tree branch. "Your turn," he says and hands off the ax.

My teacher this warm summer day is John Pigeon, a member of the large, renowned Pigeon family of Potawatomi basket makers. Since that first initiation to pounding a log, I'm grateful to have sat in on black ash basket classes with several generations of the extended family of Pigeons—Steve, Kitt, Ed, Stephanie, Pearl, Angie, and more, children and grandchildren—with splints in their hands. All gifted basket makers, carriers of culture, and generous teachers. The log is a good teacher, too.

It's harder than it looks, making the ax repeat its pattern evenly down the log. Too much impact in one spot will break the fibers; too little and the strip won't fully break free, leaving a thin spot. Each of us beginners works differently, some with sharp strokes from overhead, some with dull thudding as if we were hammering nails. The sound changes with the pounder: a high ringing note like the call of wild geese, a bark like a startled coyote's, the muffled thumping of a drumming grouse.

When John was a kid the sound of log pounding was heard all through the community. Walking home from school, he could tell who was out working by the sound of their swing. Uncle Chester was a hard, fast *crack, crack, crack*. From across the hedgerow he could hear Grandma Bell's slow *thuds* separated by long pauses while she caught her breath. But now the village grows quieter and quieter as elders walk on and kids seem more interested in video games than in tromping through the swamp. So John Pigeon teaches any who will come, to pass on what he's learned from his elders and the trees.

John is both a master basket maker and a carrier of tradition. Pigeon family baskets can be found in the Smithsonian and other museums and galleries around the world. But they are also available here, at the family's booth at the annual Potawatomi Gathering of Nations. Their table is loaded with colorful baskets, no two alike. There are fancy baskets the size of a bird's nest, gathering baskets, potato baskets, corn-washing baskets. His whole family weaves, and no one at the Gathering wants to go home without a Pigeon basket. I save up each year for one.

Like the rest of the family, John is also a master teacher, committed to sharing what has been passed on by generations who came before. What was given to him, he now gives back to the people. Some basket classes I've taken start with a neat pile of materials, all assembled on a clean table. But John doesn't hold with teaching basket weaving where the splints come ready made—he teaches basket *making*, beginning with a living tree.

Black Ash (*Fraxinus nigra*) likes to have its feet wet. In floodplain forests and edges of swamps, black ash mingles with red maples, elms, and willows. It is never the most common tree—you only find it in scattered patches—so it can take a long day of tromping over boot-sucking ground to find the right tree. Scanning a wet forest, you can pick out the black ash by its bark. You pass by maples with bark of rigid gray plates, the braided corky ridges of elm, the deeply furrowed willows, and instead seek out the fine pattern of interlocked ridges and warty knobs of black ash. The knobs feel spongy under your fingertips when you give them a squeeze. There are other species of ash growing in the swamp, so it's good to check the leaves overhead as well. All ashes—green, white, blue, pumpkin, and black—have compound leaves borne opposite one another on stout, corky twigs.

And yet it's not enough to simply find black ash; it has to be the right one—a tree ready to be a basket. An ideal basket ash has a straight, clear bole with no branches in the lower trunk. Branches make knots that interrupt the straight grain of the splint. A good tree is about a handbreadth across, the crown full and vigorous, a healthy tree. A tree that has grown directly up toward the sun will be straight and fine grained, while those that have wandered a bit to find the light show twists and turns in the grain. Some basket makers will choose only trees perched on a hummock in the swamp, while others will avoid a black ash growing next to a cedar.

Trees are affected by their sapling days as much as people are by their childhoods. The history of a tree appears in its growth rings, of course. Good years yield a wide ring, poor years a thin one, and the pattern of rings is critical to the process of basket making.

Growth rings are formed by the cycle of the seasons, by the waking and resting of the fragile layer of cells that lies between the bark and the newest wood, the cambium. Peel away the bark and you feel the cambium's slippery wetness. The cells of the cambium are perpetually embryonic, always dividing to add to the girth of the tree. In the spring, when the buds detect the lengthening of the days and the sap starts to rise, the cambium grows cells made for feast days, big, wide-mouthed tubes to carry the abundant water leafward. These lines of large vessels are what you count to determine a tree's age. They grow quickly and so their walls tend to be thin. Wood scientists call this part of the annual ring springwood or early wood. When spring turns to summer, nutrients and water become scarce and the cambium produces smaller, thicker cells for leaner times. These densely packed cells are called late wood or summerwood. When the days shorten and leaves fall, the cambium settles in for a winter's rest and stops dividing altogether. But as soon as spring is imminent, the cambium once again bursts into action, making large springwood cells. The abrupt transition between the last year's small-celled late wood and the early wood of spring creates the appearance of a line, a growth ring.

John has developed a practiced eye for these things. But sometimes, just to be sure, he'll unsheathe his knife and cut out a wedge for a look at the rings. John prefers a tree in the range of thirty to forty growth rings, each ring as wide as a nickel. When he's found the right one, the harvest begins. Not with a saw, though, but rather with a conversation.

Traditional harvesters recognize the individuality of each tree as a person, a nonhuman forest person. Trees are not taken, but requested. Respectfully, the cutter explains his purpose and the tree is asked permission for harvest.

Sometimes the answer is no. It might be a cue in the surroundings—a vireo nest in the branches, or the bark's adamant resistance to the questioning knife—that suggests a tree is not willing, or it might be the ineffable knowing that turns him away. If consent is granted, a prayer is made and tobacco is left as a reciprocating gift. The tree is felled with great care so as not to damage it or others in the fall. Sometimes a cutter will make a bed of spruce boughs to cushion the landing of the tree. When they finish, John and his son hoist the log to their shoulders and begin the long walk home.

John and his extended family make a lot of baskets. His mother prefers to pound her own log, although he and the boys will often do it when her arthritis is bothering her. They'll weave all year round, but there are certain seasons for the best harvest. It's a good idea to pound a log soon after harvest, while it is still moist, although John says you can bury a log in a trench covered with damp earth to keep it fresh. His favorite times are spring—when "the sap is rising and the energy of the earth is flowing into the tree"—and fall, "when the energy is flowing back to the ground."

Today, John scales away the spongy bark, which would deflect the power of the ax, and gets to work. When he pulls the edge of the first strip, you can see what's happening: Beating the log crushes the thin-walled cells of the early wood, breaking them down and separating them from the late wood. The log fractures at the dividing line between springwood and summer, so the strip that peels off is the wood between annual rings.

Depending on the individual history of the tree and its pattern of rings, a strip might come off carrying the wood of five years or sometimes just one. Every tree is different, but as the basket makers pound and peel, he is always moving back through time. The tree's life is coming off in his hands, layer by layer. As the hoops of splint grow more numerous, the log itself grows smaller and within hours is a skinny pole. "See," John shows us, "we've stripped all the way back to the time it was a sapling." He gestures to the big pile of splint we've accumulated. "Don't ever forget that. It's the whole life of that tree you've got piled up there."

The long strips of wood vary in thickness, so the next step is splitting the strip into its component layers, further separating the annual rings. Thick splints are needed for a big laundry hamper or a trapper's pack basket. The finest fancy baskets use only a ribbon of less than one year's wood. From the back of his new white pickup, John pulls out his splitters: two pieces of wood joined with a clamp to make what looks like a giant clothespin. He sits on the edge of his chair and holds the splitter between his knees so its open legs are on the ground and the peaked end rises from his lap. He threads a full eight- foot length of splint up through the clamp and fastens it there with an inch or so protruding. He flicks open his knife and wedges the blade into the cut end of the strip, wiggling it along the growth ring to open a cut. His brown hands grasp either side of the cut and he pulls them apart in a smooth motion, yielding strips as smooth and even as two long blades of grass.

"That's all there is to it," he says, but there's laughter in his eyes as they meet mine. I thread the splint, try to balance the splitter steady between my thighs, and then make the cut that will start the split. I discover quickly that you need to grip the splitter hard between your legs—something I can barely manage. "Yup," John laughs, "this is an old Indian invention—the thigh master!" By the time I'm through, my splint looks like a chipmunk has been gnawing on the end. John is a patient teacher, but he won't do it for me. He just smiles, smartly severs my frayed end, and says, "Try it again." Eventually I get two sides that I can pull, but they're uneven and my pulling yields only a twelve-inch splinter, thin on one side, thick on the other. John circles among us, offering encouragement. He has learned everyone's name and picked up something of what each one of us needs. Some he joshes about their weak biceps, others he pats warmly on the shoulder. With the frustrated he sits gently alongside and says, "Don't try so hard. Be easier on yourself." For others, he just pulls the strip and gives it to them. He's as good a judge of people as he is of trees.

"This tree's a good teacher," he says. "That's what we've always been taught. The work of being a human is finding balance, and making splints will not let you forget it."

When you get the hang of it, the splint pulls apart evenly, the inner faces of the splint unexpectedly beautiful: glossy and warm, they catch the light like a ribbon of cream satin. The outer surface is uneven and roughened with splintered ends that leave long "hairs."

"You need a very sharp knife now," he says. "I have to use the whetstone every day. And it's awfully easy to cut yourself." John hands each of us a "leg," cut from worn blue jeans, and shows us how to lay the double thickness of denim over our left thighs. "Deerskin is really the best thing to use," he says, "if you've got some lying around. But blue jeans work fine. Just be careful." He sits with us individually to demonstrate, for the difference between success and bloodshed is a small degree in the angle of the knife and the pressure of the hand. He lays the strip across his thigh, rough side up, and sets the knife edge against it. With his other hand, he draws the strip out from beneath the knife in a continuous motion like a skate blade skimming over ice. The shavings gather on the knife as the strip pulls by. The result is a polished surface. This too he makes look easy. I've seen Kitt Pigeon pull satiny strips as if she were pulling ribbon from a spool, but my knife snags and I end up cutting gouges instead of planing it smooth. The angle of my knife is too sharp and I cut right through, rendering a long pretty strip into a scrap.

"You're about up to a loaf of bread," John says, shaking his head when I ruin yet another piece. "That's what my mother would say when we spoiled splints." Basket making was and is the livelihood of the Pigeon family. In their grandfather's time the lake, woods, and gardens gave them most of their food and other provisions, but at times they also needed store goods, and baskets were the cash crop that bought bread, canned peaches, and school shoes. Spoiled splints were like food thrown away. Depending on the size and design, a black ash basket can sell for good money. "People get a little mad when they see the prices," John says. "People think it's 'just' basket weaving, but 80 percent of the work comes long before you weave. With finding the tree, pounding and pulling, and all, you barely make minimum wage."

With splints finally prepared, we're poised for weaving—what we had mistakenly thought was the real work of a basket. But John stops the class, his gentle voice gaining a hard edge. "You've missed the most important thing," he says. "Look around you." We look—at the forest, at the camp, at each other. "At the *ground!*" he says. In a circle around each novice is a litter of scraps. "Stop and think what you're holding. That ash tree was growing out there in that swamp for thirty years, putting out leaves, dropping them, putting out more. It got eaten by deer, hit by a freeze, but it kept working year in and year out, laying down those rings of wood. A splint fallen on the ground is a whole year of that tree's life and you're about to step on it, bend it, grind it into the dirt? That tree honored you with its life. There's no shame in messing up a splint; you're just learning. But whatever you do, you owe that tree respect and should never waste it." And so he guides us as we sort through the debris we've made. Short strips go into a pile for small baskets and decoration. The miscellaneous bits and shavings get tossed into a box to be dried and used for tinder. John keeps to the tradition of the Honorable Harvest: take only what you need and use everything you take.

His words echo what I've often heard from my folks. They grew up during the Depression, with the imperative not to waste, and there were certainly no scraps on the floor then. But "use it up, wear it out, make it do, or do without" is an ethic both economical and ecological. The waste of splints both dishonors the tree and diminishes the household budget.

Just about everything we use is the result of another's life, but that simple reality is rarely acknowledged in our society. The ash curls we make are almost paper thin. They say that the "waste stream" in this country is dominated by paper. Just as much as an ash splint, a sheet of paper is a tree's life, along with the water and energy and toxic byproducts that went into making it. And yet we use it as if it were nothing. The short path from mailbox to waste bin tells the story. But what would happen, I wonder, to the mountain of junk mail if we could see in it the trees it once had been? If John was there to remind us of the worthiness of their lives?

In some parts of the range, basket makers began to observe a decline in the numbers of black ash. They worried that overharvesting might be to blame, a decline caused by too much attention for the baskets in the marketplace and too little for their sources in the woods. My graduate student Tom Touchet and I decided to investigate. We began by analyzing the population structure of black ashes around us in New York State, to understand where in the trees' life cycle the difficulty might lie. In every swamp we visited, we counted all the black ash we could find and wrapped a tape around them to get their size. Tom cored a few in every site to check their ages. In stand after stand, Tom found that there were old trees and seedlings, but hardly any trees in between. There was a big hole in the demographic census. He found plenty of seeds, plenty of young seedlings, but most of the next age class—the saplings, the future of the forest—were dead or missing.

There were only two places where he found an abundance of adolescent trees. One was in gaps in the forest canopy, where disease or a windstorm had brought down a few old trees, letting light through. Curiously enough, he found that where Dutch elm disease had killed off elms, black ash was replacing them in a balance between loss of one species and gain of another. To make the transition from seedling to tree, the young black ash needed an opening. If they remained in full shade they would die.

The other place where saplings were thriving was near communities of basket makers. Where the tradition of black ash basketry was alive and well, so were the trees. We hypothesized that the apparent decline in ash trees might be due not to overharvesting but to *underharvesting*. When communities echoed with *Doonk, doonk, doonk*, there were plenty of basket makers in the woods, creating gaps where the light would reach the seedlings and the young trees could shoot to the canopy and become adults. In places where the basket makers disappeared, or were few, the forest didn't get opened up enough for black ash to flourish.

Black ash and basket makers are partners in a symbiosis between harvesters and harvested: ash relies on people as the people rely on ash. Their fates are linked.

The Pigeons' teaching of this linkage is part of a growing movement to revive traditional basketry, tied to the revitalization of indigenous lands, language, culture, and philosophies. All over Turtle Island, Native peoples are leading a resurgence in traditional knowledge and lifeways that nearly disappeared under the pressures of newcomers. But just as the revival of ash basketry is gaining strength, it is being threatened by yet another invading species.

John sends us off for a break, a cool drink, and a stretch for tired fingers. "You need a clear mind for the next part," he says. As we mill about, shaking out the cramps in our necks and hands, John gives us each a U.S. Department of Agriculture pamphlet with a photo of a shiny green beetle on the cover. "If you care about ash trees," he says, "you'd better pay attention. They're under attack."

The emerald ash borer, introduced from China, lays its eggs in tree trunks. After the larvae hatch, they chew up the cambium until they pupate, when the beetle bores its way out of the tree and flies off to find a new nursery. But wherever it lands, it is inevitably fatal for the infested trees. Unfortunately for the people of the Great Lakes region and New England, the beetle's favorite host is ash. Today there is a quarantine on moving logs and firewood in an effort to contain their spread, but the insect is moving faster than scientists predicted.

"So, be on the lookout," John says. "We have to protect our trees, that's our job." When he and his family are harvesting logs in the fall, they take special care to gather up fallen seeds and spread them around as they move through the wetlands. "It's like anything else," he reminds us. "You can't take something without giving back. This tree takes care of us, so we have to take care of it."

Already, vast areas of ash in Michigan have died; beloved basket grounds are now boneyards of barkless trees. There is a rupture in the chain of relationship that stretches back through time immemorial. The swamp where the Pigeons have gathered and cared for black ash for generations is now infested. Angie Pigeon writes, "Our trees are all gone. I don't know if there will be any more baskets." To most people, an invasive species represents losses in a landscape, the empty spaces to be filled by something else. To those who carry the responsibility of an ancient relationship, the empty niche means empty hands and a hole in the collective heart.

Now, when so many trees have fallen and the tradition passed on by generations is at risk, the Pigeons work to protect both trees and the tradition. They are partnering with forest scientists to resist the insect and to adapt to its aftermath. There are reweavers among us.

John and his family are not alone in their efforts to protect the black ash. At Akwesasne, a Mohawk reserve that straddles the border between New York State and Canada, black ash has yet more guardians. Over the past three decades, Les Benedict, Richard David, and Mike Bridgen have led an effort to bring traditional ecological knowledge as well as scientific tools to bear in the protection of black ash. They have grown thousands of black ash seedlings to give away to indigenous communities throughout the region. Les even convinced the New York State Tree Nursery to grow them for planting in places ranging from school yards to Superfund sites. Thousands had already been planted in resurgent forests, in resurgent communities, just as the ash borer appeared on our shores.

As the threat wings its way closer to their homelands every fall, Les and his colleagues gather the willing to collect the best seeds they can find, storing seed to keep faith with the future, to replant the forest after the wave of invasion has passed. Every species needs its Les Benedict, its Pigeon family, its allies and protectors. Many of our traditional teachings recognize that certain species are our helpers and guides. The Original Instructions remind us that we must return the favor. It is an honor to be the guardian of another species—an honor within each person's reach that we too often forget. A Black Ash basket is a gift that reminds us of the gifts of other beings, gifts we can gratefully return through advocacy and care.

John calls us back to the circle for the next step: assembling the bottom of the basket. We're doing a traditional round bottom, so the first two strips are laid out at right angles in a symmetrical cross. Easy. "Now take a look at what you've done," John says. "You've started with the four directions in front of you. It's the heart of your basket. Everything else is built around that." Our people honor the four sacred directions and the powers resident there. Where the two basket strips meet, at the intersection of those four directions, is right where we stand as humans, trying to find balance among them. "See there," John says, "every thing we do in life is sacred. The four directions are what we build on. That's why we start like that."

Once the eight spokes of the framework are twined into place with the thinnest possible strips, each basket begins to grow. We look to John for the next set of instructions, but there are none. He says, "You're on your own now. The design of the basket is up to you. No one can tell you what to create." We have thick and thin splints to work with, and John shakes out a bag full of brightly dyed splints in every color. The tangled pile looks like the singing ribbons on the men's ribbon shirts in the evening powwows. "Just think of the tree and all its hard work before you start," he says. "It gave its life for this basket, so you know your responsibility. Make something beautiful in return."

Responsibility to the tree makes everyone pause before beginning. Sometimes I have that same sense when I face a blank sheet of paper. For me, writing is an act of reciprocity with the world; it is what I can give back in return for everything that has been given to me. And now there's another layer of responsibility, writing on a thin sheet of tree and hoping the words are worth it. Such a thought could make a person set down her pen.

The first two rows of the basket are the hardest. On the first go-round, the splint seems to have a will of its own and wants to wander from the over-under rhythm around the circle. It resists the pattern and looks all loose and wobbly. This is when John steps in to help, offering encouragement and a steady hand to anchor the escaping splints. The second row is almost as frustrating; the spacing is all wrong and you have to clamp the weaver in place to get it to stay. Even then, it comes loose and slaps you in the face with its wet end. John just laughs. It is a mess of unruly pieces, nothing like a whole. But then there's the third row—my favorite. At this point, the tension of over is balanced by the tension of under, and the opposing forces start to come into balance. The give and take—reciprocity—begins to take hold and the parts begin to become a whole. The weaving becomes easy as splints fall snugly into place. Order and stability emerge out of chaos.

In weaving well-being for land and people, we need to pay attention to the lessons of the three rows. Ecological well-being and the laws of nature are always the first row. Without them, there is no basket of plenty. Only if that first circle is in place can we weave the second. The second reveals material welfare, the subsistence of human needs. Economy built upon ecology. But with only two rows in place, the basket is still in jeopardy of pulling apart. It's only when the third row comes that the first two can hold together. Here is where ecology, economics, and spirit are woven together. By using materials as if they were a gift, and returning that gift through worthy use, we find balance. I think that third row goes by many names: Respect. Reciprocity. All Our Relations. I think of it as the spirit row. Whatever the name, the three rows represent recognition that our lives depend on one another, human needs being only one row in the basket that must hold us all. In relationship, the separate splints become a whole basket, sturdy and resilient enough to carry us into the future.

While we're working, a gaggle of little kids comes by to watch. John is pulled in many directions to help us all, but he stops and gives his full attention to the boys. They're too little to join in, but they want to be there, so he takes up a handful of the short strips from our debris. His hands, now deliberate and slow, bend and twist the strips until a few minutes later a little toy horse sits in the palm of his hand. He gives the boys some scraps, the model, and a few words in Potawatomi, but doesn't tell them how to make a horse. They're used to this kind of teaching and don't ask questions. They look and look some more and then set to work to figure it out. Before long, a herd of horses is galloping over the table and little boys are watching baskets grow.

Toward the end of the afternoon, in the lengthening shadows, the work table begins to fill with completed baskets. John helps us add the decorative curls that are traditional on small baskets. The black ash ribbons are so flexible that you can embroider the surface of the basket with loops and twists that show off the glossy sheen of the ash. We've made low round trays, tall thin vases, plump apple baskets in textures and colors of every kind. "Here's the last step," he says, handing out Sharpie markers. "You've got to sign your basket. Take pride in what you did. That basket didn't make itself. Claim it, mistakes and all." He makes us line up for a photograph, all holding our baskets. "This is a special occasion," he says, beaming like a proud father. "Look what you've learned today. I want you to see what the baskets have shown you. Every one of them is beautiful. Every one of them is different and yet every one of them began in the same tree. They are all made of the same stuff and yet each is itself. That's the way it is with our people, too, all made of the same thing and each their own kind of beautiful."

That night I see the powwow circle with new eyes. I notice that the cedar arbor sheltering the drums is supported by poles set in the four directions. The drum, the heartbeat, calls us out to dance. There is one beat, but each dancer has a distinctive step: dipping grass dancers, crouching buffalo dancers, the twirl of fancy shawl dancers, high-stepping jingle-dress girls, the dignified pace of the women's traditional dancers. Each man, each woman, each child, all dressed in their dreamed-of colors, ribbons flying, fringes swaying, all beautiful, all dancing to the heartbeat. Around the circle we go all night, together weaving a basket.

Today, my house is full of baskets and my favorites are Pigeons. In them I can hear John's voice, can hear the *doonk, doonk, doonk*, and smell the swamp. They remind me of the years of a tree's life that I hold in my hands. What would it be like, I wondered, to live with that heightened sensitivity to the lives given for ours? To consider the tree in the Kleenex, the algae in the toothpaste, the oaks in the floor, the grapes in the wine; to follow back the thread of life in everything and pay it respect? Once you start, it's hard to stop, and you begin to feel yourself awash in gifts.

I open the cupboard, a likely place for gifts. I think, "I greet you, jar of jam. You glass who once was sand upon the beach, washed back and forth and bathed in foam and seagull cries, but who are formed into a glass until you once again return to the sea. And you, berries, plump in your June-ness, now in my February pantry. And you, sugar, so far from your Caribbean home—thanks for making the trip."

In that awareness, looking over the objects on my desk—the basket, the candle, the paper—I delight in following their origins back to the ground. I twirl a pencil—a magic wand lathed from incense cedar—between my fingers. The willow bark in the aspirin. Even the metal of my lamp asks me to consider its roots in the strata of the earth. But I notice that my eyes and my thoughts pass quickly over the plastic on my desk. I hardly give the computer a second glance. I can muster no reflective moment for plastic. It is so far removed from the natural world. I wonder if that's a place where the disconnection began, the loss of respect, when we could no longer easily see the life within the object.

And yet I mean no disrespect for the diatoms and marine invertebrates who two hundred million years ago lived well and fell to the bottom of an ancient sea, where under great pressure of a shifting earth they became oil that was pumped from the ground to a refinery where it was broken down and then polymerized to make the case of my laptop or the cap of the aspirin bottle—but being mindful in the vast network of hyperindustrialized goods really gives me a headache. We weren't made for that sort of constant awareness. We've got work to do.

But every once in a while, with a basket in hand, or a peach or a pencil, there is that moment when the mind and spirit open to all the connections, to all the lives and our responsibility to use them well. And just in that moment, I can hear John Pigeon say, "Slow down—it's thirty years of a tree's life you've got in your hands there. Don't you owe it a few minutes to think about what you'll do with it?"

Things to Think About When You Are Buying Clothes

Meena Kandasamy

1. Trying to escape the poverty of life in a land where agriculture had dismally failed, where their hereditary profession of being nomadic witch-doctors no longer held any meaning in a modernising society, all of my male cousins fled the village that my paternal grandparents had made their home. My father had run away from that landscape a generation before them, got a university education, married up and above his level. He had never looked back, because making-do in a city was difficult enough, but perhaps because of a fear that if he were to go back, he could never escape another time. I am a privileged child, I grew up in the city and I now live in London, I have no taste of that horror which my cousins experience. One half of them went to Malaysia to work as cooks in roadside eateries, the other migrated to Tirupur and Coimbatore to work in garment factories. My cousin works as a tailor there, doing the intricate, finishing job of sewing buttons, of doing the collars on male shirts – the kind of work that requires a fine eye and finer fingers. What can I claim to know about my cousin's life? To me, sewing is the leisurely pastime on a sunny day – it is a wraparound skirt I make from a Size 12 summer dress, or cotton pillow covers I fashion out of very large Ikea curtains. I do not know the factory floor. I do not know sewing that will feed a family. I will never know the seventy-hour working week that will one day become the money that will marry off my sisters. I thought about this when I wanted to start writing this story, but could not get the courage to share. It is an aspect of my life I hide, and I hide it very well. More than that, it is only *personal* by extension, the pain is not my own, my cousin's poverty is not a wound that I can tend, or dress, or heal. And he is not alone.

Before I write of my cousin, before I wanted to bring in any personal touch to the story, I wrote about how clothing claims lives even before it is made. I started with the statistics: Thirty-one farmers kill themselves every day, and cotton farmers headline this list.[1] This is how shiny, glitzy neoliberalism brought death – farmers switched from food crops to cash crops in the dream of export-led growth. This suicide story is the tale of western India, a land where the skies bake the earth to yield the purest white clouds of cotton, this is the land that goes by the name of suicide belt. This is where Monsanto's genetically-modified seeds, now used on about 90 per cent of India's cotton fields,[2] became, in the words of the renowned environmental activist Vandana Shiva, the infamous 'suicide seeds'.[3] This is the land of loan-sharks; where the state eases itself into an afternoon siesta, where the rural banks have been shut down, where moneylenders convert wispy cotton into sturdy nooses as they watch debt-ridden farmers hang themselves. This is a land of young widows left to look after their little children; women who work for less than two dollars a day; kids who drop out when school becomes an unaffordable luxury. These are the fields that lay themselves bare to drought, to hailstones, to calamity – crop failure is one of the many unmourned victims of climate change.[4]

2. When I think of cotton plantations, it conjures up the reek of sweat and the sound of whiplashes, the soul-crushing images of slavery and indenture. It is not history alone that holds us prisoner. I learn of how cotton subsidies in the West and the introduction of Monsanto seeds ate up the fields and the farmers in the African nations of Burkina Faso, Benin, Mali and Chad. I tell myself to not wander away, to not go global, to stick to home territory, to only tell the story of India because there are countless stories that need telling here. Most of all, because like every Indian story, caste entangles the story of clothes and clothing here.

3. In Vidarbha[5] for instance, where there are 3.2 million farmers depending on cotton for a living, it is reported that a farmer suicide is reported every eight hours. Producing more than 40 million bales of cotton a year[6] does not save India's farmers – the surplus pushes down the global prices, the success on the fields comes back to kill them. India's liberalization programme of throwing open its markets to foreign produce has not helped either: the suicides began at around the same time when Indian cotton farmers were forced to compete with farmers from other countries where agriculture is highly subsidized. Yet, it's not the farmers alone who suffer. The Rumpelstiltskins – the weavers who spin this white gold into coarse cloth – face bleak futures too.

4. Sometimes, to report on the starvation deaths and the soup kitchens that have become the plight of the weavers and their families, the news media indulge in clothing-related puns. 'Looming disaster' is a perennial favourite.

5. Failure appears to be the fate of the working class. Indian handloom, with its quaintness, its earthiness, its authenticity lends itself to designer dreams. The

fashion industry cannibalizes a craft, a culture and artisanal castes. The weavers who hand-spin these dreams battle a poverty they cannot escape.[7]

6. Propaganda is central to everything, so allow me to corrupt your clean minds with some words from *The Poverty of Philosophy*. Marx wrote: 'In acquiring new productive forces men change their mode of production; and in changing their mode of production, in changing the way of earning their living, they change all their social relations. The hand-mill gives you society with the feudal lord; the steam-mill society with the industrial capitalist.'[8]

In the country that I'm writing about, the land that this essay tries to lay threadbare, there are hand-mills and power looms, the feudal lords and the industrial capitalists, all existing side by side.

7. In India, with its caste system, even Marx – so straight, so white – has to retreat into the margins to watch how it is *not* the modes of production that change social relations, but how it is the social relations that superimpose themselves and work their way around the modes of production. Caste reproduced itself successfully within the dominion of capitalism. Dalit men worked in the poorly-paid ring-spinning departments of the textile mills (they constituted 40 per cent of the male workforce there), whereas the more lucrative weaving sheds, with the highest paid skilled workers, were closed to them (they had a dismal representation there: 0.6 per cent).[9] Dalit women, thrice oppressed by caste, class and gender, were largely relegated to the winding and reeling department. The advent of technology did not crush caste, it only created new roles, new segmentations of labour. Where the pay itself did not vary, and was equal to all labourers within a department – the work areas were segregated, with no mixing of the caste-Hindus and the Dalits, and that was how untouchability was maintained. This was the reciprocal bounty of capitalism – to respect caste, to sustain caste, to structure itself around the boundary walls of caste system.

8. How could cruelty be far behind once caste and capitalism came some place? It was not a mere coincidence that the most accident-prone areas of the mill, like the throstle department, were the places that employed the most Dalits.[10]

9. Was it a question of economics or safety alone that relegated the Dalits to the lowest rungs of the textile mills? No, it was caste with its ideas of pollution and purity too. Let me quote Jan Breman paraphrasing Salim Lakha[11]: 'The work in the mills was determined by the caste identity which the workers had brought with them to city. Dheds and Vankars, who had supplemented their income from farm labour by weaving, were put to work in the spinning shops, as were the Chamars, a leather-tanning caste. These untouchables were not admitted to the

weaving shops, which were a domain of the Muslims and of higher castes like the Kanbis. This division of labour, which developed towards the end of the nineteenth century, was justified on the basis that weavers needed both hands and their mouth to tie a knot in the thread if it broke or to suck the yarn onto the shuttle whenever a weft bobbin was replaced. If members of the untouchable castes were permitted to do this work, it would defile the resulting product. This pollution would be passed on to the subsequent stages of production. To avoid this, the untouchables were only eligible for the preceding phase of spinning.' The saliva of some people was permissible, of some people was polluting. That is how Dalits pushed out of the villages by failing agriculture, running away from feudal oppression and chasing their big-city dreams found themselves in the capitalist framework: in the spinning shops, and working where the raw cotton was delivered and stored. To quote Breman, again, 'The division of tasks in the mills closely, if not entirely, followed the hierarchy of the caste system.'[12]

10. The shop floors alone did not enforce caste – it worked its way through the entire industrial complex. The caste-Hindu workers ate inside the canteens, the Dalit workers outside. An untouchable worker who claimed to be a Muslim to get work in the weaving department was severely beaten when it was revealed that he was a Mahar.[13] The water tanks for the caste-Hindus and the Dalits were separate. Untouchability was rampant in these mills, it was everywhere.

11. To pause to breathe, let us remember the revolutionary words of Dr Ambedkar, 'Caste is not merely a division of labour, it is a division of labourers.'

12. Did trade unionism break caste, did it erase these discriminations, did it unite the workers who had nothing to lose but their chains?

In the historic 1928 textile workers strike that shut down all the mills in Bombay, Dr Ambedkar supported the communists in the strike on the ground that trade unions would recognize the right of the Dalits to work in all the departments. What was the reaction to this demand? In his own words, 'They afterwards consented, most reluctantly, to include this as one of their demands, and when they presented this to the millowners, the millowners very rightly snubbed them and said that if this was an injustice, they certainly were not responsible for it.' The following year, Dr Ambedkar would call upon the Dalit workers to not take part in the strikes, to stress upon their discriminated position in the workforce, and because it was economically unviable for the Dalits to strike when they were at the mercy of moneylenders. Caste became a fault line within the class struggle, and all of this history is woven across the history of textile in India.

13. Allow me the temptation to smuggle in something in the question-and-answer format to shed some light on the issue of untouchability in the textile

mills of Bombay. When I was looking for information, or what passes off for research – I found these little treasures in an unlikely place: in Dr Ambedkar's evidence before the Indian Statutory Commission (more popularly known as the Simon Commission, consisting of a team of seven British Parliamentarians sent to the country to examine constitutional affairs) dating from October 1928. I present before you three excerpts of his submissions before the Commission:[14]

Exhibit One:

> Q. Major [Clement] Attlee: Are there members of the depressed classes working in industry, in the cotton mills and so on?
> Dr Ambedkar: All of them. The depressed class men are all labourers.
> Q. You have not got my point; I am talking of industry. You have members of the depressed classes who work in villages, for the most part in certain occupations. But are there large numbers of the depressed classes engaged in industry?
> Dr Ambedkar: A very large number.
> Q. You would have a very large number in a place like Bombay City?
> Dr Ambedkar: Yes.
> Q. Do they cease in any degree to be untouchable?
> Dr Ambedkar: No, I should like to point out this. The depressed class man is entirely kept out of the weaving department, the most paying department. He can only enter departments like the throstle department and others.
> Q. Why?
> Dr Ambedkar: On account of untouchability.
> Q. When he is working there he is working alongside people of all castes?
> Dr Ambedkar: Not quite. The departments are discriminated according to castes. One department is entirely manned by the depressed classes; another – say the weaving department – by Mohammedans and caste Hindus.
> Q. Do they take part in the trade unions?
> Dr Ambedkar: Yes, they are beginning to do so.
> Q. With members of the classes above the depressed classes?
> Dr Ambedkar: Yes.
> Q. I wanted to get this point from you. You put forward a claim for representation of the depressed classes on the basis of numbers. Now, we have claims put forward on a different basis altogether; on, say, the labour basis. You get a cross-division in that way, because a man can be a depressed class man and he can also be a labourer?
> Dr Ambedkar: He is usually, if not always, a labourer.

*

Exhibit Two:

> Q. May I revert to a question put to you by Major Attlee? I gather the depressed classes work in the factories in isolation?
>
> Dr Ambedkar: In isolation, yes.
>
> Q. They have their own shed and their own department?
>
> Dr Ambedkar: Their own department; there are no sheds.
>
> Q. Whatever it is, they are separated from the other workers in the factory?
>
> Dr Ambedkar: I would rather put it in this way, that certain departments are exclusively assigned to the depressed classes and certain departments are departments into which they are not allowed to enter.
>
> Q. Certain kinds of occupations are forbidden to them?
>
> Dr Ambedkar: In the mills, yes.
>
> Q. I think you said they are not allowed to go into the weaving department?
>
> Dr Ambedkar: Yes.
>
> Q. If they became members of the same trade union, would the workers in the weaving department decline to allow them in?
>
> Dr Ambedkar: They would decline to allow them in. If I may mention one thing, in the recent Bombay strike this matter was brought up prominently by me. I said to the members of the union that if they did not recognise the right of the depressed classes to work all the departments, I would rather dissuade the depressed classes from taking part in the strike. They afterwards consented, most reluctantly, to include this as one of their demands, and when they presented this to the millowners, the millowners very rightly snubbed them and said that if this was an injustice, they certainly were not responsible for it.
>
> Q. It is not altogether merely a case of the employers wanting to get cheap labour and confining certain departments to the depressed classes for economic reasons?
>
> Dr Ambedkar: No, it is untouchability.
>
> Q. Would there be anything of this in the situation? The better-paid Indian, say, declines to allow the untouchable to come into his department for fear that the effect of their lower wages would be to depress wages in his department?
>
> Dr Ambedkar: No. There is no distinction on the basis of wages.
>
> Q. That does not come into it at all?
>
> Dr Ambedkar: No, not at all.
>
> Q. It is merely a question of untouchability?
>
> Dr Ambedkar: Quite so.

*

Exhibit Three:

Q: Mr Premchand: Do you know the depressed classes are employed in the
    weaving departments of the Ahmedabad mills?

Dr Ambedkar: I did not know that.

Q. I can tell you they are.

Dr Ambedkar: There again I should like to say one thing, probably they are
    employed exclusively. I can quite conceive of a situation where, for instance, so
    many looms are exclusively handed over to the depressed classes. Today there is
    a proposal also in certain mills that the depressed classes should take charge of
    the whole of the weaving department, that the mill owners should hand it over
    to them, but you cannot have part depressed classes and part caste Hindus.

Q. Chairman: The difficulty is the mixture?

Dr Ambedkar: Yes.

*

14. This was a story of exclusion and discrimination that did not belong to
Bombay alone, but had taken place everywhere else in India. In 1918, a year after
the Russian Revolution, India had its first trade union: Madras Labour Union
formed by mill-workers at the Buckingham and Carnatic Mills who worked
under extremely exploitative circumstances. In 1921, when the mill workers at
the Buckingham and Carnatic Mills went on strike from June to October
crippling the Madras economy, the Dalit workers, facing starvation and lacking
the social capital of caste-Hindu workers, were forced by circumstances to go
back to work. To pull them into line, and using the ruse of attacking scab workers,
caste-Hindus burnt 100 huts of Dalit workers in Pulianthope on 28 June 1921.
Because caste stayed in control of the narrative, it would conveniently present
Dalit workers as strike-breakers; vilify and erase their militancy, and rob them of
being recognized for their sacrifices in the working-class movements.[15]

15. Caste is about those who spin and those who weave and those who make
the clothes. Caste is about touch and caste is about spit. Caste is about exploitative
baniyas who own these mills, it is about who is allowed to work where. Long before
capitalism enters this scene of crime, caste had other rules. About wearing clothes,
about not wearing clothes, about how to wear clothes and about washing clothes.
There is nothing that is beyond the pale of regimentation by the caste system.

16. Stripping a Dalit is one of the most recurrent caste atrocities that occur in
our country. To quote from the Scheduled Caste and Scheduled Tribe (Prevention
of Atrocities) Act, it is an atrocity when a caste-Hindu forcibly removes clothes
from the person of a member of a Scheduled Caste or a Scheduled Tribe or parades

them naked or with painted face or body or commits any similar act which is derogatory to human dignity. As an everyday horror show, it finds its ways into headlines because it couples dominance with the predatory gaze. Dalit men and women are stripped and/or paraded naked when they do not follow caste diktats.

17. Sometimes, the rules about clothes extend to things that are not clothes, but accessories nonetheless. Dalits, in many villages in Tamil Nadu, were prohibited from wearing shoes or sandals, draping a towel on their shoulders, unfurling their umbrellas, riding cycles or motorcycles on caste-Hindu streets. A Dalit would have to pick up his footwear when he trod through these streets, he would have to tuck his towel or his umbrella under his armpit, he would have to alight from his bicycle and push it through. In this manner, the vicious ego of caste oppression gloats, unwilling to accept the change that is sweeping through society.

18. In the militant village of Kilvenmani, an elderly Dalit farm-worker told me of the time he had worn a red shirt to school – and his teacher had called him 'Danger' and sent him back home. In Tamil Nadu, self-respect became synonymous with the Black Shirt of the Dravidian movement. Sometimes, self-respect became synonymous with any shirt. All through my childhood, I've heard variations of this from my own father: 'I could wear a shirt because of Periyar.' A shirt served as a symbol of aspiration to equality, and more than that, a claim to what one deserved in place of being consigned to nothing.

19. Periyar E.V. Ramasamy (1879–1973) may have been responsible for millions of men like my father gaining the right to wear shirts or go to school or enter college, but most of all, he will be remembered for telling women to step out of the constraints of the many-yards sari, telling them to dress in shirts and trousers, telling them to cut their hair short, telling them to be equal to men in everything.

20. Periyar was not the only anti-caste leader who addressed the question of clothing in a caste society. When caste made rules to distinguish between the touchables and untouchables through material markers, it was the work of revolutionaries to turn the tide. Dr Ambedkar addressing Dalit women in the Mahad conference in 1928, said, 'Untouchables do not have a stamp of their Untouchable status on their foreheads. But Untouchables can be immediately identified due to their ways of living which I think have been forced upon us. Hence you should abandon all markers that will identify you as Untouchables. Your style of draping saris is one such marker. You should destroy this evidence. You should make it a habit to drape saris like the high-caste women. Similarly, the many necklaces and silver and tin bangles up to your elbow are also a mark of identification. [. . .] Change your sari-draping style before you go home.'[16]

21. And they did. Shailaja Paik writes, 'Immediately after his Mahad speech, helped by the radical upper-caste women Lakshmibai Tipnis and Indirabai Chitre from the Chandraseniya Kayastha Prabhu community, women readily draped their saris like upper-caste women, covering their legs down to their ankles.'[17] Under an oppressive system that demarcated who should wear what, dress lends itself to rebellion, and to camouflage. Dr Ambedkar would touch upon clothes again, exhorting Dalit women to wear white saris on 14 October 1956, the day on which he and close to half a million followers embraced Buddhism, refusing to die as Untouchables under a horrendous caste system.

22. Not always did men, male reformers, have to lead the struggle against caste in the matter of clothing. In a society where stripping Dalits of their clothes is a form of punishment, dress becomes a form of resistance.

In the nineteenth century, Nadar (or Chaanar) women, of the caste of toddy-tappers, prohibited from wearing jackets or blouses to cover their upper bodies in the style of upper-caste women led a successful revolt against the Travancore kingdom. This phenomenal struggle took place at the confluence of various strands of history, which also involved the church, conversions and British colonial authority.[18]

Another exemplary incident of individual rebellion is the story of Nangeli, who refused to pay the *mulakkaram*, a tax that Dalit women had to pay in the 19th century to the government of the Travancore Kingdom for covering their breasts. When the tax-collectors came knocking at her door, she chopped her breast and offered it on a plantain leaf, dying shortly thereafter.[19] It is in these snippets of our history that we realize how bloody and how brutal the caste system was and remains, and how clothes (neutral, beautiful, innocent) have been at the centre of so much control.

23. Remember. Remember, even though I extend examples from history, this is a story of the here and now, of today.

24. In 2012, three hundred homes of Dalits in three villages in the Dharmapuri district were burnt down to express indignation over the inter-caste marriage of a Dalit man Ilavarasan and a Vanniyar woman Divya. The leader of Pattali Makkal Katchi (PMK), a Vanniyar Party renowned for its history of anti-Dalit violence, said, 'Dalit boys are wearing jeans, T-shirts and sunglasses and taking our girls away...'[20] An aspiration to style became the reason for a caste-based demonisation and a witch-hunt. Think of this when you slip into your T-shirt and jeans today.

Under the Weather

Jane Tynan

1

Solitary, weightless, fragile. Alberto Giacometti's slender sculptures of the human figure are ghostly. These elongated bodies modelled in clay and cast in plaster and bronze were created in Giacometti's Paris studio after World War Two. His sculpture *Me Walking Quickly under the Rain* (1948) conveys a human body moving through inclement weather: slightly bent forward, arms swinging, a posture cast by the force of oncoming rain. We don't see the weather but know the feeling. There is something in the atmosphere. In the work, Giacometti casts himself as a lonely, fragile figure moving through the downpour, feeling the force of the rain on his body.

A body caught in the rain could be a metaphor for unspeakably bleak feelings of despair and hopelessness. Like Samuel Beckett, one of his closest friends in Paris, Giacometti created works of lone isolated figures, often walking, as he himself was known to do. The ambling gait of Giacometti's roughly hewn, sinewy figures accentuates their sense of solitude, as if they persist in spite of the wear and tear of atmospheric effects, a stoicism that recalls Beckett's line 'I can't go on. I'll go on.'[1] But 'tramping' – journeying on against an uncertain, capricious world – reflects the condition of Giacometti's walking figure and connects the work of the sculptor and the playwright.[2] Both foreground the sensation of living, of being a body, occupying space and feeling the effects of the atmosphere.

A photograph taken by Henri Cartier-Bresson of Giacometti in 1961 finds the artist himself walking in the rain on a Paris street, grimacing against oncoming wind.[3] With his coat pulled up to cradle the back of his head, he moves within a shroud-like cover against an almighty downpour that catches him unprepared. He holds a lit cigarette in one hand, while the other is nestled in his coat pocket. The scene looks watery, windy and chilly but, then again, he doesn't seem too bothered.

Figure 2 Photograph by Henri Cartier-Bresson. France, Paris, 14th arrondissement, Rue d'Alésia. The Swiss painter and sculptor, Alberto GIACOMETTI, 1961.

© Fondation Henri Cartier-Bresson / Magnum Photos.

This image reveals something about the inadequacy of clothes to defend against capricious weather. Cartier-Bresson captures a joyous wrestle between human and environment: it is not just the heavy rain beating down on the artist that registers, but the fact that Giacometti doesn't wear a raincoat or waterproof boots. His vulnerability is obvious, and yet here he is, a ludic, turtle-like figure tramping in the rain, ruggedly persisting, as if content to abandon himself to the inevitable.

2

In the 1970s, when raincoats became the norm in many households, I was a child living in the west of Ireland. As the reliability of weather forecasting improved, raincoats became a must-have item. Regular weather reports equipped us with the information to dress appropriately – or so it seemed. On television, weather charts forecasted the atmospheric moods we could expect the following day, prophecies beamed into our living room at regular intervals.

It was computer modelling into the science of predicting weather in the 1960s that made forecasting commonplace. In the UK, the jump in the credibility of weather data was directed to households but also to businesses, primarily the oil and gas industries.[4] Ireland followed. Numerical weather prediction brought science into homes, via public service broadcasting, with the promise that we would never again be unprepared. These weather reports were not always accurate, but fairly reliable – the credibility of the Meteorological Office took a dive each time they were proved wrong. Part of the difficulty, if you lived in Ireland or the UK, was the changeability of weather, the "four seasons in one day" feel of a temperate climate near the Atlantic Ocean. Unpredictability made weather reports even more urgent.

Raincoats became part of our routine: we calculated when to pack them, how much space they would take up in our bags. We all got in on the weather prediction game. In everyday conversation, older ways of predicting weather mixed with meteorological science. My rain gear followed me around like a warning of a crisis to come. I owned a yellow raincoat, a lot like those seen on fishermen. It replaced my friendly Pakamac, which, being light, red, airy and fun, was much more appealing. I couldn't make my peace with this strange-smelling coat with its thick, durable surface and large zips and fasteners, over-engineered details that proclaimed *I'm functional*. Bulky, difficult-to-fold and unsightly, the coat was more than an inconvenience: it was a denial of the ebb and flow of weather, difficult to predict and really not the disaster it was set up to be. As my mother said when we didn't want to go out in the rain, 'You won't melt.'

Then there was the feeling of these otherworldly things: their plastic, dead feel, neither animal nor vegetable, but something else, something unnatural. I had a vague sense that some unspeakable chemical process had brought these synthetic coats into being, but the specifics were hard to comprehend. Manufacturing polymers made textiles alien to the touch, but who could say no to fabrics that were improbably strong and resistant to wear and water? It was obvious that they were, as Mary Douglas said of polluting agents, 'matter out of place', an uneasy, unsettling, unstable thing.[5] They were nothing like other garments, if they were indeed clothes at all. More like imposters in the wardrobe, pretending to be at home amongst the riotous assemblage of warmth, colour, and softness. Wool has memory, I am told, which is why it shrinks in the wash. Synthetics do not. But raincoats, in all their strangeness and un-clothes-like disposition, managed to wheedle their way into our lives.

The discomfort of rainwear was singular: it felt heavy, damp and miserable. Cycling in my raincoat I was sure to sweat and when it really poured down, the water inevitably seeped through the seams, trickling down the sides of my body, into my armpits, and down the back of my neck. Sweat and warm rain mingled to create an exquisitely uncomfortable feeling. And yet, discomfort is what the whole enterprise of the synthetic rainwear trade railed against, selling commodities that promised to seal us off against unwelcome rain and wind. In a war against body discomfort, various rainwear manufacturers sought to convey safety, security and convenience.

Rather than being alleviated by the post-war boom in plastics and the fine-tuning of scientific weather forecasting, paradoxically, weather insecurity seemed to be on the rise. Ever-more sophisticated waterproof clothing doesn't really solve the problem but is very effective in creating (false) expectations of dryness and comfort too easily punctured by the intrusion of a very wet day. In a crowded marketplace, where rainwear manufacturers competed for our attention, it was no longer enough to invoke the familiar feelings of discomfort rain has on our bodies. That's just an inconvenience. To commodify weather anxiety, they had to exploit fears about ill-health. Changeable weather had long been blamed for all manner of problems, including causing the flu, and sensational ads would warn that raincoats were essential to keep sickness at bay. In a 1920 newspaper advertisement for an 'All-Weather Security Garment', I found claims that this garment would not just keep the rain off but 'Guard Your Health and Secure Comfort'.[6] But such warnings about rain getting into your bones were not just a thing of the past – they persisted. To get caught in the rain was to flirt with danger, lest you 'get a chill', as parents were fond of repeating. But rain doesn't transmit viruses, which are more likely to spread in dry conditions rather than wet. Hypothermia is a danger in extreme conditions, such as prolonged exposure to cold rain. Maybe a danger for military personnel or explorers, not kids playing in the fields. Nevertheless, this flawed reasoning was regularly trotted out, and the myth that rain made you sick endured into the age of plastics. A new spin on old narratives of weather insecurity were a gift to the outdoor leisure industry. Security. Comfort. Health. The anxious messaging lingered.

The photograph of Giacometti in Paris flies in the face of such narratives. Instead of cultivating fear of the unknown territory of everyday weather, when the heavens opened, the artist gets gloriously wet. Pulling his hoodless coat above his head, he smiles knowingly as he splashes in the puddles. Defying the science of comfort, he yields to the rhythms of what Tim Ingold calls a 'weather world'.[7] Rather than be numbed by tales of risk and catastrophe, the artist sees rain as part of the ebb and flow of things.

We are moved by the cadences of weather; it makes us more human, not less, and "weathering" captures the ongoing, continuous dialogue between living beings, earth and sky.[8] A raincoat can be a handy item, but the desire for a frictionless encounter with weather represents a disconnect. We might be irritated by its ever-changing moods, but the weather is a large and ferocious reminder of the futility of sealing the body off from atmospheric effects. Weatherproofing is a style of being in the world; it embodies the desire to be unchanged by the forces and energies of the natural environment. The response to wrap ourselves in plastic reflects the impulse to control rather than to care.

3

Rain features strongly in Somerset Maugham's 1921 short story that follows the trials and tribulations of a group stranded in Pago-Pago when a trip to Apia is interrupted by a measles epidemic. Events throw two couples together – the Davidsons, fervent Christian missionaries, and the McPhails, an easy-going doctor and his wife – and they pass the time in a local boarding house As the English and Americans visitors make contact with the local population, the Davidsons are disgusted by their dress, given their determination to proselytize against immoral dancing and immodest clothing, earthly temptations they seek to prohibit. In the story, we get insights into colonial ways of knowing, and how the quest to control and subjugate people entangles with feelings about weather. Torrential rain finds the missionaries anxiously preparing with umbrellas and waterproofs while the men and women of Pago-Pago, reportedly the rainiest place in the Pacific, go about their business in loincloths. Meanwhile the missionaries plan to Christianise the region by compelling all boys over the age of ten to wear trousers.

We see the place through the eyes of Dr. McPhail, its foreignness apparent in the temperament of raging unforgiving weather: 'It was not like our soft English rain that drops gently on the earth; it was unmerciful and somehow terrible; you felt in it the malignancy of the primitive powers of nature. It did not pour, it flowed.'[9]

Feelings of powerlessness and anger surface in the group of white people, for whom the rain 'seemed to have a fury of its own. And sometimes you felt that you must scream if it did not stop, and then suddenly you felt powerless, as though your bones had suddenly become soft; and you were miserable and hopeless.'[10] Vulnerability in the face of what they regarded as an unruly climate says more about the missionaries' fears and desires than anything about the island itself, or its inhabitants. Threatened by the ungodly rain, their impulse is to view the Samoans as immoral and in need of saving. A clash of morality is told through clothing, and the ferocity of the weather stands between the missionaries and the magnitude of their task. Covering up bodies is a reflex for those who cannot feel anything but disdain for unfamiliar weather rhythms and the bodies that know how to live with them.

The idea that we must battle the elements is not the only way to become 'weather wise.'[11] Sartorial adaptations to adverse climatic conditions, as in Maugham's story, is a tale of colonial ways of encountering weather, of meeting it as an adversary and responding with anger and despair. During World War Two, US army clothing experiments saw 'technologies and vocabularies of comfort' emerging from Pacific combat.[12] This scientific approach to comfort, though, is subjective; it only suits the perspective of those travelling to foreign 'weather worlds' without an open mind. But anxiety about weather is often about feeling different, uncomfortable, out of place. What if we have imbibed weather anxiety through habitual ways of knowing borrowed from ancestors who themselves were enveloped by fears of Otherness? The weather worlds encountered by all manner of colonial servants must have been a shock to the body, but perhaps that feeling of discomfort was only given significance because it impeded colonial and military campaigns: the weather reinforcing their lack of power in an environment over which they were trying to claim mastery. So, they tooled up to meet difference with order, control and aggression.

Such fears, materialized in clothes and equipment, is discernible in various mid-twentieth century advertisements for military clothing – one claimed that 'no rapid climatic changes catch it unawares', and 'no torrid heat or driving rain can overcome its nullifying resistance.'[13] Clothes take on a colossal task if their brief is to cancel the sensation of unfamiliar weather patterns. Supposedly resistance is the only solution, and clothes do the heavy lifting. The impulse to weatherproof the body is haunted by fantasies of dominance, whether over people, weather, terrain, or time. Most of the raincoats we wear owe something to the military sartorial experiments of the last century: the trench coat, the cagoule, vinyl and nylon rainwear all came to the market as a result of military research. But textile technology has followed a path that betrays just how much consumer culture has been imbued with military/colonial imperatives. In this vein, waterproofing could be viewed as a projection of the hostility that colonizers could not own, a sign of their desire for control without involvement, extraction without peril. Far from being a show of strength, though, in the end clothing cannot defend against anxiety, and making stronger, ever-more defensive garments betrays a brittleness borne of travelling beyond home and not knowing what to do or how to be. It conjures an image of bodies embattled by atmospheric effects and ultimately undone by hubris.

Imperial anxiety might have given waterproof coats a military edge by setting weather up as the unpredictable adversary. But whatever the origin of weatherproof gear, these stories of venturing to "unknown" places, anxiously preparing with raincoats and galoshes, being outraged by "bad" weather, and even more so by people who endure its caprices, has a miserable predictability to it.

The apparel industry promotes the idea that we are all in urgent need of security solutions to the weather's natural rhythms. According to Arne Naess, we now expect to encounter landscapes with the help of various consumer 'outdoor recreation' goods, invariably designed to seal us off from inclement weather.[14] Synthetic fabrics are a large part of that offering. The raincoat resists weather worlds and promises a frictionless outdoor experience, with none of the inconvenience of being in and of the landscape or connecting with people who know its rhythms.

Weatherproofing the body might not be new, but the synthetics boom has brought its own problems. Treated wool, oilskins, rubber, and various other processes were created to proof garments in the centuries before synthetics came along. All had their downsides. Rubber, in particular, had a reputation for being smelly and unhygienic. Even treating wool frieze relied on toxic chemicals to create water-repellence. But the acceptance of garments made wholly of synthetics to resist rainwater is dangerously reliant on narratives of alterity. We are still deeply ambivalent about being in weather, a discomfort that led to the over-production of non-renewable fibres and further entrenched us in fossil fuel dependence.

Cultural imaginaries of discomfort and insecurity surface in the very textures of water-repellent outerwear. Smooth like a skin but disturbingly without life or memory, which brings me back to the place the loathsome raincoat had in my childhood. A then-relatively new solution to the discomforts of rain, synthetic fibres, like a lot of new conveniences, brought hope. But they also brought a disturbance into everyday clothing, their unsettling texture placing us outside of nature. Raincoats bespeak the endless pliability of matter that can be made to do exactly what you want it to do, but once these fibres are stabilised you must live with their toxic reality forever in the ecosystem. In every sense, they are matter out of place.

4

In the 1980s, when Italian students came to study at university in Dublin, they came equipped with Barbour jackets or colourful raincoats and wore them at all times, even when it wasn't raining. Why, we wondered, did they need so much stuff? We didn't really notice the drizzle. Heavy rain, when it came, was another matter. But in our nonchalance, we either had inferior gear – heavy dour raincoats – or none at all.

We never really had a good reason to be so negligent. But we had excuses: you couldn't predict the rain on any given day, waterproofs were awkward, and umbrellas invariably got lost. We lived in our weather world and the Italian students, likely briefed in advance about Ireland's changeable days, dressed in anticipation of a weather world unfamiliar to them. Some days they were proved right. The heavens opened and it poured down. For our part, we might amble through the wet streets, hiding in doorways, joking about the silliness of our predicament; but we were ultimately surrendering to the inevitable: the blithe unpredictability of weather on our rainy island.

A Stitch Between Reality and Imagination

Thao Thai

Imagine two strips of satin, unwieldy and impossibly liquid, slipping through your fingers. Through mechanical propulsion and your own gentle pressure, the fabric dips under a needle with a clicking sound, then out again, magically united by a stitch that acts like punctuation, a series of staccato hyphens. The satin waterfalls over the edge of the table, the greenest green you've ever laid eyes on.

From the right angle, the two pieces of satin are joined by an unpuckered crease, as if they had always been meant to lie together. What emerges is a breathless combination of imagination and physicality. The mind sees the thing, and the body brings it to life. It is such a common and extraordinary experience.

My mother told me that when I was a toddler, I roamed wild in my grandmother's fabric shop in Vietnam. She said, in lieu of childcare, I would often tag along with family members while they worked in the store. They'd bribe me with candy and scraps of silk, which I'd loop around my head like a rainbow wigs. All day long, wobble underfoot, listening to the haggling and the gossip, gobbling sesame candy offered by the parade of aunties.

We don't have pictures of the store, but having been to fabric stalls in my hometown, I can picture it: a shadowed hallway filled to the tarped ceiling with the most exquisite bolts of fabric you can imagine. In my imagination, I see watercolor silk in those vibrant '80s shades of fuchsia and ice blue; shirting fabric so crisp a fold could cut skin; tightly flowered calico for two-piece house sets; and sheer cotton that wafts dreamily over a child's sleeping form.

My aunt became a criminal in the family fabric store. If she spied something pretty being delivered—pink eyelet trim or buttons that resembled little gemstones—she'd steal it for me, slipping her finds into her pocket with a wink. Days later, when I appeared wearing a new dress with shiny, familiar buttons, my grandmother cut her eyes at us. She scolded. But then she'd finger the Peter Pan collar on my dress and reluctantly praise my aunt for her artistry. Craft and beauty, in our home, often trumps the murkier questions of ethics—at least, the low-stakes ones.

Most of the women in my family are expert seamstresses, the kind that don't use patterns at all. They can look at a Macy's mannequin through narrowed eyes, then go home to draft the same blouse—for a fraction of the price—from bits of leftover fabric. In Vietnam, it wasn't uncommon for a person to take sewing lessons outside the home. Ready-made clothing was expensive and slightly rarer in the '60s and '70s in our small town, at the time when my mother grew up, so it was imperative to learn how to clothe your family affordably. My mom says she was forced to spend three weeks sewing a straight line before her very stern instructor finally allowed her to advance.

After we immigrated to America in the nineties, we bought two appliances first: a rice cooker and a sewing machine. I often fell asleep to the solid, comforting thump of that sewing machine, breathing in the dust from threads that blew into the air, then settled like alighting dragonflies. To be a sewist—and I mean the creative kind they are, not the haphazard kind I am—requires a kind of dauntless imagination.

You have to be able to see what things *could* be: how a flat piece of spandex can become a body-skimming bathing suit to turn heads, how a pile of satin and lace becomes a wedding gown for a hopeful bride. Because sewing is, after all, a form of hope. If we dress for identity, as well as the lives we wish for, then there is power in shaping the garments that enclose our fragile bodies.

Though my mother gave me a sewing machine of my own at the age of eight, I didn't have the patience to follow through. It sat unboxed for decades. In the meantime, the women in my family sewed less. Their jobs became demanding, their eyesight strained. My mother still piled her fabrics high—she loved collecting polka-dotted cotton and fussy lace trimming—but they were largely ignored, a reminder of a life when sewing was pleasurable and creative, rather than another pull of time in a day bereft of it. For my part, I filled my days with books and writing, deadbeat boyfriends and trifling purchases from Wet Seal. Life sped along.

In my thirties, I became a mother. During those fraught early days, I couldn't read much at a time without my eyes glazing over, my focus slipping away. I certainly couldn't write. But when I gazed at my new baby, clad in a panda-printed onesie, I felt an urge to create something for her. I remembered my aunt's baby dresses for me, each so exquisite and carefully sewn that they felt like wearable art. I wanted to give that to my child.

We'd just moved to a new town, a developing farm community with picturesque houses and sprawling acreage and a palpable undercurrent of xenophobia. There, I was lonely and sometimes scared. My mother, hundreds of miles away. My aunt, spending much of her time in Vietnam. Both offered encouragement as I began sewing, but I wanted to have them next to me, breaths warm on my shoulder as I tried to thread a needle. I needed their stern proficiency, their depthless wells of compassion.

Sewing, too, had always been safety for me. At first, I tried learning the basics online, through YouTube, but I'm the sort of learner that thrives on dialogue. I called the local fabric store and pleaded with the owner, Miss Robin, to allow me to take a private class with her.

That weekend, I toted my inexpensive Brother sewing machine to the sewing store—tucked into a tiny street with a donut shop and a greasy diner—and spent two hours learning the basics of my machine and all the stitches that would serve me along the way. Miss Robin was matter-of-fact, but patient. "Give yourself grace," she said. "Everyone starts somewhere." It was hard for me to understand this, having been only exposed to master sewists, but I saw that there was value in becoming a beginner again. Every desperate tear, every frustrated crumple of fabric, becomes another notch forward, another symbol of perseverance. I tried to channel my mother, who spent three weeks sewing a single straight line over and over again until her instructor was satisfied. I took heart.

Soon, I was able to sew a crooked, A-line dress for my baby from a pattern from Miss Robin's fabric store. It hung too large on her, but my family praised me for my careful stitches, though it was doubtful they could see that level of detail through the snapshot I sent. I kept going, moving onto the much fussier knit fabrics that caught under my presser foot. I sewed matching baseball tees for us and empire-waisted baby dresses and even tiny bloomers to go under them. I began collecting fabric, too. As the years went on, I sewed so much that whole seasons would arrive, bringing with them a completely hand-sewn wardrobe for my daughter. Sometimes I made things for myself, but that never felt as fun. Everything's better in miniature.

Now, my daughter is six, and I don't sew quite as much as I did in the mania of her babyhood. In my makeshift basement studio, there are industrial shelves that hold teetering piles of fabric, visited less and less. She tells me that her style is "sporty," and prefers loose-fitting tees from Target to the vintage-inspired dresses I usually sew. And for my part, I have less time than I once did, too, now that I write full-time.

The comparisons between writing and sewing are perhaps too obvious. Both are acts of creation, relying on pattern and ingenuity to produce a new thing in the world. A garment, a sentence, is composed of common elements rearranged in specific and fateful ways. Both require dedication and precision, and often, many, many instances of redrafting. In my mind, the two practices are positioned as opposites: I sew when I'm blocked on a piece of writing. Sewing feels solidly practical and easily quantifiable, in a way that at least my writing often isn't. But in reality, sewing and writing have always been inextricably linked for me. They both act as a kind of language, a way to relate to the external world.

Once in a while, a certain fabric grabs my attention, or I have a vision for something spectacular, and I can't help but go back to the sewing table. Right now, I have my eye on a tie-dyed fabric for a full-skirted spring dress with flounce sleeves. I see her swirling in the sunshine, a miraculous storm of color and youth and joy.

I share my idea with my daughter and her face brightens. "Now?" she asks. "Can you go make it now?" Spring is ages away, I protest. She smiles and shrugs, knowing as I do that sewing is about possibility. Hope. Making a tie-dye dress in the dead of winter is a gesture of yearning and also, a resolute conviction that brighter days lie in wait. If we imagine it, it will come.

Paradise Engraved

Krys Osei

Sweeter After Rain

'*Here is the magnificent African artist, Miriam Makeba!*'
The screen fades to black, the audience applauds in harmonious synchronicity, and the emblematic South African artist and activist appears centre stage. In a sleek figure-hugging leopard print gown, statement yellow gold-tone earrings, and her natural Afro-textured hair, she emits an ethereal glow as she performs her vibrant single 'Pata Pata' – the international, chart-topping hit that, in 1967, emblazoned her legacy in world music alongside her proudly African diasporic fashion identity. Her signature look exemplified the transnational 'Black is Beautiful' cultural movement of the 1960s.[1]

Many years later, my mother smiles from ear-to-ear as she watches Miriam Makeba, one of her favourite artists, perform on YouTube in our family kitchen in Accra, Ghana. I watch her and get a glimpse of how music foregrounds memories. For her, consuming Miriam Makeba's music and aesthetic while growing up in the Grassfields of Northwest Cameroon was an act of pleasure that redefined her love for geography and proximity to nature. Although engaging in subsistence agriculture anchored a sense of belonging, my mother came to understand the fragmentation of home, identity, country and the arbitrary borders and land division marked up during colonisation through Miriam Makeba's vocalisation. I realised that her admiration of Makeba, who lived in exile, facilitated a creative response in her from the tender age of four. Playing with sticks in the sand, she would sketch detailed maps of her dream town – consisting of farms, neighbourhoods, schools and shopping centres – symbolic even then of her inclination towards geography, reimagining the possibilities of space, and the drive to reaffirm her cultural value there on the ground of the Anglophone region where her family lived.

In the truest sense, her admiration of Miriam Makeba was also a radical act of defiance against tradition and the legacy of patriarchal governance that embargoed educational, economic, and personal development opportunities in her life and those of my grandmother and great-grandmother. My grandmother fought for my mother to stay in school, in sharp defiance of the local expectation for young girls to pursue marriage, as women were subjugated to domestic servitude and were limited in what they could achieve.

So, my mother went from climbing breathtaking mountain peaks to relocating to the capital city of Yaoundé for university. Perhaps it was her intimate connection to nature that began to reveal the stark inequities of the world during that time: how certain populations have obstacles – literal mountains – to ascend, while others have roads paved and sidewalks assembled to support their livelihoods. When she arrived in the University of Yaoundé campus library, she was shocked that there were no books in English and that none of her teachers were bilingual. If she dared to submit an assignment in English, it was an automatic failure. For 18 months she was alienated in a space of linguistic enclosure. My mother carried the legacy of Miriam Makeba throughout those months by remembering her melodies and prose. From her lyrics on the ills of apartheid, which reflected parallel state-sanctioned Black human suffering internationally, to her timeless sense of style, which my mother references in her own dress even now, Miriam Makeba exemplifies a dynamic image of Black African femininity produced in South Africa that continues to facilitate a sense of communal pride for Black women around the world.

Mama Said

Mama said in the Cameroonian Grassfields, all-girl agricultural groups planted and harvested for six weeks to raise money for school fees, books and uniforms

In summer they banded together:
Cocoyam, plantain, okra and cassava
Papaya, mangoes and avocados

To greet the small miracle of grandma's open market stalls

Rest is declared on Saturday and Sunday

Because

We braid hair and knit for leisure
But mama says the tropics teach you that you are always carrying something with you

Circa 1968

I write outpouring the wisdom of my mother: gardening is a form of translation from her agricultural beginnings

Welcome to my translation

Circa 2020 something

Adornment as Memoir

I am guided by the emotional durability of objects and the tactility of storytelling. How, in a race towards adolescence, my teenaged, bedazzled Sony Walkman featuring a splash of rhinestones, my penchant for crafting 'do it yourself' denim wallets out of the back pockets of worn-out jeans, marked a form of material lineage I was yet to recognise. A material lineage that is embedded within the wax-printed cloth my mother inherited from her mother, and in turn, I have inherited from her. Wrapped at the waist, the gathered fabric dances in canary yellow with glimpses of citrine. The frayed edges unravel a tale of migration: the manipulation of free-flowing cloth allows the possibility to make a place for yourself in the world, amidst the changing location of "home". This material lineage extends beyond the physicality of the cloth itself to an expansive inheritance of beauty, meticulous care, and self-determination.

Cloth: draped in the memory of silhouettes my mother and grandmother adorned in past times.

In 2023, during a virtual managing symptoms group, we were asked by the hospital psychologist to select one word to describe the reality of living with chronic inflammatory disease. With hesitation, the word *disorienting* rolled off my tongue and blended into the wider chorus of 'D' words asserted by other participants: *disabling; debilitating; demoralising*. I nodded in agreement as the session continued.

Today, on this 2020 something Monday, my revised word of choice is *daunting*, which may, or may not be, a sufficient expression to capture my wounded fear of simply not being able to complete heart-led desires and expectations of my labour due to the unpredictability of my health, as frantic pauses, breaks and dispiriting flashes of pain rupture the boundaries of sequential time. Staging my body as compass, I map the illegible coordinates of remission and relapse, trace the fragments of self-compassion and welcome the discomfort of solitude, as I gently stylise my grandmother's fabric with vintage gold-tone costume jewellery. Revisiting photographs of my family, the wardrobe pieces they donned forms an archive. This archive tells a wider narrative of movement, their draped textiles a literal – and figurative – model of tailored freedom. These objects are imbued with migratory history, a collection of worn garments, photographs and specific sewing tools telling genealogies of diasporic heritage and stylised survival. I have incorporated some of these pieces into my own wardrobe; others remain safely stored away. All of them speak memories of their initial owner. From a brown distressed leather bag that belonged to my Ghanaian father, which functioned as my go-to bag during undergraduate years studying political science, to twisted navy blue yarn bracelets and metal knitting needles crafted by a local welder in Cameroon that belonged to my maternal grandmother, to the parallel images of my mother on her first day at Howard University and my father's arrival in New York City in 1982. They tell of the art of making a home from possessions carried across continents, while timestamping my parents' transition into the readymade clothing marketplace.

Self-fashioning has allowed me to remix the possibilities of time. I reach for billowy silhouettes and am drawn to the malleability of languid fabrics. Lipstick is a playful staple: MAC Cosmetics 'Whirl' matte lipstick has been consistently applied for a decade. Cloth as a spiritual anchor further serves as an instrument with which I melodically build a home within the grief of otherness and bodily difference.[2] On a gorgeous spring day in 2016, throbbing waves of abdominal cramps sliced through me, bringing my internal music and embodied harmony of dress to an abrupt halt. My internal compass was heartbroken, jammed. As I stood in front of the Atlantic Ocean, and the sun quietly descended, symptoms of the illness arose, enraged, persistent.

The evolving circumstances of my health have transformed the hospital into a different home. Yet this home is an eerie landscape of unresolved striving through the pursuit of remission, hampered by the volatility of repeat hospitalisation, unsuccessful treatments, the hopeful frenzy of a clinical trial and an assortment of past, present and future invasive surveillance procedures.

Monet, Napier, and Trifari were the vintage gold-tone costume jewellery brands I began to purchase off eBay as a high school student. The pleasure and play of glamorous, affordable and durable earrings were a departure from the delicate 14-karat gold hoops that had previously strictly graced my earlobes. My wrists adorned in voluminous bracelets with textured etching, drawing on the decorative power of jewellery. This young woman, who composed worlds through geometric embellishment, developed a signature look that glistened through shapely designs.

After my diagnosis, my once steadfast relationship with clothing remained destabilised throughout the dramatic flares of chronic illness. I came to realise that clothing as an expressive vehicle had become less viable as a method of experimentation, as I weathered weight fluctuations that sparked feelings of anguish. Reflecting on the boundlessness of my grandmother's draped textile fabric, wearable in a hundred ways, teaching me the lesson of how one can creatively resuscitate their own survival apparatus, I discovered the restorative contours of fine jewellery. This invigorating sense of renewal stems from the continuity of jewellery's size. Rings were an expressive device that I had previously only tentatively embraced, but was drawn to during illness, making the design process a space for experimentation. The accumulation of scuffs and scratches on each ring, gracefully transitioning them to a patina finish, is tethered to their permanence, their ability to withstand the daily wear of my assorted health challenges. The continuity of each ring's presence, a daily adornment, provides stabilised reassurance within an unstable body.

A member of the concierge team at the made-to-order jewellery store told me that her father was a gastroenterologist, as we slowly made our way up the staircase, and I disclosed my fatigue from a recent treatment in the infusion unit. I was there to discuss having a ring custom-made, but once comfortably sat against a plush cushion, an 18-karat rose gold, bezel-set oval pink sapphire ring met my gaze in the showroom. Nestled inside an elongated forest green jewellery box, the gemstone's variable colour palette of apricot rose evoked the warmth of my mother's Crepe Myrtle flowering trees – her unique thumbprint and record of tropical memory in the United States.[3] Adjacent to the pink sapphire ring was an 18-karat yellow gold, emerald-cut aquamarine solitaire ring that plunged me into a deeper reminiscence. I envisioned the pastel-leaning shade of teal as the fabric, sourced by my Ghanaian father in Lomé, Togo for his best friend's wedding, in the late 1970s. The aquamarine gemstone also recalled the storytelling properties of the denim bell-bottoms my father would have tailored in Accra as a 1960s pastime. The jewelled pairing of pink sapphire and aquamarine in the showroom opened a pathway of speculative bridging, allowing me to map my inheritance of clothed memories onto fine jewellery.

Perhaps transforming my sorrow into wearable statements is a resolution to honour everything my body has – and will – continue to carry me through.

Bloom in Amaryllis, Twirl in Marigold

Before immigrating to Washington, D.C. in August 1982 and eventually marrying my Ghanaian father, my mother spent considerable time within the halls of the American Embassy in Yaoundé, Cameroon. From discovering the illustrious voice of Diana Ross and the towering discography of Motown Records, she was routinely exposed to the iconicity of Black American cultural touchstones, while delving into the glossy pages of popular magazines that marketed the fantastical application of cherry red lipstick and the decadent glamour of Hollywood film studios. The online images of university campuses were also part of an illusion that steered her desire to be in the United States. The yearning to leave was as if she was running away from something and stemmed from her lack of academic achievement at the University of Yaoundé, as everything was in French. As my mother grew up and lived in the English-speaking region of Cameroon where French was never introduced, she was catapulted into a dispiriting learning environment that did not reflect the bilingual status of the country.

In July 2021, while rummaging through a velvety, mauve-toned trinket box in my mother's closet, I discovered the back of a photograph dated September 1982 with a handwritten note that read:

September 1982
Just arrived into the U.S.
The same outfit I had when I entered the Dulles airport.

In the photograph my mother is serenely sitting centre in the frame, surrounded by other English-speaking Cameroonians newly arrived in Washington D.C. She is wearing a warm-spirited, tailor-made print ensemble, which awakens my reflection on the intimate ways Black African women engage in placemaking through dress.[4] As I meditated on her cursive script, I wondered how, as a geography undergraduate attending Howard University, she adapted to uncharted territory through clothing, and what ordinary objects served as extraordinary anchors to preserve her tropical aliveness in the metropolis.

My Cameroonian mother is the architect of her own freedom through resolute worldmaking design. This has primarily manifested in the beauty she cultivates in her garden. The infusion of colourful decoration as a reparative template throughout my life can be understood as a working translation of my mother's survival apparatus: the cultivation of flowering plants in gardens throughout space and time. I remain close to the tension and tenderness of how Black women affectively, and with great care, stylise towards the feeling of home, the succulence of beauty, and remixed desires for freedom. This armoured work, undertaken by Black women, throughout time, is enveloped in beauty.

An elaborate rose printed evening gown, a sculpted tangerine wrap dress with magnified ruffle detailing, and an emerald-green satin ensemble, gathered at the waist, with billowing posture. My mother has always created fashion collages of Black women from her magazines, snipping pictures of models wearing the clothes she wishes to have tailored for her when in Accra. She carefully arranges the clipped images of these glamourous Black women on her posterboard. Her tailor, Christine Nkansah, owns her own shop and lives within walking distance of our family home in Tema. My mother has been getting wardrobe pieces made by her since August 2019. Emphasising the main attraction of choosing styles and silhouettes that are uniquely sewn for her body, she is drawn to lavender shades of lace and Kente print textiles.

Over the phone, I asked her: How do you resonate with glamorous images of Black femininity and womanhood portrayed in magazines?

She replied: A lot of it is through the Black women models, on a level that is deeper than just their aesthetic presentation. I look at how the styled colours complement our different skin tones and use that as a guide when shopping at a department store.

Krys: How do you feel when you encounter different clothing styles that can be reimagined through local fabrics sourced in Ghana?

Mama: Clipping out different fashion styles that are modelled by Black women, and having the clothes made in Ghana, draws me back to the continent where I came from. Everyone makes clothes, and my mother knitted sweaters for us as there was no place to buy them. There were no second-hand markets in our village.

Krys: Is there a connection between grandma's knitting practice and your style of adornment, through both ornamental horticulture and self-fashioning?

Mama: Her knitted sweaters and tending to the farm signalled how Cameroon is a labour-intensive society where things need to be done. A lot of things require you to get involved, including the extent to which people walk to the markets. Growing up, you also quickly learn that it is a cash-based society. The wearer saves money to buy the fabric, and the wearer saves money to pay the seamstress. We had one major seamster in our village, Uncle Zachariah, and we started planning our Christmas outfits in October.

Krys: How do you select the different fabrics used for the potential styles?

Mama: I go to Makola Market to look for fabrics as the starting point. I'm drawn to gold, red, and the earth tones. I'll send you a picture later to show you, but the outfit I'm wearing today is golden-yellow with vertical stripes of green.

Krys: Golden-yellow reminds me of amber. Yes, please send me photos! What do you love the most about fabric selection in the market?

Mama: I love that I'm in control of the colour selection of the outfit to be made, even if it's just a slight shade variation. Tropical people are very colourful, and having multicoloured clothing sewn brings me back to the source.

Krys: Do you see a connection between your agricultural upbringing and the wider cultural value of sewing?

Mama: Yes, definitely. If you can't grow the food, somebody else is growing it, and you go buy it. By design, clothes are the same way. Everything always goes back to the source. Somebody makes the clothing, and you go buy it, or you go and buy the fabric and somebody sews it.

Krys: When you left Cameroon and travelled to the US in 1982 as an undergraduate student, how did you transition into the readymade clothing marketplace?

Mama: Oh, it was a complete culture shock, and I often felt detached from the clothing itself. When I came [to Washington, D.C.] to attend Howard, I had no choice but the buy and wear what was being sold in the city. I did have a few pieces made, but the overall pricing was financially out of reach. Life moved fast, and there were too many buses and trains to catch. I truly wondered if I would ever feel normal abroad.

Krys: Were there specific material objects in the US that anchored a sense of home while you navigated the hardships?

Mama: I used the wax-printed wrapper given to me by my mother when I was leaving Cameroon as a blanket. It was packed in my suitcase and journeyed with me from Douala-Paris-Washington, D.C. aboard Union de Transports Aériens. The radio also felt familiar – most of Africa is radio and people still gather to listen.

Krys: Are there any evocative memories of radio transmission that come to mind?

Mama: I remember that anything to do with South Africa was barred, including travel. South African radio didn't come to us, and the country was blocked from the rest of the continent because of apartheid. There was no relationship because of racism, until apartheid was broken. We learned about it in school; how Black people were being treated like animals. But sometimes, when Miriam Makeba performed in Kenya, the radio would come through to us, and the sound of her voice held us together.

I remain enamoured by my mother's methodical patterns of translation, from farming in Cameroon to gardening in the US. Her geographic adaptation of cultivated beauty is wondrous and mighty in its visualisation of endurance. When I ask her about which flowering plant encompasses the aesthetic principles of decorative repair in her garden, akin to the self-making properties of fine jewellery for me, she takes a brief pause to reflect on her devoted catalogue of botanicals and our shared material lineage which is exhibited through beauty and distinct colourways.

Mama: I would have to say the Crepe Myrtle due to its stability and self-maintenance. They just grow and bloom flowers. You don't have to do much with them because they are a statement of endurance. It's a flowering plant that withstands the winter while dormant, but like clockwork, it opens up again in April, and before you know it, it starts blossoming in June, to beautify the background in which they have been planted. And for that reason, the Crepe Myrtle is very dear to me. Oh, how I love them. I remember when I first planted them and they bloomed the first year, a woman who was passing by came and told me that when you plant one tree, it will always stay with you. The birds carry and spread the seeds.

Krys: They bring so much glamour to the garden. The cherry red and magenta pink flowers are beloved. In what ways does your migratory cultural geography speak to the intimacy of survival?

Mama: I was raised in a farm environment, which is sacred to me. We were poor, but there was always an abundance of food to eat. When I came to Washington, D.C., as a student, I was in survival mode, and my whole day was like scavenging, just trying to make it through the day, working multiple jobs, 70+ hours a week. Although I was never sure what my tomorrow would bring, seeing yards full of flowers presented a glimmer of continuity, and I found liberation within my imagination. I had no idea where the flowers came from, so I began to observe. On a Spring Day, I witnessed landscapers arranging flowers – situating them at different angles, adding different colours, mulching, edging, and compacting the dirt. And I thought to myself: 'This is what I did on the farm! I can do this!' I had found a decorative anchor.

Krys: You found a song of liberation within the flowers . . . and used your imagination to recontextualise farming through flowers, which carried you. Your ingenuity in itself is a coded language of decorative repair.

Mama: It's amazing, the ingenuity of Black women, as we have been through so much. We always find a way to come around and sustain. The soil will always remember, and the plants are a testament. I think the Black experience is like that. I started cutting brochures out of the *Washington Post* in the Sunday paper, where they used to have inserts. In the Spring they would have flower gardens, and I used to take that insert page and cut out the featured flower beds, and that's how I started to learn about ornamental landscaping, replaying what I did in Cameroon with crops on the farm. I translated that into landscaping for flowers, you know? Annuals, perennials, it was all so exciting, because the cultivation of soil is what my mother and grandmother taught me on the farm, and now I can translate the grief of separation into flowering plants and gardening outside, to reimagine my sense of self. This is where I am today, this is where you are today. You and I will always be propelled by tropical memory.

The Men Who Dressed Me: Buscemi, Cash and Dad

Honor Wilson

The first time I knew I was a man was when I watched Steve Buscemi in *Fargo*. There's one particular scene that sticks with me still: Buscemi's character – the weaselly, pencil-moustachioed Carl Showalter – bent crooked and blood-stained in his turtleneck, wheezing with impeccable sleaze to his dead-eyed accomplice, 'You should see the other guy.'[1] In that instant I was bewitched, body and soul. Later, as the credits rolled, I rushed to the set of drawers in my university bedroom and rifled through until I found one of my old binders. Rolling it on before putting back on my shirt, I then, for a long while, simply sat on the floor and watched myself in the mirror, euphoric and terrified.

Of course, this wasn't my first trans-awakening, though I wish it was. In a pinch it's the story I tell people, but the reality is I had already come out in 2020, a full two years prior to my Buscemi-revelation, but that was a bad time. Turns out I had dropped something of a bomb upon my unwitting parents, who, despite having always previously prided themselves on my unconventional aspects (the hair-dye, the aversion to dresses, the politics, the unabashed bisexuality) found this development beyond their acceptable realm of "different". 'We don't understand,' was all they'd say. Well, neither did I.

Not wanting to make them uncomfortable (God forbid!) I slunk back into the closet two months later, grew my hair out, invested in some lingerie and laughed the whole thing off as just some hazy lockdown-induced gender crisis, until the night I decided to expand my cinematic tastes with *Fargo*. Not long beforehand I had broken up with my boyfriend, suddenly understanding why it had enraged me so much whenever he complimented my figure, adoring the very same things I had loathed since puberty, every squeeze or heavy pet seeming to carry the immense, sickly weight of *gender*, like he was pouring hot glue over me to help the femininity stick better. The binder helped it all slide off, a plate of armour that kept everything flat and up for debate.

Due to my chest size, there are only so many things binding can help with. I've always preferred colder weather over hot, but especially so since coming out. Summer involves risking heat stroke in your old faithful hoodie and baggy trousers, your lungs straining for air as sweat drips under your vest, running over every curve you're desperate to forget. In preparation for a holiday in Lake Como with two friends (both cis women) I bought a vintage pair of swimming trunks from Hugo Boss, though they never saw the water. But when it came time to swim, I abstained. My fun had been ruined an hour prior when I looked at a picture my friend took of the three of us and I saw that I was very much *not* channelling the same brick-jawed masculinity of the Hugo Boss models frequently seen smouldering in their adverts. Due to the hot weather and Ryanair carry-on limit, I had had to deplete my layers, so in the picture the slight lump of my binder was out and proud for all to see, though I was far from proud. Most likely, no one noticed, but I did, and that's all it took to confirm my fear that I wasn't actually convincing, that everyone was merely indulging me and my quaint game of dress-up. The femininity had reared its lurid head, leaving me to sulk on the shoreline while my friends splashed about in their bathing suits.

It was a confusing dichotomy, being pleased with my body one minute and then outright disgusted, thinking I was Hasselhoff bounding along the beach in *Baywatch*, then Shirley MacLaine in her 'barely-there bikini' (to quote journalist Lilah Ramzi) in the 1964 film, *What a Way to Go!*[2] I had short hair, hairy legs, was wearing men's trunks, and yet I still had to bind if I had any relative hope of passing. What more could I do? My chest has always been a point of insecurity, even before transitioning. As a teenager I would routinely scroll through the breast reduction surgery page on the NHS website, wanting nothing more than for my clothes to hang off me like they did on the improbably lanky store mannequins. At an age where I was still only thinking in binary terms, boys were ones and girls were zeroes, and so badly did I want the height and slenderness of a 1. So, seeing scrawny, screeching Carl Showalter scrambling through the Minnesotan snow with darkly comedic effect years later hit me something like a tidal wave. To this day, I continue to collect turtlenecks with his character in mind.

But why Buscemi? Well, I found comradery in his being 'funny lookin'.[3] A fervent, whiny, wiry hitman, hilariously disproportionate next to his 6' 2" partner, Gaear Grimsrud (played by Peter Stormare), rang home for someone who often feels like a shrill estimation of the cis men I find myself standing alongside when ordering at a bar or waiting for a bus. By many standards (usually heterosexual, cisgender ones), I too am a pretty funny lookin' man. A similarly relatable role of Buscemi's is the naïve bowling-enthusiast Donny in *The Big Lebowski* (1998), a character from yet another Coen Brothers romp and who is described by film scholar Jeffrey Adams as an 'indeterminate' shadow, devoid and strangely lacking in a film otherwise chock-full of zany characters.[4] Again, the absurdity of Buscemi, whenever stood next to his more immense castmates, John Goodman and Jeff Bridges, hits close to home. The gag of his personalised bowling shirts that, upon closer inspection, boast a different name each time can be metaphorized as a trans man assuming the different identities of the men whose shirts he finds in thrift stores. This interpretation is wholly steeped in my own experience, based on my decision to buy second-hand clothes from charity shops and thrifting apps, such as Vinted and Depop, in an effort to be environmentally conscious whilst excusing myself from the discomfort of shopping in the strictly gendered floors of name-brand stores. If I'm lucky, Mum will shrink one of Dad's Savile Row knits in the wash down to my size or I'll score a not-entirely-stained graphic tee at the local British Heart Foundation. I prefer wearing clothes that I know, at least at some point, a man might have actually worn rather than the blank slates hanging at H&M or Zara, aisles of polyester husks which I feel too green in the ways of masculinity to fill.

Buscemi is only the tip of the iceberg. I have a collection of men, amassed over time. Any popular figure under 6 ft. is automatically added. Kieran Culkin, Kendrick Lamar, Bob Dylan, Buster Keaton, to name just a few. I am one centimetre taller than Al Pacino and I cling to this desperately. I found it important early on in my transition to remember that even most cis men don't fit the stereotypical constraints of "man". On the train I'll look for small hands, big eyes, soft jaws, full lips. When it's not features, it's fabrics. It's jeans, rolled-up shirt sleeves or heavy brass belt buckles. And black. More often than not, I'm wearing something black, too. Such loyalty, beyond a temporary emo phase in secondary school, was inspired by a picture of Johnny Cash, snapped outside Folsom Prison in 1968.[5] The iconicity of the photo comes through in a description of it by journalist Liza Corsillo for *GQ*:

'His posture – right toe pointed like a thoroughbred horse, right hand grasping the metal gate, and the residual cloud of cigarette smoke frozen in front of his chest – is the stuff of Renaissance paintings.'[6]

This was a guy who could hold his own on a stage in front of a hall full of inmates, playing concerts at Folsom and San Quentin State Prison, who could be both stoic and poetic, hardy yet all the while maintaining a level of interiority I admired. The photograph outside Folsom Prison is another staple in my personal Fashion Hall of Fame, the classic all-black suit with blood red lining giving him the appearance of a blue-collar Dracula. Like Buscemi's pipsqueak sleaze as Showalter, Cash's dark, brooding country persona, lamenting about the wrongs of the world in deep baritone, struck a chord. His slick, shiny black hair, generously heeled loafers and dramatic suit had been another awakening, and so into the collection Johnny went. Any all-black outfit comprised of a button-down shirt and straight-leg trousers I wear is in homage to him, even though my dad says it makes me look more like a waiter than the singer-songwriter. In sixth form I discovered Cash's cover of Shel Silverstein's 'A Boy Named Sue' and continue to interpret it as a transmasc anthem; the narrator's loathing, brawling and eventual reconciling with his father for giving him a girl's name having in part inspired me to keep my own birth name post-transition. That, and the fact that, last Christmas, my uncle gifted me a red leather travel wallet embossed in gold with my initials, and no other "H" name seemed appropriate.

Once I decided to commit to the whole trans thing, I marched myself into the centre of my university city, determined to spend the last of my student loan on Man Clothes, only to be utterly horrified by the options. It was khakis and button-ups as far as the eye could see. Where were the aisles for the dandies of the world? Drawn from my dad's extensive coffee table book collection, I used to pore over *Reigning Men: Fashion in Menswear, 1715-2015*, which detailed everything from the Macaroni Englishmen of the 1760's, with their foppish character and lavish style, all the way through time to the lacy denim suits of Vivienne Westwood's Fall 1992 'Always on Camera' runway show. Where, oh where, I asked on my knees in the men's section of TK Maxx, are the clothes for the funny lookin' men?

Perhaps my shock would have not been so profuse if I had had a more casual reference for masculinity in my father. This was the man who, once it finally clicked, accepted my transness with an immediate gift of a pair of wooden shoe trees from Jones Bootmaker, followed by an extensive lecture on the dos and don'ts of menswear. Don't wear a belt a different colour to your shoes, don't match black with navy, take suits to the dry cleaners and keep jeans far, far away from the washing machine. Even in girlhood, I envied my dad's tie collection. The frequent wail of men's fashion is its restrictiveness, seen firsthand in the way the boys at my school would wrench off their ties the second the final bell rang, and echoed by *The Guardian*'s Phineas Harper when he wrote that, 'modern menswear is too often a parade of gloomy conformity, produced by an industry that contemptuously sees male shoppers as predictable and dull.'[7] I, however – prior to my self-actualisation and subsequent experimentation with clothes, at least – delighted in it. As a teenage girl, overwhelmed by the variety on offer in the women's section, the idea that a man need only wear a suit to be considered somewhat fashionable was appealing. A tie does all the heavy lifting, a single splash of colour wielded in a slip of fabric echoing earlier times of splendour, of the Elizabethan ruff or Lord Byron's cravat. Like Cash's crimson suit lining, ties speak of identity subtly. A prime example is found in my dad's collection: despite never being one to spend superfluously on himself, he clearly invested in these ties. Intricate patterns from Gucci, Versace, Hermès, Harrods and Liberty, all of which I hope to inherit. For my graduation, though not wanting to outshine me on the day, he nevertheless permitted himself a Gucci tie swimming with multi-coloured sketches of fish. Perhaps it is not so much his ties I wish to inherit as it is his masculinity. In wearing his ties, I might, in some way, convey to the world what I have inherited from my father, especially now that I am on hormones and my face, already inclined towards his features even as a girl, now bears more similarity to him than ever. With no pictures of dad as a young man to hold as a reference, it is in things like the ties that I can relate to him and, in him teaching me how to tie them, that he can make up for those rocky years where he didn't understand me.

The longer I explore my identity, the more I find I enjoy not the binarism but the ambiguity of being transgender. Recent debates calling for politicians and gender studies professors to "define" a woman are as exhaustive as they are unnecessary. Trans people are lambasted for adhering to antiquated gender norms yet in the same breath are insulted if they are seen – by needling, self-imposed cis authorities – to not be putting enough effort into passing. Trans women face the worst of this, trans men less so. Everyone can understand wanting to be a man, but no one can comprehend why you would actually choose to be a woman. Whilst some trans people may only be satisfied adhering to a strict binary, as far as I've encountered, this is a minority sentiment. The trans people I know frequently relish the gaps of things, the second takes, the question marks, wriggling into these pitfalls in understanding and making them wider; wide enough for anyone to fit and play inside. Writing in the 1980s, Elizabeth Wilson remarks that recent decades have seemingly forgotten the 'sacred' androgyny of previous eras, leaving fashion as one of the few spaces one can still play with aspects of gender: 'Fashion permits us to flirt with transvestism, precisely to divest it of all its danger and power'.[8]

I am scheduled for top surgery in the coming weeks and, beyond the obvious relief of no longer being at risk of spinal injury and lung damage (a hazard of continuous chest binding), I most look forward to seeing what the surgery welcomes in, what exciting new gaps it may open for me to explore. Despite having sold or donated most of my "girl" clothes, I have kept aside some pieces – a blouse, a skirt, a pair of fishnets – stowing them in the back of my wardrobe, not to see the light of day until after surgery, when I hope I will feel confident enough to wear them. The irony is not lost on me: it took becoming a man to finally feel like I can dress like a girl, but irony is a staple of the genderqueer experience. It is slippages, fragments. It is the *Coronation Street*-inspired drag worn by the members of Queen in the music video of their 1984 hit 'I Want to Break Free'.[9] It is the bedazzled Christian Siriano eyeball fluttering its eyelashes over Janelle Monáe's breast at the 2019 Met Gala. It was the delightful, neon hedonism of the Club Kid culture of late 80s and early 90s in New York City. It is the uncertain 'have a good day, Miss', muttered by the pharmacist as he hands me my testosterone. It is the bustier I intend to wear after my surgery where I will be, deliciously, ironically, sans bust.

Never have I been so eager to be cut open. As the day of my surgery approaches, I often recall trans model April Ashley, recounting her sex-reassignment surgery in the television documentary, *What Am I?*: 'As I went under the anaesthetic, my doctor [Georges Burou] said "Au revoir, Monsieur" and when I woke up, he said "Bonjour, Madame".[10] The idea of waking up as a new person is at once both dazzling and petrifying, not unlike what I felt that night with *Fargo*, meeting myself for the first time in my bedroom mirror. Nevertheless, I am keen to meet the man I will be after my procedure; it has been a hard fight to find him, and he and I must make up for lost time.

Sartorial Misdirection

Rosie Findlay

A Body round thy Body

One of the rectories we lived in when I was a child had a tree in the garden where cicadas loved to wrestle out of their bodies. Unhooking the husks they left behind was a careful job. Poised on the length of my palm, each empty cicada light as a dried leaf and as recently alive. A ghost you could stroke with your fingertip. My dad, my brother and I would spray-paint them gold and silver for our Christmas tree.

I later learned cicadas bury themselves underground to grow into their adult bodies. That what we collected was their bones, which protect their growing wings until they're ready to tear open their backs and struggle out. Their body-skeleton even has vents allowing them to breathe – some communion, then, between the shelter of their bodied interior and the fresh, open world.

By the time I became interested in clothes, we'd moved house again, leaving the tree and its occasional treasure behind. Remaining constant for my family was the church, both a place and a community that wove through me, who, in turn, burrowed happily into Sunday night services, youth group and Bible studies. My faith was as simple and strong as milk. When I focused on God, I felt total unity, symmetry in myself. Singing the words of a centuries-old hymn, I was sheer spirit and feeling. A beam of light both rising and falling, lifting as I expanded with joy, and deepening, deepened, with presence. This shining sense could pierce me when a verse cut through, or in prayer, when we were alone together, God and I, both invisible in my room. I wasn't separated from my body, and God was in me, and it was good.

But somewhere in the number of those days, I went from a girl in a body to a woman with a body and the symmetry was upset. Carried with the unwelcome changes of adulthood was the realisation that the world's relation to me had changed. My body became a stranger and for the first time, the way other people saw me felt present and intrusive. It wasn't only that their gaze pinned me into myself in a specific, confusing way, but that I didn't know how to evade it.

Highlighting my nascent self-consciousness were the talks administered at church, reminding me and every other girl that we had a problem on our hands. Nothing could feel less erotic than sitting cross-legged on the floor of the church hall hearing a leader explain we should wear t-shirts into the surf so not to cause our teenaged brothers in Christ to stumble. Our friends, familiar as puppies, were recast as a threat and our bodies the weapons that would be turned against us. Clothes were the answer: they hid, and in hiding made acceptable. *Clothe yourselves in righteousness.*

I refused to wear a T-shirt to the beach: to even think of it was to feel the dead weight of wet clothes on a scorching day, exacerbating my sullen hips and embarrassing breasts. But the danger had been marked: to appear in the world in unconscious immediacy, me in my body, here and visible, was to have control taken away. But even as an uncertain teenager I was stubborn, and this particular restriction, in my hands, became an escape route. Clothes as a way of effacing and resurfacing, clothes as elision, clothes as hiding in plain sight.

A gift came in the post. My aunt in Cairns signed up to *Vogue Australia* because they were giving away a watch with every subscription. She wanted the watch more than the magazine, so she sent it on to our house each month. Every worshipper remembers the moment of their conversion, and this was mine: standing barefoot on the chilly tiled floor, holding onto the pages like the hem of the future. I didn't know then what fashion would come to mean to me, but I saw in these glossy clothes a way of materialising my longing. I'd scrutinise each page, drinking the line of a miniskirt slung in frills across a hipbone, and the elegant slouch of grey grandpa pants tied with a silk chiffon bow. A one-shouldered Chloé dress, rearing white horses foaming against turquoise, slung across an insouciant shoulder. I studied spaghetti-strap tops that floated empire-line from the bust, and sporty neon Versace dresses so tight and slick they looked painted on, and jeans styled back to front and bleached to a fine fray. Desire is often likened to fever because of its hot abandon, but what of the nausea of unrequited wanting, and its inflamed anguish? Most of the brands weren't stocked in Australia, and those that were were so impossibly beyond my reach that the yearning they produced seemed as inherent to them as their astonishing prices. Yet these clothes and how they were worn in the magazine offered a look and an attitude: here were women who looked at home in themselves as they strode down catwalks and glared at the camera: they didn't have to care about who saw them because they were so self-sufficient. These women were on the page to be looked at but remained unfazed, untouched, because they existed somewhere else entirely.

These photos trained my eye. Now when I went shopping with my pocket of money from working at the video store I knew by instinct what I needed. And I searched for it. My local shopping centre, home to a thousand surf shops, lost all appeal. I scoured the newspaper's fashion pages for notices of sample sales by Australian brands. I would journey from the southern suburbs into Zetland, a wasteland of squat warehouses with tiny windows, filled with silk seconds and haughty PR girls who resented having to work the card machine. I'd ride the train to Central, reading my book until the doors opened on Foveaux Street, a vertiginous hill with a studio halfway up where Akira and Zimmermann held their sales on the third floor. You had to be buzzed in. They only took cash. Inside awaited a profusion of rails and hangers and boxes of bikini bottoms. Shy, I'd spend the entire time in a deep blush as older girls, who looked to me like models, dug through on their knees, and by them I also kneeled, all of us looking for just the thing.

If I found a way to imitate a catwalk look that lived in my imagination, I would experience a kind of floating escape. The clothes I unearthed ascended me somewhere rarer. A charged space beyond how I usually experienced myself and closer to the promise of who I wanted to be: a person liberated from burning self-consciousness, a person who was inscrutable, and therefore free. The fashion looks I saw in the magazine handed me the knowledge to build, to borrow from Thomas Carlyle's 'Sartor Resartus', *a Body round my Body*. These clothes felt like a vision of style that remade me, marking me as separate and safe, hidden and defiant.

Getting the Picture

A friend recently told me that in Northern Ireland, when someone dresses in a way that is out of step with everyone else, it's said that they *have notions*. We seem to have agreed somewhere along the way that it is unseemly to be preoccupied with clothes, so to encounter someone who appears outfit-first can be to sense a kind of threat. The eye-catching clothes symbolise something and if their meaning is elusive, the shortest route leads to vanity. Likening a person in a big look, as I've heard they say in Polish slang, to a rat who's dressed for the opening of a sewer, or asking them, voice dripping, what they are *wearing* or, *what we've come as today*, or *you didn't pay* money *for that did you* calls profligates back by reminding them of the shame they should have felt before leaving the house *dressed like that*.

Dressing is deeply social, marking our collective humanity. Our clothes signal in multiple, complex ways where we belong and who we belong to. So garments that reveal that you have one foot in another world are often perceived as a rejection of your community, or as an effort to project yourself as bigger and better than them. The question of where the intention is directed is important. As art historian Anne Hollander writes, *it is the inner theatre that is costumed by the choice in clothes, and this is not always under conscious management. The public may not always be intended, much less able, to get the picture.* Whatever in the social mix a person is resisting, the distinction marked by their clothes is not about self-elevation but about ameliorating the quality of their existence. Whether consciously adopted or not, a strategy of sartorial misdirection is an effort to make being in the world more bearable while carrying the confusion of yourself. It draws attention to the surface, for both onlooker and wearer, away from all that can feel helpless, painful, unresolved or dangerous.

Some say that our faculty of reason is what distinguishes us from other animals, but as psychotherapist Eve Golden reminds us, we're the only species that requires clothing to exist comfortably in the natural world. In 'Clothes, Inside Out', an essay weaving psychoanalytic thought with a meditation on what clothes do to and for us, she describes clothing as both artefact, protecting and delineating us, and idea, *contribut[ing] to the language of imagery by which we think of and speak to ourselves*. When we put on clothes, we are dressing our psyche as much as the rest of our body. A favourite jumper can comfort and warm in equal measure. In writing that clothes help keep *separation and merger, inclusion and exclusion, conformity and individuality, closeness and distance, concealment and display [. . .] adjusted to tolerable levels*, Golden acknowledges something fashion theorists know intimately: that clothes always rest on the interface of opposites. While in the world and of it, clothes are separate to us and yet they become part of us. Clothes enter the space of our body and fold against it, becoming our threshold and therefore inextricable from our experience of being in the world.

So let us see extravagant clothes as turning the volume up on closeness and distance, concealment and display, as they throw others off the scent and in their distraction, reveal something about us, even if the message remains elusive. Driven by instinct, things we half-know about ourselves, or things we don't want other people to recognise, clothes offer a facilitating environment in which to exist. They help us feel our way towards a coherent sense of self as they point others over there, away. Look here! they say. Let them stand in, for now, for me.

A Way of Honouring those Sartorial Traditions

Last summer, without really thinking about it, I posted that I thought extravagant clothes can be a way of hiding or escaping complicated feelings about yourself. I invited anyone who felt the same to write to me and, if they wanted, we could talk.

How the people who replied defined 'extravagant clothes' varied but their stories all touched on difficult feelings: of shame, confusion, pain and temporary self-alienation. As we spoke, we saw how clothes had presented a way of holding and speaking those feelings, transforming them into a skin that was more comfortable to wear, offering beauty, release, invisibility and, sometimes, recognition.

I first met Cella at an academic conference, where she wore a green carnation pinned on a velvet frock coat to give her paper on Oscar Wilde. She told me that she first started dressing to the theme of her presentations in high school, when she realised that dressing up in some way, even if it was just to mess around with her uniform, released her from her fear of public speaking. Picture Cella striding across campus in a recent favourite look: for a seminar on the late Victorian New Woman, billowy tweed Rationals, a silk cravat and boater.

Cella has always been particular about what clothing says about her: even as a child, she wanted to match her clothes to her emotions. Dressing was a way of *embodying complex feelings but without directly expressing them*, she said. *My dress is at once expressive and illegible, save by those who know me best. My complex feelings are hidden in plain sight. Dress is how I understand the world and assert my place in it.* The vintage dresses from the 1940s, 50s and 60s that she favoured as a teenager morphed into a form of nineteenth century dandyism in her twenties, flourishing through patterned blazers, silk shirts and brocade trousers. We were unknowingly in lockstep in our different cities, each dressing into a collection of fashion references; but Cella's was a bespoke library of David Bowie's glamorous androgyny, the Artistic Dress movement, high Victorian dandies and the New Woman's defiant panache. Cella was feeling her way towards a version of androgyny that side-stepped the aesthetic of teenage boyhood; instead, her androgynous dandyism was classically elegant, a little masculine. Her collection of 1970s power suits grew, culminating in her purchase of a neo-Edwardian tailcoat. *I felt myself when wearing that garment.* Cella hadn't come out as queer and had no plans to, comfortable in knowing who she was without feeling that she had to share it with anyone else.

Yet all that time, the nature of the conversation she was having with her clothes remained semi-opaque, until a pivotal moment towards the end of her

PhD. Cella was invited to an overseas conference and decided to get a bespoke suit made while she was there. A dressmaker and tailor herself, she had the suit in her head, and loved the process of having it measured and cut, the fitting of the baste, white stitches dashing the lines of the jacket, holding it all together. The length and breadth of her limned in fabric. It took three days for the tailor to make.

The suit was loosely inspired by a 1940s photograph of her grandfather in his thirties, wearing a grey double-breasted jacket and wide-leg, almost Oxford bag trousers with a deep cuff. Cella's version was a classically cut two-piece, dark navy worsted wool self stripe, with narrow trousers sitting on her natural waist. Single-breast, single-vent, three buttons, with a three-button cuff and a narrow lapel, because she didn't want it to look too "fashionable". Yet it was lined with acid green and blue shot silk, a flash of juicy colour inside the tidy fit. *When I put it on, I felt this incredible sense of relief and confidence and how I felt in my body, how I understood myself to be, coalesced.* She turned to face the mirror and saw herself. *And in that moment, I knew how to say it – I want to come out. It all fits together, it all feels right.*

The next night, still charged with the clarity wrought by the suit, Cella came out over dinner to her supervisor. Patty, who had gone with her to the tailor to try the suit on for the first time, already knew: *it was obviously the suit, I could just tell. Your whole body relaxed; your face opened up. You looked like a different person.*

Every time Cella wears the suit, the same feeling returns. Soon after, Patty gave her another Edwardian coat, which she had bought right after her own coming out. This gift from her queer family is material lineage, connecting Cella to Patty and to their queer forebears. *I could see myself doing that with the suit too – gifting it to a young queer person in my family one day.*

The Fugitive and the Stable

In the opening montage of his documentary *Notebook on Cities and Clothes*, director Wim Wenders narrates white typewritten text as it slides up the screen, backlit by dark blue static.

> We are creating an image of ourselves,
> We are attempting to resemble this image . . .
> Is that what we call identity?
> The accord

Between the image we have created
Of ourselves
And . . . ourselves?
Just who is that, 'ourselves'?

When they commissioned this film in 1989, the Centre Georges Pompidou asked Wenders to make a short film about fashion. What he produced was a rumination on how images and identity inform each other in fashion and cinema. Its central subject is the philosophy and practice of Japanese fashion designer Yohji Yamamoto, who speaks about his desire to make clothes that protect the people who wear them. His ideal, as a designer, is that *people can live life with this clothing.*

In one scene, Yamamoto sits in his studio as he explains this intention. Surrounding him are cool white walls and black clothes, some hanging on a rail, some on dress forms. He wears black, too, a collared shirt, sleeves pushed slightly up as he gestures with his cigarette. He tells how working people in the early nineteenth century relied on their winter coats to survive the extreme cold. *You need a thick coat on you, then this is life, this is real clothes for you. This is not for fashion. The coat is so beautiful because you feel so cold and you can't make your life without this coat, for example. It looks like your friend, or it looks like your family. And . . . if people can wear my things like in that way, then I could be so happy, because . . .* He smiles and gestures, as if to say, that's all there is to it.

Yohji Yamamoto is the fashion designer whose work is most important to David, who cited this film as a personal touchpoint in our conversation. He contacted me after seeing my post, and during our phone call, he described his teenage self as a poor, skinny and brown boy who did not fit in at school. He was interested in clothes but without access to them because his family didn't have the money to spare. He owned two sets of clothes: those he wore to school and the pyjamas he changed into when he got home.

When he was thirteen, David was diagnosed with Crohn's Disease. Crohn's wears cruelly on the body, an inflammation of the bowel leading to fatigue, weight loss and malnutrition, among other symptoms. While David's diagnosis seemed to explain his perpetual thinness, it also exacerbated his feelings of not fitting in and concentrated his disdain for his body. When, as a teenager, he started earning disposable income, David gravitated towards the brightest clothes he could find because the more colourful they were, the safer they felt. *Clothes became a way to create more distance between me and other people. If I can get people to look at the clothes, they're not looking at me.*

When he wore vibrant colours, he felt as though his body didn't matter as much. Topshop and American Apparel were beacons: David would stalk the shopfloor, hunting for the most vivid version of whatever they had. When getting dressed, he'd put together anything that clashed: a hot pink sweater with lime green skinny trousers one day, head-to-toe red and electric blue another. A pastel camouflage hoodie. A pair of bright orange suede trainers. David's aposematic style created a smokescreen for the bullies laying in wait on the streets of his neighbourhood. They started calling out to him about his clothes instead, which was both a relief and the intention. His outfits were *something to know me by that's in my control. I don't feel like I have control of my body, my health, my mental health. But that's always been my relationship to clothing and fashion: impression management.*

But even in the midst of his brilliant colours, David felt he was dressing for other people, not himself. He photographed his outfit every day to document it, always angling the camera so his face was obscured. Looking back at the photos, David could chart how good he felt in himself on any given day based on the clothes he was wearing. The more colourful, the more excessive, the worse he felt and correspondingly, the more bravado he exerted to conceal his feelings.

When he was twenty-one, David's doctors told him he would have to be hospitalised for treatment. He had to take time out from university and sold almost all of his clothes. He decided to start again from scratch and this time, to only wear black. I asked why black, and he said that he'd always wanted to wear it but told himself, *later*, something to anticipate. David's feelings changed when he felt that his illness was taking everything away from him. *I thought, why not embrace it now? It's a luxury and an extravagance to just wear a single colour. It's attention grabbing but not.*

Black gave him distance in both directions: reaching out, an inscrutable forcefield; reaching towards, wrapping David against himself. *I'm still trying to create distance. I was never comfortable with my body or who I am – it's an ongoing journey.* But he did glimpse something of himself in the words and work of other black clothes aficionados. One of them was Wim Wenders. In *Notebook on Cities and Clothes*, the director describes his first encounter with Yohji Yamamoto's designs as *an experience of identity.* His voice speaks over a scene of the two men playing pool, Wenders lean and boyishly clean-cut in a steel-blue shirt and jeans; Yamamoto casually elegant in black as he leans forward to crack apart the triangle. The narration places us in a shop's changing room, where Wenders is trying on a shirt and a jacket that seemed both *new and old at the same time. In the mirror I saw me . . . only better; more me than before.* The clothes reminded

Wenders of his father, and his childhood, as if his personal memories invigorated the warp and weft of the cloth. *The jacket was a direct translation of this feeling and it expressed 'father' better than words. What did Yamamoto know about me? About everybody?*

Feeling similarly saturates David's experience of clothes. At one time in his life, he didn't look into a mirror for a year, deciding what to wear based on whether the clothes felt right. When I asked what feeling right felt like, he said, *they help me feel more like myself, and I don't know how else to put it.* He gave the example of the security bestowed by a pair of black Yohji pants that belt across his waist, quietly speaking strength, a soft anchor. And his Ann Demeulemeester shirt, offering a feeling of being seen and met. When he put it on for the first time he wondered, *how does she know my body this way?*

Yohji Yamamoto kneels on the floor of his studio, dress forms and assistants visible in the background as he contemplates a model, off-camera in one of his designs. Wenders' warm voice explains his realisation that Yamamoto *expressed himself in two languages simultaneously. He played two instruments at the same time: the fluid and the solid. The fugitive and the stable.* I am reminded of David, clothing himself every day in the depths of velvet shadow. He's known for always wearing black, distinctive but inscrutable. His clothes swoop and drape, the touch giving form, the material giving shape. An elegance that steadies.

In Symmetry and Solitude

When I think of my teenaged self, I remember most keenly how full of feeling I was. As forceful, as buoyant as a shaken-up bottle of lemonade. I couldn't have explained then why my clothes felt so necessary, or why I felt so wrong and stunted on the rare times I tried on "normal clothes", like my friends at church wore. I didn't have a language to name the feeling, which was shame. But it was there in the surge of humiliation and helpless fury that only the sight of myself in a bikini could prompt. And in the mortification of being told a boy liked me, even one I had thought cute until that moment. And did I question why I covered my school diary in photos of fashion models looking aloof and hot in clothes? Collect the litany of shoulds and shouldn'ts and must nots, and *pray about it*, and *you're fearfully and wonderfully made*, and *your body will cause others to sin*, and *your body is holy*, and *yes, God loves you, but He loves you best when you obey*, and *understand that to obey is to be truly free, truly known, truly loved*? I could have laid them out one by one, these messages I took to heart, to see what they added up to. But instead, I held their contradictions close and believed them all.

For me, they were proof of God's mystery, his inherent difference from our way of making sense. If Jesus can be fully God and fully man at the same time, anything is possible. I trusted him to sort me out, and that my wordless, feelingful tangle would unspool, in time, in his hands. And in the meantime, as I kept unfurling into sudden womanhood, I had to somehow not only command the tumult but live with it, learning to breathe through everything I was taught and everything I tried to be, and all of the mystery I inherited, and all of the grace, and all of the pain.

It was a lot to carry. Easier to find coherence and delight in the clothes I chose for myself. They made acceptable a body I didn't really know how to inhabit with any freedom; the ways my outfits seemed strange in my suburb materialised my sense of not fitting in, of feeling ravelled and not knowing why. In clothes, I met strangeness with strangeness. They dressed me with a kind of distanced power. My style also put distance between me and the girls I compared myself to and knew I could never really emulate, seeming so assured, so comfortable with wanting and being wanted.

Joy came on Sunday mornings, when the sprawling playground of Bondi Public School would fill with stalls filled with everything from irregular bricks of soap to amateur paintings of the beach, and most importantly, vintage clothes. These clothes were technically second-hand, rather than vintage but they were *good*. The stalls were hidden around the back, in the courtyard, a maze of polyester dresses and blouses drifting in the breeze above suitcases of T-shirts, soft as time.

I preferred to venture there alone, the intensity of my desire flooding my field of vision and powering me through the daymakers hovering over cuffs made of bent spoons. I wouldn't slow down until I had my hand on a hanger, blood beating in time with the sun on my back, the rhythm of right passing to left. Eyes glancing up and down. Touching to feel how scratchy, how soft. To see something I wanted was to involuntarily catch my breath. Solitary gymnastics as I wrangled it over my perspiring shoulders, twisting, bag sliding down to hobble my knees. And then I'd ask the slightly sick, knife-edge question: *how much?*

I remember everything I bought there, even though most of it has drifted away by now, to charity shops or into someone else's wardrobe. A tiny chocolate and gold Louis Vuitton coin purse that was definitely fake. Bright blue fisherman's pants that wrapped me hip to hip into a flat parcel of cloth and girl. A hand-knitted pale pink acrylic jumper with a tiny pie-crust collar and enormous leg of mutton sleeves that narrowed into tourniquets, making it hard to bend my arms beyond 90 degrees. But the most vital of all, and long-gone now, was a pinafore dress that seemed to me the apotheosis of all that was cool in Sydney, fashion, and life. It was faded buff brown, made of cotton worn stiff by someone else, with a tiny waistband and a full skirt. Its bib-front was straight and rectangular, making me look like I was constantly holding a manila envelope against my chest. It felt artless, cool and *model off-duty*, the highest compliment I could feel in a garment thanks to the fashionspeak I faithfully absorbed. I would wear it over a white ribbed singlet and a pair of hot pink thongs, and feel myself expand, filling with a helium sense of pride and fulfilment. The pinafore transformed me into a girl from the magazines. I didn't look like her, but I felt like her. By approximating the longed-for look, I dressed myself into a dream that was better than a dream, because I could slip my yoke and live inside it.

Sunday night would come, and I'd choose something I bought and get dressed. The fizz of the thing that burnishes a new facet of you. I'd step through the arches into the church building, saying hi to John, the church warden who would wait by the door in an ironed shirt and tie to greet us all. The band would be warming up, my friends already gathering in our pew, fourth from the front, on the right, which the rest of the congregation always left free. The plastic-covered brown Bibles, the cream pleather pews with all their stuffing worn away. Maybe as I moved down the aisle, I'd see my friend Kieran, grinning at me. *Nice outfit, Rose. What are you dressed as tonight: an eighties babysitter?* And I'd grin back, happy, at home for now. My clothes a secret weapon, a secret language, a delight that was just for me.

'The Cool'

Yomi Șode

In her novel, *Fool's Errand*, Robin Hobb says, 'Despite my pain, I felt not the regret of an ending, but the foreboding of the beginning.'[1] As the grey hairs slowly but surely crept up on me, Hobb's quote came back: I felt like I was shedding this old, layered skin, not to leave behind, but to hold and look on from time to time. Occasionally turning it over in my hands; wondering in this journey of 'The Cool', whether I enjoyed the most precious parts of those younger years, enough to let go and embrace this new phase I was entering.

Roughly nine years ago, I attended a one-year-old's birthday party with my partner and our first child. As we journeyed, I navigated through roads that sometimes felt too narrow to pass through.

The mood at the party was chill. My son left his buggy and ran freely into a garden space I envied. Most people wouldn't realise this, but I am awkward at most social gatherings. So, I become the helicopter parent, checking in to see if my child is safe but really, it's an excuse to avoid speaking to a single soul. The issue on my side, though, is a more-than-capable child not needing his parents at all, waving at me from the sidelines while I secretly wait for him to tag me in for assistance. I'm in my head for the duration we are there, roaming the room, thinking. At times, snapped out of silence by my partner. 'You good?' She asks, as I count the third man wearing a V-neck jumper. I turn my head again, counting. *Four, five,* I carry on, 'Six, you see this?' My response is sharp. Six men wearing V-neck jumpers. By the look of it, all of them are fathers, and all of them look like this is the last place they want to be. My immediate thought was that if the future of fatherhood looked like this, then I did not want it!

That evening, I joked about it with my partner, swearing blind that I would never be caught dead wearing a V-neck like those men. Days later, I found myself unable to shift the feeling. I had questions. Questions regarding my identity, purpose and comfort. Looking back towards those men and searching for where their characters went. Yet they were comfortable and settled while I was irritated and anxious. 'It's just clothes,' my partner said, and she was right. I was projecting something I couldn't distil in the moment because even though she said, *it's just clothes*, I flashback through time, wanting to prove why it *wasn't* a case of it just being clothes. This was a me problem.

I arrived in England around nine years old. And, as expected, it was cold. I remember the snow falling over Peckham that morning. Dropping over and through the cracks of the many high-rise buildings, looking at my mother as we waited for my aunty to come home, with not much of a plan. Fast forward some months and I'm living in Camberwell and enrolled in a new primary school. The opportunity to assimilate and meet other students was right there, but my awkwardness became apparent, not to mention the fact that I spoke very little English. My mother was excited though and quickly went shopping to purchase the clothes that I would wear on my first day.

The morning I first walked into Comber Grove primary school, I wore an oversized orange, black, green and white striped t-shirt, over matching cycling shorts. I also wore pink and white Puma Discs. These trainers were special because they had no laces: you simply twisted the discs to tighten or loosen. Prior to walking inside my then-school, I had no idea about 'The Cool'.

In Nigeria, our school uniform consisted of a generic polo shirt and shorts in varying shades of brown, and sandals on our feet. The pressure was less on clothes – there were no brand-heavy items to show off – but more on grades and behaving well in class. Walking into the school in Camberwell on the first day was like hearing the needle scratch across vinyl. Each student in the playground looked at me strangely, othering me before I even opened my mouth. Their clothes were branded with logos that became more familiar in months to come. Though I was wearing branded trainers, it wasn't in the top three of branded trainers. Even the colour code of choice – for instance, girls mainly wearing pink, but not boys – was new to me. My first day was spent indoors with Mr O' Brian, my English teacher, who tried to stem the flow of my tears. He asked whether I was ok, trying his best to explain to me how mean kids can be. All I could do was nod my head.

My presentation now is not out of preference, but more out of not wanting to be a laughingstock to others – it's about standing out, on my terms, my autonomy. An unfortunate birth rite in keeping up appearances by being conditioned to be on your *A game* all the time. Now as an adult, it's less about being a laughingstock, you just never know what is around the corner: the CEO of a company walking into the elevator you waited two minutes for, or your crush casually sitting, watching, as you leap through the closing doors of the train. You never know what's around the corner, but you have to be ready. Maybe this was one of the reasons I was so fixated on the men wearing V-necks at the party, happily and not feeling the need to stand out. They felt less pressure to stand out, whereas I could almost taste the trauma of my past, ironically wanting to stand out from the rest, but not in the wrong way (according to me).

My idea of dress over the years has changed as I've poured more and more Britishness into the mixing pot holding my Nigerian-ness. Thinking back, I would have loved my elders to plead with me to hold onto the scraps of my identity, rather than letting it go so freely. What children of the diaspora know well is the pressure their parents felt in normalising their kids within White Britain. This often meant they ensured their child spoke 'proper English,' and didn't teach their mother tongue in fear that the accent may push through whenever they spoke. Again, not a thing of choice but of survival. My aunt, for example, didn't sit my mother down to lecture her about why I should marry a White woman when I was older out of preference – she wanted me to prosper and thought this was the only option.

Growing up between Peckham and Camberwell (with a short stint living in Bethnal Green), I was fortunate to be around a mix of cultures. Black African/ Caribbean, White British, South/East Asians. Slowly, my Nigerian identity was located in specific places. Òwàmbè on Saturday evenings, church all day Sunday. These moments – that I would love to relive now – were often lonely experiences back then. For the parties, my mother would dress me in Nigerian attire, bùbá and sokoto. There's extravagance when attending these gatherings: amidst the food, celebrations and music, there's the style. The random photographer that was not invited yet finds himself taking images of people, then charging £10 for printouts, or the multiple people exchanging pounds to dollars to spray money on the celebrant while they show us youngers the way it's done on the dancefloor. The extravagance in African customs was my normal. You felt it when an elder pinches the sides of his agbada before spinning on the dancefloor. The air gathering underneath soon lifts their agbada, making our elders look larger than life. You would know when Nigerians step in the room because of our clothing.

I think back to these golden moments, watching on as the adults enjoyed themselves until the morning. Wanting to get out of these clothes and hurry home to wear more of what my friends were wearing, or what I saw on TV. My Nigerian identity then was not framed to me as something so rich and sacred. It was just *there*. It wasn't in my face like the adverts selling various clothes and food, and it wasn't long before I wanted the inside of my fridge, stacked with various stews in reused ice cream tubs, to look like Georgie's fridge, which had no reused ice cream tubs. The European aesthetic began to drown out my language, my style, and overall, the culture I was born into.

The culture of England that I grew up in was very Black British and working class. The attire was less bùbá and sokoto, and more Nike, Adidas, Moschino, Versace, Valentino, Prada, Iceberg jeans, Evisu, and Avirex jackets. Brands you saw on TV on Monday, before spotting one of the olders wearing it within the week. Brands that seemed out of reach until you saw someone in proximity wear it. You notice the girls pay extra attention and mandem pay more respect. I only window-shopped for these designer items because they were too expensive; but if you were lucky enough to save up the money, you would buy, then remix every piece of clothing in your wardrobe to pair with them. These brands opened a gateway to 'The Cool'. In 'The Cool', you were welcomed with open arms. In 'The Cool', you jumped queues while watching everyone else wait. The acceptance was there almost immediately without having to work for it. Your clothes said enough. Cue people cooing over you wearing the latest trainers or jacket, while somewhere on the periphery were others who longed for the same attention. Some who never noticed you before now marking a target on your back.

When Frank Lucas wore his $100,000 full length chinchilla coat to a star-studded Mohammad Ali fight in 1971, he had no idea that from that night, his life would change forever. Lucas, when interviewed years later, even noted that his choice of clothing that evening was a 'massive mistake.'[2] Up until the evening of the fight, Frank Lucas was relatively unknown. Nobody knew of the massive drug empire he had built, connecting imports of heroin from Southeast Asia, bypassing the Mafia and known cartels. Yet, here was this unknown man in his coat and matching hat, in better seats than celebrities like Diana Ross and Frank Sinatra. By the time the fight was over, the main question in the minds of the NYPD, the mobsters, and the many who were there that evening was, *who is that guy?* It could be argued that that one move led to the downfall of Lucas's entire empire. He also caught the attention of crooked police officers who began to blackmail him for their compliance. Frank Lucas was eventually arrested in 1975 and sentenced to 70 years in jail. Unimaginable to think that a piece of clothing could do such a thing. After all, the intention is to look good in what you wear, to show it off because you have earned it, and knowing the people around you will shower you with praise because you look good. But at what cost?

Growing up, it's not as simple to just say, *I can wear these new pair of Nike 110's freely down the street* without being mindful of the corners taken at x hour, and in which borough. Whole fights have broken out, leading to serious harm, because someone stepped on someone else's white trainers. People may argue that dirt can just be washed off, but the context may involve months of saving to purchase those white trainers. We start to better understand the impact of class, poverty and ego in relation to expensive items. I cannot tell you a time I have freely enjoyed wearing expensive items without the thoughts that they may be taken from me. I explore this anxiety in my poetry collection, *Manorism*.[2] Again, this thing of survival. Maybe it explains why I wear clothing that is not heavily branded. People watch. Some place you on a pedestal; others want to push you off it.

Currently, social media influencers are littered all over our screens. They attend every event, they pose on the red carpet, donning the latest clothing items and getting their Getty images hours later. My first proper experience of this felt explosive. Dressed by Dior, the attention was overwhelming. An official invitation to their Autumn/Winter fashion show. The lead-up to the event felt overwhelmingly good: I had a tailor, champagne, even an assistant to fit my shoes. I was told to not lift a finger in my dressing. My assigned seat made me feel special; the show was out of this world. I got a glimpse into what is normal life for celebrities. The images were released over the next few days. They got all the views and in my head all I could think was, *but I only write poems*. Some normality came once the courier arrived to collect the clothes. However, the Dior show was a mere flash in the pan of my real life. The next time I was invited to something similar, I experienced a new internal pressure to keep up appearances. In a similar, but also not so similar turn of events as Frank Lucas, by wearing the Dior suit, I had unintentionally invited people to spot me in the room. The following years would be met with 'Yomi! I was wondering what you were going to wear tonight'. The parallels of a life we desire versus the lengths we go to meet that desire can, in some cases, lead to damaging outcomes. I have fallen victim to a type of pressure, checking I don't pay the price with my bank balance and good credit. The same social media influencers glossing the red carpets will eventually realise the financial implications of the upkeep of their presence. In this lifestyle, notoriety is a gift and a curse. Something I briefly was in the whirlwind of until I leapt out!

In 2013, I arrived back in Nigeria, after more than 20 years. I spent the majority of my time on my grandmother's compound, not really having the opportunity to immerse myself at home, on my terms. So, when I was invited back to perform in 2017, it felt like a beautiful moment to do the things I couldn't do in 2013.

It's hard to explain the idea of belonging. It's even worse when trying to lean into the customs of the environment that surrounds you. The running joke is that children of the diaspora forget their foundations. Even now as a father, it pains me slightly when my kids do backflips for fish and chips or pasta yet turn up their noses at the mention of certain traditional dishes like pounded yam or egúṣí. I spot my projections firing off on all cylinders, *they are not African enough, this is embarrassing on my part*, forgetting that kids are fussy and allowing myself to make peace with their preferences. The food, the clothes, the culture. Growing up as an African in Britain, there's no fixed placement regarding the idea of home, so when arriving on Nigerian soil, finally, on my terms? A part of me welcomed the peace in feeling settled, without people questioning whether I belonged.

For the time I was in Nigeria, I decided to wear traditional clothing. This was intentional. I sent my measurements to my aunt roughly three weeks prior to travelling. The tailors in mainland Lagos work extremely fast. What would take the tailors in London roughly two to three weeks would be done in two to four days. The work rate is different because of the mass of orders they receive. Bespoke from the styling to the embroidery. It reminds me of a barber customising your haircut to the image you show them. The same goes for these craftsmen who bring your vision to life, using a plethora of fabrics – ankara, brocade, atiku and much more.

Wearing these clothes made me feel at home. Comments such as 'Oh that's fancy, where is it from?' or 'Is that hard to take off?' wouldn't come at me because my landscape was different. However, the surprise came when I was in a conversation with a group of boys. Word had spread that I was visiting from the UK to perform, and in their disappointment, they wondered why I was wearing clothes that reminded them of themselves. Seeing me wear my bùbá and sokoto was triggering as it didn't show them anything to aspire to outside of the world they were living in. Instead, they asked why I wasn't wearing any Adidas or Nike on my feet. Why was I not wearing any Gucci or Louis Vuitton as they see on the TV and in London? 'It's an expensive lifestyle, and I'm home. I want to wear this.' If there was a final nail in the coffin, the look on their faces hammered it right in.

I would later find that traditional wear is more something the purists and elders wear. Not so much the younger generation. There are one or two days in the week where trad clothing is worn out of courtesy, as opposed to choice. I thought back to my first day of school in England, knowing nothing of these pressures existing in Nigeria. Now, it seemed those same pressures had found their way here, and oddly I'd othered myself, again, at home.

Fast forward four years to 2022. I received a lovely email from the Victoria & Albert Museum about a project called 'Fashioning Masculinities', an exhibition looking at the art of menswear and masculinity over the years. My poetry collection was due to be published later that year, and the worlds aligned in relation to the themes I explored in the book. Their offer was to work with a group of young male creatives in responding to the exhibition and to explore the idea of masculinity, clothing and identity as part of the programme, culminating to a public performance at V&A Lates. What was clear from the outset was that I was keen to explore the idea of masculinity changing over time for me, even more so now as a father.

The writing programme involved a series of workshops that would lead to in-depth writing. What the group did not know was the catharsis that I was also taking myself through. I ran a session on the colour pink and its relationship with men. I drew on examples from Hip Hop culture and known rappers like Cam'ron, who wore pink in all of his supposed alpha male-ness and ego. How this was what normalised the colour for me back then. This was 'The Cool'. The workshops generated talking points on power and softness, being bare skinned or wearing countless layers. We discussed the language of suits and the feeling of wearing a good quality suit. Some vowed to never touch a suit in their life – they liked their comforts in just being – while some couldn't wait to wear one. They wanted to be seen and looked upon as a somebody.

The standing ovation they received on the night of their performance was incredible. I felt proud, not because of their poems, but of the journey that led to their poems. In the debrief, one of the participants asked whether I dressed to be seen or not. 'I'm not sure', I responded. I think he saw the confusion on my face because I couldn't find an answer. The reason was more complex.

'Despite my pain, I felt not the regret of an ending, but the foreboding of the beginning.'

While I love the idea of the random men in V-necks carrying on with life, I've pretty much been raised with a sense of making my presence known – to wear the fur coat, essentially. This (as I've come to realise over the years) is as much political as just existing as a Black man in Britain. Blending in the background not being an option. The elders have instilled the same talk to most of us from young, regarding our time in England: *Get the best test results and make your family proud,* or to consider being a lawyer or engineer as career choices. A poet was nowhere in their thoughts or grade scale of salaries. I couldn't answer the question posed to me by the young poets because it was layered. I stared at those men at the birthday party, and I was hit with my age and my responsibility on this earth going forward. It sounds big, because it was. It felt like a chapter closing and a new one beginning.

My only issue with those men was the mirror of myself that I was faced with. The many years I've had to navigate my presence, and sometimes wondering whether there was a point I truly felt free in that celebration. Who wants to live with that kind of anxiety hovering over them? As an adult, I can look back, celebrating moments of absolute joy and thanking the heavens for the closest of calls. As a parent, I have to exercise not imposing these experiences to them. This new chapter I'm now reliving through my children. The branded hoodies I wore when I was younger, my son now wants to wear. He feels the history as he runs his head and arms through the top. He smiles in knowing it once belonged to me. My heart thumping with anxiety because of his excitement in wearing them, but also the risk wearing those items of clothing posed. The trials and tribulations I went through back then, now trusting that my son and my daughter will have to navigate this world in their own way, while I'm there on the periphery, hoping not to hold on to any loose threads as they grow.

On Losing Something Precious: Of Talismans and the End of Love

Stephanie Danler

For a certain kind of woman, her biography is in her jewelry. I am aware of women for whom jewelry is an accessory. Their trinkets are purchased based on trends and are retired at the end of a season. I'm not talking about that kind of jewelry or that kind of woman. This woman is the opposite of superficial, as she over-invests her objects with meaning. A woman who wears talismans. From them, she starts to believe there are things irreplaceable.

*   *   *   *

I was in Mexico for a wedding, in that prestigious enclave called Tulum with its baby powder sand and echoes of Bushwick and Silverlake. I don't usually drink tequila. It was a wedding where the bride and groom were so in love that the ground glowed. Where clouds gathered as the ceremony ended and everyone danced in the rain, sweating, the humidity plumping away our fine lines. The last my friends saw of me I was running towards a dark stormy sea to swim. They knew I was alive later because I liked a slew of photos on Instagram.

It was one of those nights that bled into one of those flights the next morning. I'm a terrible flyer and I fly all the time. But when they announced that it would be a bumpy take-off from the hellacious Cancun airport, I doubled down on my Xanax. An hour later I was in tears and paged the flight attendant to my seat, ding, ding, to tell me that I wasn't going to die. "Being in the air isn't the most dangerous part of flying." What a fucking answer.

The two ladies next to me wore matching sequined hoodies from Señor Frogs and were passed out. I cried silently in the window seat, hands braced in front of me. I couldn't read, I couldn't listen to music. My wrists were seizing up. The only thing I had left was to organize my purse. Receipts, mints, Nars lipsticks. I'm still alive, I said, sweating, look at my tools for living. I opened my jewelry bag that I always carry on in my purse. I wear eight rings, some stacked, on a daily basis. I'd done my best "beach casual" and only worn two for the weekend. I touched them all and came up with seven. The plane bounced and there were only seven rings. My wedding ring was gone.

The loss of a piece of jewelry is a specific grief, one that can't fully justify itself. It is final. It comes with an aura of irresponsibility. And though we know that it is an essentially irrational attachment, it is weighty, financially or historically. Every time there is the slap of absence, the sense of incompleteness, when we lose these "things." It contains a verdict—that we aren't quite worthy. That none of us have the ability to retain.

A wedding ring being the most obviously devastating loss. A universal symbol of love. It's supposed to bind you to your partner, mark your fidelity. It's supposed to contain more than the sum of the metal and stone and more than the sum of our fickle hearts.

At the time of its disappearance, I hadn't been married for years. But the band was from 1919, engraved with an Art Deco design, with little shreds of diamonds on top (the woman who sold it to me said it would bring light to my hand). It hadn't cost much. After I separated, I moved it to my right hand, and when my eyes brushed over it I said to myself, We were really beautiful, weren't we? Weren't we.

*   *   *   *

Once on a December night, I snuck out of my apartment mid-dinner-prep, abandoning my friend mid-kabocha-squash-chopping. I went to a dark bar and met a man for one beer. He was in another relationship with someone else, and I was in and out the city, but if we had even twenty minutes that month, we gave it to each other. Lunch breaks, runs in the park, drive-by hugs. Occasionally we met to ride the subway, side by side, untouching. He handed me a box and in it was a rose thorn, cast in rose gold, on a chain. Delicate, sharp. "Roses are bittersweet," he said.

I wore it everyday for months, while our affair swelled and ebbed, while I booked more plane tickets away from him or he retreated into the silent, white box of his real life. I saw the necklace in the mirror, or in photographs, and said, Look how brave I am. Affairs do this to people. Pain becomes the barometer of love, instead of joy.

I lost that necklace for three hours in a nothing beach town in Sicily. I did not remember taking it off. It was—by far—the most panicked I have ever been about a piece of jewelry. My friend was with me. She watched me fly around the room, calling the front desk, thrashing through my suitcases, demolishing the bed sheets, and in that tentative voice that she uses when I am long gone from the world, said, "Maybe it's a sign."

"Of what?" I screamed at her. Rageful.

Significance is as mutable as wind. Barthes, writing about objects that get entangled in desire, said, "What does my reading of it depend on? – If I believe myself about to gratified, the object will be favorable. If I see myself as abandoned, it will be sinister." We always receive the confirmation we desire. To be a writer is to be a reader of objects, of gazes, of houses, and it is a dangerous occupation.

A sign to leave him? A sign that I didn't deserve love?

When I found the necklace I didn't put it back on immediately. I waited ten minutes in which I stared at it on the sheets and thought, *I dare you, I dare you to leave me again.*

*   *   *   *

I called my aunt, the jewelry oracle in my family, to tell her about my wedding ring.

"Why on earth were you still wearing it?"

"Well, I wear it sometimes," I said, as if that explained something "It's a beautiful ring."

"I'm not debating its aesthetic merit. It's loaded. You have to look at your jewelry and ask yourself, why am I so attached to this?"

"I get it. I'm not hung up on my ex-husband."

"I know you're not. So what are you hung up on?"

It was a good question and I was silent.

"My first wedding was hideously expensive, at the Hotel Bel Air, and it still wasn't enough for his mother, who made us have two receptions. I was one year out of law school, and Joel, my first husband, slightly hated me because I had passed the bar and it took him three more times. Not the brightest bulb." She sighed. "That one I lost to the maid."

"Were you sad?"

"You need to start taking Paxil. I wasted almost forty years wanting to kill myself, and life is short."

"I'm not sure I totally understand," I say. But I do.

*   *   *   *

Do you remember the insanity of that trip to Venice? We were twenty. We went for Carnival. I know there was a group of us because they are in the photos but

I don't remember them. The trip was last minute (and your idea, all the trips were your idea). We had to stay on Lido because Venice was all booked up. We took the water taxis to the big island in the freezing February wind. A girl named Lisa asked to wear my cheap hoop earrings from Forever 21 and I said, Sure, we could switch. She pulled out her diamond studs, and I unclipped my hoops. We had a huge room with multiple beds. I stayed away from you when I was sober.

I remember you in the Piazza San Marco, you kicked a water bottle, it hit a cop and we ran. I remember needing to pee and running into an alley and while I was in the middle of it, the busboys of a restaurant started bringing out the trash. I was too drunk to stop peeing so I laughed, and they called their friends to come laugh at me, and you came down the alley and pulled up my pants. I remember a crowded Irish bar that was full of Americans, and you were in the booth behind me, you were directly behind me, and I laid my head back and looked at you, and you laid your head back, I was done trying to stay away from you. I remember you covering me with streamers. I remember the black shuttered windows of Venice, the fetid canals, the deadening facades, and I asked you where the real people were. I remember stealing wine from the closed restaurant of the hotel, I remember spilling red wine all over your bed sheets, I remember that you were too drunk to get hard, I remember coming when you went down on me, I remember thinking I shouldn't come loudly because someone was sleeping five feet away, I came loudly, I remember you telling me to stay in your bed, but you remember me saying I wanted to stay. You held me the entire night and when I woke up I knew from the way we were tangled that it was serious.

I do not remember when I lost one of Lisa's diamond earrings. I have no idea where that ended up. It had been her grandmother's, who had passed away a few years earlier. I remember apologizing as she got into a water taxi to leave and I remember shaking with my hangover and anxiety. The day was bright. Then she was gone and I was back to thinking about you and me. But in the decade since I have thought of her often and with sadness.

*　*　*　*

Like most writers, I live in fear of disappearance. I've been writing all of my life, and I understand my interests (presence, light and temperature, telling lies, the body, sex, how language obscures more than it reveals, etc.), but also what compels me to get out of bed in the morning: Fear. I'm terrified of losing the intensity of this world.

*　*　*　*

A boy left salt-and-pepper diamond earrings on my doorstep once. He had made them. We'd stopped seeing each other at that point, but he let himself in with a key I had meant to take back. It was the same week I found out I had a lump in my breast that they were hoping was cystic but wasn't, was nothing to be scared of, but also was nothing they could explain, and the same week that I vacated my apartment in Williamsburg and loaded my books on a truck headed for Los Angeles. The Boy-Jeweler wanted to see me and I said no. He was quite young, quite talented, and believed that the feelings we had when we were together (pleasant, warm, loving feelings) were all that mattered. Sometimes he made pronouncements like, "Change is our only constant," and I would think, you have no fucking idea what you're talking about yet. But he connected me to something I had thought dead—my younger self that had no concept of failure. When I found every difficulty an obstacle, not a life sentence.

The earrings posed a conundrum. Though I couldn't possibly keep them, he knew I would keep them. I am not only fond of jewelry, I'm fond of jewelry given to me by men that have been inside me, or that I've penetrated, in my own less innocent way.

I forget that I'm Catholic because I'm not religious, but I was raised and educated in the church. Occasionally it's reflected back at me when I decorate myself with these pieces, the pageantry, the penchant for self-recrimination. Do you see what you did? I ask myself.

Do you see that I'm wearing a collection of my failures? And while my body forgets, do you see how my jewelry reminds me that I survived?

Sometimes it's as if keeping the pain present justifies the unbearable beauty of my life.

* * * *

I have small gold hoop earrings that were given to me by my grandmother when I was six-years old. They were "Italian gold" she said, like I knew what that meant, and like every object in her orbit, it came with a story. She and my grandfather had walked by them on display in a shop in Venice, Italy. My grandmother commented that they were a strange size, a thick small hoop (a size she would later deem unflattering to an adult and a better fit for a kindergartener). When they were about to board the boat that would take them to the train station, my grandmother became hysterical and knew she was supposed to have those earrings. My grandfather ran to buy them (I can see him much younger, with his dark mustache, holding onto his hat as he ran across the narrow bridges). The store was closing, the boat was leaving, the train was pulling out of the station, but he captured them for her. His eyes always teared when he noticed me wearing them.

The earrings were de-quired twenty-six years later, at 5am, somewhere between the bedroom and the shower of a cottage in Laurel Canyon, while I rushed to pack for a flight. I checked the mirror and my face looked wrong. I so rarely took them off that I noticed the unbalance immediately. I grasped at my earlobe, uncomprehending. I felt my grandmother's watery, Scotch-scorched blue eyes on me, disappointed, receding in a gondola. *You're dead* I said to her, defensive. *Everything you left me is mine to lose.*

*   *   *   *

A few days after I got back from the Tulum wedding I was cutting lemons from a tree, wondering if I would ever write again, wondering if I would ever feel safe. My phone interrupted me. It was a friend who had been at the wedding.

"Did you pray to St. Christopher?" she asked. Cuca, their nanny, has been with her husband's family since he was a child, and is often referred to as the St. Christopher of Santa Monica. Cuca is preternaturally calm in turbulent air. She knows how to cure a child's cut with a slice of tomato. Back in Tulum, she was taking the baby off the beach, at a hotel I hadn't even stayed at, and noticed something flicker in the sand (it will bring light to your hand, the jeweler said to me). Cuca put my wedding ring on her pinkie and forgot about it for two days.

When I got it back I put it in a dish on my desk. If loss is a punishment, return is an absolution. My relief had flooded the house. But not just relief, something more ambiguous. I was vindicated. As I had unpacked from Tulum, the ring never appearing, I said, It's ok. Let go. And as I had paced the house in denial, I also said, I know it's not gone. This is a misunderstanding. I will be better. I will be trustworthy.

"Do not put it back on," My aunt said when I told her of its return. "It's a sign."

"It's not," I said, "It's just a pretty thing."

I spent a lot of time asking about lost jewelry after that. Every woman I know has a story, the ring in the garbage disposal, the earrings fallen through subway grates, the vanished brooch, that haunts them. When I asked them how long it took them to accept the loss, they often said, Oh I just can't think about it. It was a month in which I also spent a lot of time staring out of a window. A time in which I touched all of my things nightly, guarding against a vague, persistent fear that comes when I spend too long inside, when I believe I am being watched over by someone, and not kindly. I want to not think about the losses. I saw them all: These solitary pieces that slipped into the ether, the diamonds shorn of power, the platinum that abandoned us. I don't blame them, as I don't blame anything that retreats to safety.

A Leg to Stand On: Prosthetics, Metaphor, and Materiality

Vivian Sobchack

Matter has been given infinite fertility, inexhaustible vitality, and at the same time, a seductive power of temptation which invites us to create as well.
— Bruno Schulz, *The Street of Crocodiles*

It is this submission which is offered as a sacrifice to the glamorous singularity of an inhuman condition.
— Roland Barthes, "The Jet-man," in *Mythologies*

Let me begin again with the fact that I have a prosthetic left leg—and thus a certain investment in and curiosity about the ways in which "the prosthetic" has been embraced and recreated by contemporary scholars trying to make sense (and theory) out of our increasingly technologized lives. When I put my leg on in the morning, knowing that I am the one who will give it literal—if exhaustible—vitality even as it gives me literal support, I don't find it nearly as seductive a matter—or generalized an idea—as do some of my academic colleagues. And walking around during the day, going to teach a class or shop at the supermarket, neither do I feel like Barthes's "reified hero", the "Jet-man": a mythological "semi-object" whose prosthetically enhanced flesh has sacrificially submitted itself to "the glamorous singularity of an inhuman condition."[1] Not only do I see myself as fully human (if hardly singular or glamorous), but I also know intimately my prosthetic leg's essential inertia and lack of motivating volition. Indeed, for all the weight I place on it, it does not run my life. And thus, as I engage a variety of recent work in the humanities and arts, I am both startled and amused at the extraordinary moves made of and by "the prosthetic" of late—particularly since my prosthetic leg can barely stand on its own and certainly will never go out dancing without me.

Particularly, shall we say, "well equipped" to do so, I want both to critique and redress this metaphorical (and, dare I say, ethical) displacement of the prosthetic through a return to its premises in lived-body experience. However, this return will not be direct—but rather by way of what might be called a "tropological phenomenology."[2] In *The Rule of Metaphor* Paul Ricoeur writes: "If there is a point in our experience where living expression states living existence, it is where our movement up the entropic slope of language encounters the movement by which we come back this side of the distinctions between actuality, action, production, motion."[3] Thus, in what follows, I will pay as much attention to language as I will to lived bodies. This is because there is not only an *oppositional tension* but also a *dynamic connection* between *the* prosthetic as a tropological figure and *my* prosthetic as a material but also a phenomenologically lived artifact—the *the* and the *my* here indicating differences both of kind and degree between generalization and specificity, figure and ground, aesthetics and pragmatics, alienation and incorporation, subjectivity and objectivity, and between (as Helen Deutsch and Felicity Nussbaum put it) "a cultural trope and a material condition that indelibly affect[s] people's lives."[4] Thus, it is not my aim to privilege here autobiographical experience as somehow "more authentic" than "less authentic" discursive experience. Experience of any kind requires both bodies and language for its expression, and both autobiographical and discursive experience are real in that they each have material causes and consequences. It is also not my aim here to hobble flights of scholarly or artistic imagination and deny them the freedom of mobility that I have come to dearly cherish. In this regard, although I will return to my own prosthetic leg at a later moment—as well as to the prosthetic legs of an extraordinary woman who has made both the metaphorical and the material dance to her own choreography—such an anecdotal move is not meant to overvalue the "secret" knowledge possessed and revealed by the cultural other who has a real prosthetic but, rather, meant to ground and expand the tropological premises of "the prosthetic" as it informs the aesthetic and ethical imagination of the humanities and arts. Perhaps a more embodied "sense-ability" of the prosthetic by cultural critics and artists will lead to a greater apprehension of "response-ability" in its discursive use.

I

Sometime, fairly recently, after the "cyborg" became somewhat tired and tiresome from academic overuse, we started to hear and read about "the prosthetic"—less, in its ordinary usage, as a specific material replacement of a missing limb or body part than as a sexy, new metaphor that, whether noun or (more frequently) adjective, has become tropological currency for describing a vague and shifting constellation of relationships among bodies, technologies, and subjectivities. In an important essay called "The Prosthetic Imagination" that investigates the scholarly uses and abuses of the prosthetic, Sarah Jain writes: "As a trope that has flourished in a recent and varied literature concerned with interrogating human-technology interfaces, 'technology as prosthesis' attempts to describe the joining of materials, naturalizations, excorporations, and semiotic transfer that also go far beyond the medical definition of 'replacement of a missing part.'"[5]

We have, for example, "prosthetic consciousness" ("a reflexive awareness of supplementation")[6] and "prosthetic memory" (the public extroversions of photography and cinema that cast doubt on the privilege of interiority that once constructed individual subjectivity and identity).[7] Then there is the "prosthetic aesthetic", which "extends our thinking on the relationship between aesthetics, the body, and technology as an a priori prosthetic one."[8] We have also "prosthetic territories", described as "where technology and humanity fuse"[9]; "prosthetic devices," such as "autobiographical objects," which are "an addition, a trace, and a replacement for the intangible aspects of desire, identification, and social relations"[10] ; and "prosthetic processes," such as "contemporary aging," which point to a "postmodern state [that] is clearly a prosthetic creature cobbled together out of various organic and cybernetic sub-units."[11] And, then, there is a recent issue of *Cultural Anthropology* that produces what might be called the "prosthetic subaltern" in two essays, respectively entitled "Stumped Identities: Body Image, Bodies Politic, and the *Mujer Maya* as Prosthetic" and "Desire and the Prosthetics of Supervision: A Case of Maquiladora Flexibility."[12] Indeed, as Diane Nelson (author of one of the essays) points out in her introduction to the issue's focus on prosthesis and cultural analysis: "The prosthetic metaphor is drawn from recent work in cyborg anthropology, feminist studies of science, philosophy, political economy, disability studies, and neurophysiology. . . . [P]rosthetics mediate a whole series of those binaries we know we need to think beyond, but which still tend to ground our politics and our theory (self/other, body/technology, actor/ground, first world/third world, normal/disabled, global/local, male/female, West/East, public/private)."[13]

This is a tall order for a metaphor to fill. Furthermore, somehow, somewhere, in all this far-reaching and interdisciplinary cultural work (and with the exception of disability studies), the literal and material ground of the metaphor has been largely forgotten, if not disavowed. That is, the primary context in which "the prosthetic" functions literally rather than figuratively has been left behind—as has the experience and agency of those who, like myself, actually use prostheses without feeling "posthuman" and who, moreover, are often startled to read of all the hidden powers their prostheses apparently exercise both in the world and in the imaginations of cultural theorists. Indeed, most of the scholars who embrace the prosthetic metaphor far too quickly mobilize their fascination with artificial and "posthuman" extensions of "the body" in the service of a rhetoric (and, in some cases, a poetics) that is always located *elsewhere*—displacing and generalizing the prosthetic before exploring it first on its own quite extraordinarily complex, literal (and logical) ground. As Jain points out in her critique, "So many authors use it as an introductory point—a general premise underpinning their work about the ways in which technoscience and bodies interact," and thus the "metaphors of prosthetic extension are presented as if they were equivalent in some way, from typewriters to automobiles, hearing aids to silicone implants. . . . Both the prosthesis and the body are generalized in a form that denies how bodies can and do 'take up' technologies of all kinds."[14]

There is, then, a certain scandal to this metaphorical displacement and generalization—not because my (or anyone else's) literal and specific experience of prosthesis is sacrosanct or because the metaphor obliterates the political atrocities of mass amputations by landmines in Cambodia or by civil war in Sierra Leone.[15] Rather, the scandal of the metaphor is that it has become a fetishized and "unfleshed-out" catchword that functions vaguely as the ungrounded and "floating signifier" for a broad and variegated critical discourse on technoculture that includes little of these prosthetic realities. That is, the metaphor (and imagination) is too often less expansive than it is reductive, and its figuration is less complex and dynamic in aspect and function than the object and relations from whence it was—dare I say—amputated. As Steven Kurzman (himself an amputee) summarizes in the aforementioned special issue of *Cultural Anthropology*:

> Rather than develop a metaphor based on ethnographic material about artificial limbs or other prosthetic devices (e.g., breast implants, dental implants, joint implants, and so on), [scholars] develop a theoretical model to explain a problem arising out of a completely different topic and then *retroactively* define it in the world of amputation and artificial limbs. . . . Prosthesis simultaneously occupies the space of artificial limbs, metaphor, and discursive framework. The metaphor becomes unsituated and an instance of totalizing theory, managing to be both everywhere and nowhere simultaneously.[16]

In this regard it is useful to think more specifically, if briefly, about the *function* of metaphor. To be fair to all of us who use metaphor (and who doesn't?), we must acknowledge that metaphor is, by tropological nature, a *displacement*: a nominative term is displaced from its mundane (hence literal, nonfigural) context and placed, precisely, elsewhere so as to illuminate some other context through its *refiguration*—that is, by highlighting certain relations of structural or functional resemblance that might not be noticed without the transportation of a foreign object into an otherwise naturalized scene, an analogy is constituted. However, as Paul Ricoeur notes (quoting Pierre Fontanier), it is important to emphasize that metaphor "does not . . . refer to objects"; rather, "it consists 'in *presenting one idea under the sign of another that is more striking or better known*.'" (57).[17] Thus, primarily based on the relation of *ideas* rather than *objects*, and on structural and functional resemblances rather than physical similarities, metaphorical usage does not owe any necessary allegiance to the literal object— such as a prosthesis—that generated it. Nonetheless, it does owe necessary allegiance to a "common opinion" about the object and context that needs to sufficiently acknowledge the resemblance in order to "get" the analogy. As Ricoeur sums up: "[R]esemblance is principally a relationship between ideas, between generally held beliefs"—and thus, not only does analogy operate between ideas of structure and function rather than between objects as such, but the "idea itself is to be understood not 'from the point of view of the object seen by the spirit' but 'from the point of view of the spirit that sees'" (57–58).[18]

It is not surprising, then, that from the point of view of the "spirited" individuals who use prostheses in the most literal (rather than literary) sense, there are some major problems with the prosthetic metaphor as it is seen (and used) by those whose point of view is positioned elsewhere, in some theoretical rather than practiced—and practical—space. In this regard (and following on the work done by Jain) Kurzman emphasizes not only the short shrift given to actually substantiating the theoretical use of the metaphor (that is, justifying the analogy through careful comparison and contrast of specific structures and functions), but he also emphasizes two major and consequential reversals and reductions that have attended its current theoretical usage that do not correspond to the common opinion of most of us who actually use prostheses.

First, despite the fact that the metaphor emerges from an apparent—and critical—interrogation that is meant to disrupt the traditional notion of the body as whole, unlike Donna Haraway's nonhierarchical and hybrid cyborg, the metaphor of the prosthetic and its technological interface with the body is predicated on a naturalized sense of the body's previous and privileged "wholeness."[19] Furthermore, this corporeal wholeness tends to be constituted in purely *objective* and *visible* terms; body "parts" are seen (from an "observer's" point of view) as missing or limited and some "thing" other (or some "other" thing) is substituted or added on to take their place. What is elided by this predication (and point of view) are the phenomenological—and quite different— structural, functional, and aesthetic terms of those who successfully *incorporate* and *subjectively live* the prosthetic and sense themselves neither as lacking something nor as walking around with some "thing" that is added on to their bodies. Rather, in most situations, the prosthetic as lived in use is usually *transparent*; that is, it is as "absent" (to use Drew Leder's term) as is the rest of our body when we're focused outward to the world and successfully engaged in the various projects of our daily life.[20] Ideally incorporated not "into" or "on" but "as" the subject, the prosthetic becomes an object only when there's a mechanical or social problem that pushes it obtrusively into the foreground of one's consciousness—much in the manner in which a blister on our heel takes on an objective presence that is something other even though it is our own bodily fluid and stretched skin that constitute it. It is, thus, not the existence or use of a prosthetic that determines whether one feels one's body disrupted. Indeed, in common use, as Kurzman writes, "[a]rtificial limbs do not *disrupt* amputees' bodies, but rather reinforce our publicly perceived normalcy and humanity. . . . [A]rtificial limbs and prostheses only disrupt . . . what is commonly considered to be the naturally whole and abled Body" (380–381).

Second, Kurzman points to the way in which the theoretical use of the prosthetic metaphor tends to transfer *agency* (albeit not subjectivity, as with the cyborg) from human actors to human artifacts. Paradoxically, this transfer of agency indicates a certain technofetishism on the part of the theorist—however closeted and often antithetical to the overt critique of certain aspects of technoculture for which the metaphor was mobilized. As an effect of the prosthetic's amputation and displacement from its mundane context, the animate and volitional human beings who use prosthetic technology disappear into the background—passive, if not completely invisible—and the prosthetic is seen to have a will and life of its own. Thus we move from technofetishism to *technoanimism*. For example, Alison Landsberg, in "Prosthetic Memory," cites an Edison film, made as early as 1908, called *The Thieving Hand*, in which an armless beggar is provided with a prosthetic arm that once belonged to a thief and, against his will—but not the arm's—starts stealing.[21] A similar agency is cinematically granted to the prosthetic arm belonging to *Dr. Strangelove* (Stanley Kubrick, 1964)—and here we might note that, in terms of body parts, more arms and hands (which in fantasy often slip and slide between the severed limb and the prosthetic) have been granted agency by the cinema than legs. (Perhaps, and I speculate, this is because, having an opposable thumb, a hand has essentially a broader and more dramatic range of acting skills.)[22]

According to this seductive (and culturally recurrent) fantasy of the uncanny and wilful life of limbs and objects, not only can my prosthetic leg go dancing without me, but it also can "will" me to join it in what, in effect, is a nightmarish *danse macabre*. And, here, in the context of both technofetishism and technoanimism, I cannot help but recall my beloved *The Red Shoes* (Michael Powell and Emeric Pressburger, 1948). Antedating both my own encounter with a prosthetic leg and our current culture of "high-technophilia" (which might regard shoes as a fetish but certainly not a technology), the film, based on a Hans Christian Andersen story, concerns a young ballerina, torn between love and art, who gets her big break in a ballet in which she plays a woman who longs for a pair of red slippers that, when she finally gets to put them on, force her to dance until she dies from exhaustion. Such transfer of human agency to our technologies allows our artifacts to come back with a vengeance. Thus, in amused response to reading a theoretical essay on the prosthetic rife with technoanimism, Kurzman imagines his "modest collection of below-knee prosthetic legs" (kept in a box in his basement) developing "a collective consciousness of oppression," when they realize that he had "been using them to complete [his] identity," and "march[ing] upstairs to have a word with [him] about it" (380).

In effect, the current metaphorical displacement of the prosthetic into other contexts because of its analogical usefulness in pointing out certain (if vaguely specified) structural and functional resemblances between ideas also—and mistakenly—displaces agency from human to artifact and operates, as Kurzman puts it, as a "silencing dynamic of *disavowal*." Contemporary scholars (and many artists as well) are unwitting technophiles who, despite their critiques of global technoculture, too often "represent prosthesis and phantom limbs as agents, and amputees are present only as stumps and phantoms, which metonymically embody our lack of presence and subjectivity. Amputees . . . become 'the ground': the invisible, silent basis of the metaphor" (383).[23]

Kurzman's use of the term *metonymy* here seems to me critical to our understanding not only of the negative reaction that many prosthetic users have to the current "prosthetic imagination" but also of the specific figural differences and consequent relational meanings and functions that "the prosthetic" discursively serves. Metonymy is a figural operation quite different in function, effect, and meaning from metaphor (even as it is often imprecisely subsumed by it). It is even more significantly quite different from *synecdoche*, with which it appears almost—and problematically—symmetrical. These differences not only often discursively slip and slide into each other in ways that are confusing, but they also form the expressive and dynamic ground of the varying, confused, and ambivalent ways in which prostheses are seen in their relation to the human beings who use them.

In this regard Ricoeur (again glossing Fontanier) is particularly helpful. He not only differentiates the figural operations of the three species of tropes—metaphor, metonymy, and synecdoche—by their respective relations of *resemblance*, relations of *correspondence* (or *correlation*), and relations of *connection* but goes on to explore these relations and their consequences in more detail. Earlier I pointed out that predicated on relations of resemblance, metaphor operates to construct an analogy, presenting "one idea under the sign of another," primarily through highlighting similarities between the structural or functional aspects of objects rather than between the literal objects as such. Hence the prosthetic as a metaphor easily—and often—takes on adjectival form, characterizing and qualifying other nouns rather than serving a noun function itself: "prosthetic memory," "prosthetic territories," and so forth. Unlike metaphor, however, metonymy and synecdoche *do* primarily refer to objects—albeit quite differently. Constructing relations of correspondence or correlation, metonymy "brings together two objects each of which constitutes 'an absolutely separate whole.' This is why metonymy divides up in turn according to the variety of relationships that satisfy the general condition of correspondence: relationship of cause to effect, instrument to purpose, container to content, thing to its location, sign to signification, physical to moral, model to thing."[24] (Here, in relation to the prosthetic, we can see this variety of relationships played out across the relevant literature as well as in the culture at large. For example, as Kurzman notes, the way in which agency is transferred from the amputee to the prosthetic is clearly metonymic in character; the cause-effect relation between two "absolutely separate wholes"—a human and an artifact—is exaggerated and becomes not an ensemble but the seemingly complete transference of force or influence from one species of object or event to another.)

Synecdoche, unlike metonymy, constructs relations of connection through which "two objects *form an ensemble, a physical or metaphysical whole, the existence or idea of one being included in the existence or idea of another*"; this relationship of connection, Ricoeur writes, like metonymy, also divides up into a variety of subordinate but constitutive relations: "relations of part to whole, material to thing, of one to many, of species to genus, of abstract to concrete, of species to individual."[25] What is particularly important not only to an understanding of tropes but also to the troubled—and troubling—figural usage of the prosthetic is that, however symmetrical the functions of metonymy and synecdoche may appear, metonymic correspondence and synecdochic connection are radically different and "designate two relationships as distinct as *exclusion* ('absolutely separate whole') and *inclusion* ('included in . . . ')."[26] In relation to Jain and Kurzman's critiques—and to the perceptual and discursive conflict between "the point of view of the object seen by the spirit" and "the point of view of the spirit that sees"—the metonymic discourse of scholars describing the prosthetic *objectively* as an absolutely different species from the body is exclusionary and is at odds with the synecdochic discourse of amputees who describe their prosthetic *subjectively* as of the same "species" as the body that has incorporated, and therefore included, it. Thus, there is significant figural movement from metonymy to synecdoche, from *the* prosthetic viewed abstractly to *my* prosthetic leaning up against the wall near my bed in the morning to *my leg*, which works with the other one and enables me to walk. And here, I would suggest, it is worth pausing to note how the notion of my "other" leg functions in the previous sentence: that is, my "real" leg is suddenly become the "other." But this is a false—and hence justly confusing—opposition, as well as a telling reversal of figure and ground. My "real" leg and my "prosthetic" leg are not usually lived as two absolutely different and separate things since they function as an ensemble and are each a part of my body participating in the whole movement that gets me from here to there; thus, they are *organically* related in practice (if not in material) and are, to a great degree, *reversible* each with the other (my leg can stand in a part-to-whole synecdochic relationship with my body and vice-versa). This is to say (to refer back to Ricoeur and Fontanier) that, as I live them subjectively (and ambiguously), my two objective legs "form an ensemble, a physical [and] metaphysical whole, the existence [and] idea of one being included in the existence [and] idea of another."

Nonetheless, to be fair in regard to the tropological tendency to see the prosthetic (and sometimes to live it) in metonymic relation to the body, it is important to note here that the inclusiveness of synecdochic connection is not always as complete in existence as it is utopian in desire. Robert Rawdon Wilson writes: "Any consideration of prostheses has to take into account their potential failure and, even, the conditions under which they might go wrong or turn against their users. The consciousness of machines always includes . . . a dimension of fear. There is also fear's most intimate radical, an element of potential disappointment: the prosthesis may not work, or may work inadequately, or may entail unwanted consequences."[27] Although I really never feel like my prosthetic leg (or, for that matter, my eyeglasses when they're dirty) possesses the agency or subjectivity to "turn against" me, I will admit that it does have the capacity to become opaque, to turn into a hermeneutic object that I have to pay attention to and interpret and do something about (other than transparently walk with it). That is, my leg is transformed metonymically at times to another (inhuman) species of thing—the prosthetic resisting its formerly organic function in an ensemble of action directed elsewhere. In these moments it becomes an absolute other. This can happen suddenly—as when, losing a certain amount of suction in the socket that holds my leg in place, I feel (quite literally) a bit detached from the leg and have to press the valve on its side to recreate a vacuum. Or, as is more often the case, it can happen gradually—as when, over a long and hot day of walking, a combination of sweat and the pressure of the edge of the socket against my flesh begins to chafe and, if I don't "do" something about it, causes an abrasion.

The point is that, like the turns and effects of language in use, my experience— and view—of my leg (indeed, of the rest of my body) is not only *dynamic* and *situated* but also *ambiguous* and *graded*. That is, whether and to what degree I live (and describe) my prosthetic metaphorically, metonymically, or synecdochically is dependent on the nature of my engagements with others (how they see or avoid it or talk about it abstractly, or if I worry whether I can keep pace with them), with my environment (when I'm in unfamiliar territory the question is always "How far can I walk on it?"), with my mood (how physically attractive or frumpy do I feel overall and what part of myself will I single out for praise or blame?), and my project (how do I write about "my leg" or "it" within the context of cultural studies?). In sum, what Jain and Kurzman and I find problematic about the tropology of the prosthetic is, first, its vagueness, if not inaccuracy, as a metaphor meant to foreground the similarity of its structures and functions with various other ideas and institutional practices—and, second, its objectifying and often stultifying tendency to privilege and essentialize metonymic and oppositional relations that separate body and prosthetic, thus neglecting or disavowing not only the synecdochic relations that posit the cooperation and connective union of body and prosthetic in world-directed tasks but also the complex and dynamic ambiguity of all these possible existential and tropological relations as they are situated and lived.

II

Let me now turn, as earlier promised, to focus on a few specific prosthetic legs— first my own rather mundane one and then the much more flamboyant ones of double below-the-knee ("BK") amputee Aimee Mullins, a successful model and record-breaking paralympian sprinter, who has subsequently gone on to celebrity as a motivational speaker, a writer, one of *People* magazine's "50 Most Beautiful People" in 1999, and, most recently, the leading lady of *Cremaster 3* (2002), the latest in artist Matthew Barney's series of art-house films filled with "impressive prosthetics and special effects."[28] As you will see, this move to the specific and material does not leave the realm of tropology but, rather, animates it—and the "human-technology interface"—with the complexity, ambiguity, and desire revealed not only in "discourse" but also by "real bodies" living both real and imaginative lives.

Here, then, I want to stay grounded in (rather than displaced from) the materially, historically, and culturally situated premises of "the prosthetic"—even as "the prosthetic" also engages an experiential and discursive realm larger than that of its merely literal materiality, situation, and logic. As will become particularly evident—and dramatic—in the case of Aimee Mullins's legs, such grounding of (and taking the scare quotes off) the prosthetic does not disavow figuration (which, in any case, cannot be avoided); rather, metaphor, metonymy, and synecdoche are put in the service of illuminating the nature and experience of our prostheses instead of the prosthetic serving to illuminate something else (and elsewhere). Furthermore, even in my own mundane instance, focusing on the specificity of the prosthetic in its primary context functions also to highlight the contingent and uncanny play of its (and my) tropological and existential possibilities. That is, the prosthetic's many inconsistencies in use and its combination of elements that are theoretically paradoxical yet creatively functional not only account for the fascination it holds for others but also open up imagination and analysis to an expanded range of both action and description.

Thus, beginning with my own situation, I want to take the general and vague trope of "technology as prosthesis" that Jain and Kurzman criticize and *reverse* it—turning it back and regrounding it in its mundane context, where, like my prosthetic leg, it stands objectively in common opinion as the general and vague trope of "prosthesis as technology." This reversal, however, neither rejects the supposed purpose of the initial metaphor, which, according to Jain's description, "attempts to describe the joining of materials, naturalizations, excorporations, and semiotic transfer that also go[es] far beyond the medical definition of 'replacement of a missing part'"—nor does it do away with figuration. Rather, viewing the prosthesis as technology allows me to stake out (and stand) my ground in the *materiality* of the prosthetic and its incorporation—and, in the process, to playfully reconnect such figurative descriptions as "standing one's ground" with their quite literal "underpinnings."

In the summer of 1993, as the result of a recurrent soft-tissue cancer in my thigh, my left leg—after three operations, literally as well as metaphorically, "a drag"—was amputated high above the knee. For six months or so, while my flesh was still healing and I was engaged in strenuous preliminary rehabilitation, I got about using crutches (and here we might wonder not only how—but also if—crutches "hold up" in today's high-tech prosthetic imagination). Finally, however, my body was ready to go through the arduous plaster casting, fiberglass molding, and microfitting of a prosthetic leg so that I could begin to learn to walk again— a fairly lengthy and complex process that imbricated both intensive mechanical adjustment and physical practice. There were all sorts of physical things I had to learn to do consciously in quick sequence or, worse, simultaneously: kick the prosthetic leg forward to ground the heel, tighten my butt, pull my residual limb back in the socket and weight the prosthetic leg to lock the knee, take a step with my "own" leg and unweight the prosthetic leg as I did so, tighten my stomach and pull up tall to kick the prosthetic forward, and begin again. This, nonetheless, took a great deal less time than I feared it would, given my middle-age, general physical clumsiness, and my almost wilful lack of intimacy with my own body. Although it took much longer for me to develop a smoothly cadenced gait, I was functionally walking in a little over a month.

A prosthetic leg has many components and involves dynamic mechanical and physical processes, as well as a descriptive vocabulary all its own. To date and beginning with my very first prosthetic, as an above-the-knee ("AK") amputee I have had four different sockets—these molded of fiberglass and "thermo-flex" plastic to conform, over time, to the changing shape of my stump. The first socket was secured to my body tenuously through a combination of suspension belt and multilayered cotton "socks" of different thickness, which were added or subtracted depending on my fluid retention, the weather, and my slowly changing shape. The sockets that followed about a year later, however, were secured snugly through the suction I referred to earlier. Now I put the leg on by pulling my flesh into the socket with a "pulling sock" and then screw a valve into a threaded plastic hole embedded in the fiberglass, depressing it so that all the air escapes and my stump and the socket mold themselves each to the other. I have also had three different metal knees made out of aluminium and titanium, all of which were attached to a small wooden block, itself bonded to the socket. The first was a mechanical knee with an interior safety "brake" that could be set to freeze at a certain angle so as to stabilize me in "midfall" inflexion, the second a double-axis hydraulic knee that I didn't like because its reaction time seemed to lag behind my increasingly accomplished and fluid movements, and the third my current single-axis hydraulic knee whose extension and inflexion move transparently (at least most of the time) in isomorphic concert with my own bodily rhythms.

Over time there have also been two different lightweight metal leg rods that, replacing my tibia and fibula, run from the knee down into the foot—the first a dull silvery aluminium rather like the stuff of my crutches, and the second a glowing chartreuse green titanium that I sometimes think a shame to hide. (Before the cosmetic cover was added, I remember an eleven-year-old boy coming over to me in admiration and envy, crowing "Cool . . . Terminator!") Ultimately, these metal rods, like the rest of the leg and thigh, were covered with sculpted foam that my prosthetist lovingly shaped to complement, albeit not exactly match, my fleshy leg. (The prosthetic thigh is a bit thinner than my real thigh since it's not as malleable as flesh is in relation to clothing.) And then I've also had two feet although I've only needed one at a time—both of hard rubber composition with an interior spring that allows me to "roll over" and shift my weight from heel to ball even without an ankle joint, both the same model "Seattle Foot." (Prosthetics often have place names like the "Oklahoma Socket," the "Boston Elbow," the "Utah Arm.") Given my replacement and accumulation over time of all these prosthetic parts, I now have a complete spare leg in the depths of my closet behind some winter coats I have no need for in California and, somewhere in the trunk of my car, there's an extra socket (put there and never taken out after I got a new lighter-weight one). Finally, along with the crutches that I use in the early morning before I shower or late at night when I wake up to get a drink of water or go to the bathroom, I have about six or seven metal, plastic, and wooden canes. Because my remaining femur is extremely short—little more than two inches in length—I need the cane for stability; it basically counters the slight torquing and consequent "wobble" of the pliable mass of flesh within my socket and thus helps ground my walk (but, again, we might ask if canes count in today's prosthetic imagination).

I've paid as much as US$79.95 for the best of my canes (they can run into hundreds of dollars when they have silver handles shaped as the heads of hunting dogs so as to disguise physical need as aristocratic attitude), but I really do not know precisely how many thousands of dollars my prosthetic legs cost. Since I am one of a fortunate few who belong to a health maintenance organization (HMO) that covers such expenses and sends me no bills, I have been spared contemplation of the enormous and quality-of-life-threatening sums of money spent on producing, purchasing, and maintaining my prostheses.[29] Nonetheless, my research tells me that it is likely that my full (and rather ordinary) "AK" leg cost no less than US$10,000–$15,000, since a top-of-the-line carbon fiber

"BK" prosthesis used for sports competition (with a special Flex-Foot its inventor also calls the "Cheetah Foot") costs at least US$20,000 per leg. Should I wish it (which I don't), I could request that my HMO approve the purchase and fitting of the latest Bock "C-leg"—one in which microprocessors, strain gauges, angle detectors, hydraulics, and electronic valves "recreate the stability and step of a normal leg" and, as the *New York Times* reports, was a "lifesaver" for Curtis Grimsley, who used the leg "to walk down from the 70th floor of the World Trade Center on September 11th."[30] On the other hand (or leg?), the HMO might refuse me—not only because the "C-leg" costs US$40,000–$50,000 but also because I'm a woman of a certain age who is generally perceived as not needing to be so "well equipped" as someone who is younger (and male).

Indeed, like the movement it enables, prosthetic technology is highly dynamic and always literally incorporating (in both the bodily and business sense) the newest materials and technology available. Nonetheless, it is worth noting (as does Dr. Richard A. Sherman in a booklet written for amputees): "Just like any other machine, [prostheses] get out of whack and break with time and use. They need to be kept up properly and tuned up. The newer devices have computers, muscle tension and motion sensors, computer-controlled joints, tiny motors, etc. You can expect them to give you and your prosthetist more problems and have more 'down time' than relatively simple mechanical prostheses."[31] As it is, I have to see my prosthetist at least once a year: the mechanisms need checking and cleaning and my cosmetic foam cover always needs some repair or "fluffing up."

I hope, by now, that you—the reader—have been technologized and quantified into a stupor by what is a very narrow and "objective" register of meaning, the bland (or at least straight-faced) enumeration, detailing, and pricing of my prosthetic parts (whether on my body or in the closet) intended to ground and lend some "unsexy" material weight to a contemporary prosthetic imagination that privileges—and, like the eleven-year-old boy quoted above, is too often thrilled by—the exotic (indeed, perhaps erotic) *idea* rather than the mundane *reality* of my intimate relations with "high" technology. (Hence my wonderment about the prosthetic status of my "low-tech" crutches or canes.) Missing here (albeit suggested) is a description of the variety of phenomenological, social, and institutional relations I engage that have been partially transformed by my prosthetic: my consciousness, for example, altered at times by a heightened awareness not only of such things as the availability of "handicapped" access and parking but also of the way in which city streets, although still the same objective size, have subjectively expanded in space and contracted in time so that responding to traffic lights now as I cross the street creates a heightened sense of peril and anxiety I never felt before my amputation.

Missing, too, is the way in which learning to walk and incorporate a prosthetic leg has made me more—not less—intimate with the operation and power of my body: I now know where my muscles are and am physically more present to myself. I also enjoy what for me (previously a really bookish person) always seems my newfound physical strength, and I have discovered my center of gravity (which, in turn, has transformed my entire comportment in ways that include but also exceed my objective physical bearing). And, then, too, there are the encounters I've had with others that my prosthetic leg enabled—for example, a support group I attended at the request of my prosthetist (who had just started it and wanted to show me off in my short skirt and one-inch heels as a success story). There I met the most extraordinary individuals who might not otherwise have crossed my path: an older quadriplegic man who, for years, had been locked away by his parents and now, with some assistance, was living on his own for the first time; a whining, self-pitying woman who had lost one of her legs "BK" to diabetic gangrene and obviously "got off" on being in a position to tearfully order her husband to respond to her beck and call; a furious young woman, just graduated from college, whose legs were crushed in a car accident and whose boyfriend had just broken up with her but who went on (still furious), with two "AK" prosthetics, to become a Special Olympics athlete. And, of course, there was my prosthetist—who knows my aging body and my ageless will perhaps more intimately and approvingly than has any other man in my life.

My objective description of the prosthetic as technology also doesn't begin to touch on the great pride I've felt in my physical accomplishments or the great delight I take both in the way my prosthetic leg can pass as real and the desire I have to show it off. This paradoxical delight and desire have led to a strangely unselfconscious and exuberant exhibitionism that always catches me by surprise. As Kurzman points out: "In a social context, artificial limbs are ideally invisible in order to facilitate mimicry of nonamputees and passing as able-bodied," yet many "amputees are proud of their ability to walk well and pass, and often disclose because one's ability to pass is most remarkable when people are aware of it. . . . Prostheses do become visible, but often under amputees' terms of pass and trespass" (379). Indeed, I often find myself revealing as a marvel what the prosthetic leg is cosmetically supposed to hide (that I have a prosthetic leg), and, even more often, I tend to talk about—and demonstrate—the coordinated and amazing process of walking that we all don't normally think about but that the prosthetic leg is able to foreground and dramatize both to myself and for others.

These paradoxical desires and delights become particularly dramatic in relation to Aimee Mullins—both her legs and their "figuration" (discursive and literal). Consider, for example, the following passages from an article on Mullins by Amy Goldwasser that appeared in 1998 in an issue of *I.D.: The International Design Magazine*:

> Men devote themselves to Aimee Mullins' legs. Two men, in particular, have made it their business to know every millimeter of the expanse that runs from Mullins' knees down to her heels. One of these men can tell you precisely how many foot-pounds of torque she stores and releases with every running stride. The other can speak authoritatively about the spacing of hair follicles on her shins and the width of her Achilles tendons. Then there is a third man, who is a glass-blower. "He wants to make glass legs for me. Isn't that amazing?" Mullins says, genuinely awed by the poetic offer. "He said, 'Cinderella had a glass slipper, I could give you glass legs.'"
>
> In a modern literal twist to the old tale, it's not the beautiful heroine's hand but her legs that have inspired such courtly attention. And the kingdom at stake spans fewer than four feet, the lower-leg prosthetics, left and right, that Aimee Mullins wears. Mullins, 22, was born without fibula bones in her shins. Both of her legs were amputated below the knee at age one, a decision her parents made when doctors told them that otherwise she'd be confined to a wheelchair. On what Mullins refers to as her "sprinting legs," she is an elite athlete who holds world class records in her class in the 100- and 200-meter dash and long jump. On her "pretty legs," she is the only amputee in the country who looks magazine-model ideal in miniskirt and strappy sandals. If design can be seen as the quest for human solutions, then the challenge of creating legs to meet Mullins' biomechanical and beauty needs is an irresistible one to engineer and artist alike.[32]

What we have here is certainly the "high technology" of practical prosthetics. However, even more apparent—and to jaw-dropping degree—is the particular and contemporary "technological high" that comes not only from imagining but also, in Aimee's case, from realizing prosthetics tropologically. For example, Van Phillips, who designed Mullins's "sprinting legs," says of the Sprint-Flex III foot that is the legs' most prominent component: "I like to call it the Cheetah Foot because if you look at the hindquarters of the cheetah, the fastest animal there is, it's basically a C-shape" (Goldwasser, 48). And then there is Mullins's own description of her "pretty legs": "They're absolutely gorgeous. Very long, delicate, slim legs. Like a Barbie's. Literally, that's exactly how it is." Even though Barbie dolls are anatomically impossible (the breasts too big and the legs too slim to support the torso), Mullins finds "the doll ideal is liberating rather than limiting"; her "cosmetic prostheses make her a leggy 5'8'," and she has an "arch that demands two-inch heels" (Goldwasser, 49). And this "liberation" is experienced not only by Mullins alone but also by Bob Watts, the prosthetist who materialized her desire for "Barbie legs." He tells us, "These are sort of my fantasy legs. With a single amputee, it's easier to get an artificial leg to look like the sound leg. But when you're making two legs, it's twice as much work. But there's twice as much freedom, because there's also no reason why you can't make them absolutely identical and ideal. Aimee offered me an opportunity to produce the perfect female leg" (Goldwasser, 49).

The mind boggles—not only at the complicit male and female gender fantasies literally materialized here but also at the complex and paradoxical desires uncannily articulated through and by the prosthetic. Cheetah legs? On the one hand (or is it leg?), this materialization is all about the desire for the superhuman power and prowess afforded by highly specialized technology; on the other, its highly specialized technological enhancement of human motion and speed in sprinting paradoxically foregrounds the human costs of such technologically achieved and focused animal power. Thus, what is gained on one side is lost on the other. Mullins finds sprinting easy, and she finds "it's standing still that's hard." As the article points out, "One limitation of legs that move like the fastest animal on earth: the fastest animal on earth is more stable than Mullins when not in motion." Thus, in photo shoots featuring her as an athlete, Mullins tells Goldwasser: "The photographer has to hold me and kind of prop me in position before I fall over" (49).

And then there are those fabulous glass legs. Unrealized in 1998 (but not, as we will see, in 2002), they form the basis for a grandiose Cinderella story in which a romantic prince looks for an ideal woman with just the right legs (or lack of them) so he can outdo previous narrative heroes and their glass slippers with something more and bigger. But the prince here is also a prosthetist—revealing both his and the imagined prosthetic's confused substrate of desire and fear. That is, the very physical and social transparency that prosthetists wish to achieve and amputees to experience with their artificial legs entails in such an extreme figuration slippage not only in the aesthetics of transparency, delicacy, and thus "femininity" but also in the awful fragility of glass.

Except for the glass legs, the tropes articulated here discursively ("Cheetah foot" and "Barbie legs") are also materialized *literally*—but, materially realized, as legs, they maintain their figurative status as tropes nonetheless. That is, like language used figuratively, they are literally "bent out of shape" both in context and material form. Furthermore, as realized figures, they not only literalize both male and female gender fantasies but also confuse such categories as human and animal or animate and inanimate in precisely the ironic way that Donna Haraway's cyborg was originally meant to do. This confusion is embraced quite matter-of-factly by Mullins, who, recalling a technology and design conference she attended, tells us:

> The offers I got after speaking . . . were from animatronics designers and aerospace engineers who are building lightweight but strong materials, and artisans—like the guy who works for Disney and creates the skin for the dinosaurs so that it doesn't rip when their necks move. . . . These ideas need to be applied to prosthetics. . . . With all this new technology, why can't you design a leg that looks—and acts—like a leg? I want to be at the forefront of these possibilities. The guy designing the next generation of theme parks. The engineers. The glass-blower. I want everyone to come to me with their ideas.
>
> (Goldwasser, 51)

Aimee Mullins—at least in this article in 1998—is entirely sincere but hardly naïve. That is, however ironically paradoxical and politically incorrect, for Mullins's practical purposes, the prosthetic fantasies articulated here are all potentially liberating: indeed, Aimee Mullins's "Cheetah legs" have allowed her to set world sprinting records, and her "Barbie legs" have allowed her a successful career as a fashion model.[33]

III

There is something truly uncanny about the literalization of desire—whether prosthetic or discursive. We find it utterly strange when figures of speech and writing suddenly take material form, yet, at the same time, we find this strangeness utterly familiar because we wished such existential substantiations through the transubstantiations of thought and language. Thus, it was both uncannily strange and familiarly "right on" when, quite by accident and within two weeks' time, I suddenly encountered both "Barbie" and Aimee Mullins in two extraordinarily suggestive prosthetic scenarios—both discursive and both very real. Here we find not only prosthetic figuration literally and materially realized but also the literal and material prosthetic reversed on itself reflexively to become figurally the trope of a trope. First, listening to the radio, I learned that Ruth Handler, Barbie's creator, had died—the news obituary flatly recounting how, after achieving corporate success at Mattel Toys, she was ousted from its leadership for "covering over" the company's "losses" but then, a survivor of breast cancer, had gone on to establish a successful company that manufactured "prosthetic breasts." Impossibly breasted Barbie on those unsupportable legs, cosmetically "covering over losses," a hidden mastectomy, prosthetic breasts—this admixture and further reversal of the literal and figurative, the projective and the introjective, reflexively refers back to earlier figurations and makes metaphor, metonymy, and synecdoche seem, by comparison, figurally straightforward.

And, then, a week later, I read that Aimee Mullins had finally gotten her glass legs—and more. Browsing through a current issue of the *New Yorker*, I came across a short piece on the New York "art-house" opening of artist Matthew Barney's latest addition to his epic *Cremaster* cycle. Suddenly, there was Aimee:

> Hardly less daring was the gown worn to the première by the movie's leading lady, Aimee Mullins: a beige, floor-length number with a deeply plunging backline skimming buttocks that could star in "StairMaster 3." Mullins, who is a double amputee, plays a number of roles in the film, including one in which she wears a backless dress over a pair of translucent high-heeled legs, and another in which she is changed into a cheetah woman, stalking her prey—Barney, in a pink tartan kilt and pink feathered busby—on hind legs that end not in human feet but in feline paws.[34]

This literalized figuration goes far beyond the narrower compass and function of the usual prosthetic imagination—whether that of the cultural theorist or that of a prosthetic user like me. Indeed, I can barely keep pace with Aimee Mullins's legs here. Figuratively, they won't stand still. Not only are there the "glass legs" (made, however, of clear polyethylene), now literalized to function figurally in a movie. But there are also the "Cheetah legs," the literal prosthetic Cheetah foot now figuratively extended to incorporate and transform the whole woman. And, further, there is leading lady Mullins off-screen at the première "teetering slightly" in strappy sandals, because, she explains to the reporter, "these legs have, like, Barbie feet, and the heels of the shoes are an inch too short."[35] Indeed, in Barney's film she also has legs fitted with shoes that slice potatoes and, as a giant's wife, "legs cast out of dirt and a big brass toe," and another set of transparent legs "ending in man-of-war tentacles."[36] Again, we are far beyond simple irony here, far beyond metaphor, metonymy, and synecdoche. Indeed, we are both discursively and "really" in the tropological realm of *metalepsis*: the "trope of a trope." This is not simply repetition at a metalevel. Rather, as Harold Bloom (glossing tropes and the "psychic defenses" that inform them in his *A Map of Misreading*) writes: "We can define metalepsis as . . . the metonymic substitution of a word for a word *already* figurative. More broadly, a metalepsis or transumption is a scheme, frequently allusive, that refers . . . back to any previous figurative scheme. The related defenses are clearly introjection, the incorporation of an object or instinct so as to overcome it, *and* projection, the outward attribution of prohibited instincts or objects onto an other."[37] Here, with Aimee Mullins's legs (both onscreen and off) we have both—and simultaneously—incorporation and projection, an overcoming and a resistance, an unstoppable "difference" that is not about negation but about the alterity of "becoming." Aimee Mullins's legs in all their variety challenge simple figuration and fixity. Here the literal and the figural do not stand on oppositional ground, and the real and the discursive together dance to Aimee Mullins's tune—and choreography.

As for me, despite my awe and admiration for Mullins and the complexity of her life and projects, I have no desire to keep pace with her. I tend to locate my difference and variety elsewhere than my legs and just want to get on with things both mundane and extraordinary. Indeed, I remember long ago attending that first meeting of the support group at which my prosthetist proudly showed a video of amputees (without Cheetah legs) racing in the Special Olympics. As I sat there, I watched the people around me—and knew that all they wanted, as I did, was to be able to walk at work, to the store, and maybe on a treadmill at the gym. In sum, I've no desire for the "latest" in either literal or figural body parts. All I want is a leg to stand on, a limb I can go out on—so I can get about my world with a minimum of prosthetic thought.

Rummaging: Losing and finding myself in clothes

Ellen Sampson

This is not an essay about dressing. I am not even sure it's an essay about shopping. It is an essay about desire, about selection, about limitlessness and (of course) my complicated relationship with clothes.

I have always loved clothes, not so much individually or on my body, but en masse, in heaps and piles, a chaos of possible and potential selves. My desire for excess sits at odds with my personal aesthetics – relatively minimal – and the zeitgeist. This love of excess is both ethically questionable and deeply unfashionable: fashion writers whisper about quiet luxury, sighing over Lemaire and The Row. We are told to be selective, to curate our wardrobes, to display a minimal and delectable taste. We are meant to be considered in our choices, our sense of style a straight line cutting a path through a world overloaded with things. We are meant to know precisely and definitely how we wish our clothes to shape us.

I do not know how to do this. It is a skill that, even in mid-life, I have yet to acquire. That is not to say that I am anti-taste or actively pursuing bad taste, but that there is something in the process of eschewing selectiveness, of allowing myself to become diffuse within piles and racks of clothes, which is profoundly freeing. That I am happiest in these moments of anticipation and searching before anything has become fixed.

Dressing-up box

It started, of course, with a dressing-up box, a wooden chest that sat on the dining room floor. My parents, educators trained in the early Seventies and passionate about the power of creative play, assembled a fantastical and discordant array of treasures. Things selected to trigger a burgeoning imagination.

a faux fur coat with the sleeves mysteriously removed,
numerous single shoes,
my paternal grandmother's pink and gold brocade Sixties evening dress, its straps
held in place with rusted safety pins.
the delicate navy tulle stole trimmed in jet black marabou, which I mindlessly
destroyed
and most precious, a sequined pink chiffon Ra-Ra dress, which had allegedly
belonged to Eighties pop star Lene Lovich, arriving at our house by way of a
circuitous chain of Campaign for Nuclear Disarmament friends.

This box of delights was my entry point to the sensory and emotional resonances of clothes. The ways that they could make you feel in both senses of the word. Not simply the sensory pleasure of too-large shoes and slippery nylon gloves or the frustration of buttons, but the piquancy of covetousness, jonesing with desire; the fulsome and visceral flush of pride; the catastrophic obliteration of loss. A shy, stubborn and occasionally angry child, only clothes could match the strength of my feelings.

Later, I spent my pocket money at church jumble sales on objects that would inevitably cause my parents to sigh and roll their eyes. A huge green net ballroom dancing skirt: rustling acetate and layers and layers of ratty tulle. So big I could climb inside it, a Christmas tree with skinny pink legs. A delicate 1930s cut glass necklace, which I hid under piles of *Country Living* magazines so that no one else would spot it whilst I pleaded with my mother for a pound. These objects were my gateway to other ways of being, things which could manifest other worlds, spaces I inserted myself in order to imagine myself somewhere else. These were not my stories; they were someone else's, but I could collect them, touch them, and try them on for size. I was learning that you could make yourself out of bits and parts, materialising identity through a patchwork of things.

Through my dressing-up box and these early acquisitive forays, I was learning the pleasures of being surrounded by clothes. A sense that in this surfeit of tactile and imaginative interactions, my emerging and nebulous sense of self was being held in place. That these potential aspects of my *body schema*, these multiple non-corporeal fabric layers, had the capacity to thicken or strengthen me, binding me and holding me in place.[1] As though through these tangles of garments, I was forming an additional skin, something distinct from but akin to Anzieu's *Skin-ego*[2] or Bick's *Second skin*;[3] psychic skins, which 'can be felt to hold together the parts of the self which have as yet no coherence.'[4]

Charity shop

My predilection for rummaging, honed through jumble sales and bring and buys, reached its peak in my twenties, when, like the women in the fairy tales I am so fond of, I was driven by an almost insatiable hunger – a need to both shape and lose myself through a tangled mess of clothes. Emerging from the strictures of a small town's gaze, and grappling with an unsteady relationship with my body, I wanted nothing more than to remain undefined. Not unnoticeable, per se, but slippery and agile, able to navigate, court, deflect others' gaze. I have a photograph of my wardrobe from this time, a rack of clothes in a terrible basement flat from which we would soon get evicted. The excess is startling, meters of discordantly bright vintage dresses unified only in their incoherence. Florals jutting up against garish brocades, sample sale finds heaped on top of charity shop polyester St Michael blouses. I hunted endlessly and compulsively, taking detours and marking charity shops in a battered *London A to Z* map, and once famously spontaneously alighted a Helsinki tram without my travel companion because I had glimpsed what appeared to be treasure through the window of a Red Cross shop.

I am never entirely sure how to describe my particular relationship to clothing and consumption at that time. I would not, I think, have described myself as a shopaholic, or at least not in the conventional sense, because for me acquisition was not tied up with a search for status, and I was not, for the most part, spending beyond my means. Instead, it was the search that provided something for me, the pleasure of the hunt. Although I find my precise motivations for my frenzied searching difficult to pinpoint, the experience of finding something I loved was often akin to limerence, the fantasy-based and unrequited love that Dorothy Tennov describes: a sudden moment of connection followed by an extended and unmediated holding in mind. The ways that, as Magdalena Peterson McIntyre writes in her exploration of shopping and desire, 'certain garments emerged as a source of the possibility of thoughts and feelings. A yearning glimpse of a new exciting life [. . .] a hope to be affected.'[5]

It was, I think, the potentiality of it, the chance that one might stumble across something incredible at any moment, that some potent, albeit used and possibly damaged object would suddenly present itself asking to be yours; and promising to fulfill a present if previously unacknowledged need. Like many, I was ambivalent about my appearance, unsure if I liked what I saw. As I tried things on, I would take glancing looks in the mirror before discarding them and moving on, only briefly registering fit and feel. I was, instead, beholden to the anticipatory potential of dress. I craved the possibilities contained within these shops and clothes, the very happenstance nature of their acquisition, the fact that in the moment of acquisition nothing was certain or fixed. The ways that, as Christina Moon observes in her beautiful essay on the anticipatory potentials of dress, clothes 'conjure beauty into being along with new potential, a new feeling or identity.'[6] So that both the spaces in which I shopped and the garments I found functioned as something akin to what psychoanalysts term, transformational objects, objects 'identified with the [potential] metamorphosis of the self'.[7] Whilst the capacity of objects to mediate and facilitate fantasy is an almost inevitable aspect of shopping, the more I reflect upon the pleasures of searching through these chaotic and, at times, discordant spaces and of rummaging through the excesses of my wardrobe, the more I feel that my clothes functioned in a way that moves beyond fantasy. The unsorted, unfiltered quality of both my wardrobe and the places in which I searched created a particular kind of space for me. In these processes of rummaging, picking, testing and holding, however briefly, these objects and spaces offered a particular kind of containment, one in which nothing was required to be fixed – a space which allowed my desire to be simultaneously held and to remain unfocused, diffuse and unconstrained.

To return to Anzieu's writing on the Skin-ego, in which he presents the body's porous surfaces as central to the functioning of the psyche, offering a 'containing and unifying wrapping around the Self; as a protective barrier for the psyche; and as a filter of exchanges and for the recording of the earliest traces' – perhaps this excess created for me a loose but elastic form of holding, a space of containment which allowed me to be held to but remain unrestrained; to stay in the mutable, and perhaps more childlike, psychic space where nothing was required to be fixed.[8] Containment is a central concept of psychoanalytic theory, both in the context of an individual's capacity to manage uncertainty and in the context of being held. For Donald Winnicott and Wilfred Bion, in particular, holding was central to infant development. This holding was both literal and metaphorical: a caregiver's physical holding of the infant and their psychic holding, through attending to the infant's needs – holding them in mind. 'This function is exercised biologically by what Winnicott [. . .] calls "holding", i.e., by the way the mother supports the baby's body. The psychical function is formed through interiorising the mother's holding'.[9] Although we often think of being held as a form of constraint, it can also offer a kind of freedom, as though without the work of having to keep oneself together one can simply be. Just as I enjoyed the anonymity the city gave me, the ability to slip seamlessly between spaces, and selves, without notice, the diffuseness of my dressed identity, my refusal to commit to the strictures of a particular style, afforded me a sense of limitlessness, a space to play.

For Winnicott, play was central not just to childhood wellbeing but was the foundation of all creativity. He 'located this important area of experience in the potential space between the individual and the environment, that which initially both joins and separates.'[10] Our earliest and most fundamental creative expressions are, of course, playful. We pick things up and put them down, draw them close to us only to watch them rolling away. We conceal ourselves behind objects and hands, laughing as we suddenly reappear. When I think of my wardrobe, the charity shop and my chaotic jumbles of clothes, I think that what I have been doing all along is playing a mental game of dress up, upon which the material realities of the world cannot intervene. Meeting these garments in an interior space, unrestrained by the bounds of the body and the realities and challenges of life. Like a dressing-up box, these spaces and objects gave me a space to play, to try out and test multiple selves, allowing me to remain in the space of potential – the clothes waiting for me to decide who to be. As I ran my fingers through my wardrobe, or across racks of clothes, I toyed with them in my imagination, asking:

Who was the woman in the Alexander McQueen pencil skirt? How could she come into being?
What sort of person would viably wear a turquoise plaid cape?
What might you do whilst wearing blood-red boots?

I did not want just enough, I wanted too much: a surfeit of possible identities and selves. I did not want to eschew one identity just because I had not managed to become her yet. The clutter of these spaces softened the sharpness of decisions, of attempting to define a new self. Muted the volume of the incessant questions: *is this who I am? Is this what I want to be?* The unfixity of my chaotic wardrobe asked nothing from me but the space to hold my clothes.

This iterative process of searching and playing, of living in flats and rooms cramped with multiple potential selves, continued for years. Empty dresses languished on chairs, stockings and sweaters spilled from drawers, shoes cluttered the floor. Simultaneously comforting and oppressive, my clothes were near my body, but not on my body, lying in wait, ready to be worn. That is not to say that I didn't cull, that I did not become increasingly attuned to what was and not me. I read and reread decluttering manuals, articles about capsule wardrobes, and definitive lists of what one needed to own: three pairs of trousers or the perfect pair of jeans. There is an obvious freedom in this shedding, a Puritan pleasure in letting go, as though self-acceptance can come from winnowing away the parts of the self which no longer fit. Yet, letting go of that potential was always challenging. I separated out these possible and past identities, the garments my changing body and life no longer corresponded to. A Seventies parrot print Bri-Nylon blouse, floor length yellow taffeta, a plethora of neat white gloves. I would place them in storage or donate them to friends, but oftentimes, they would sneak back in, a Greek chorus of past selves. And even when they were gone from me, it was as though they never truly left; I still thought of them, continued to hold them in mind.

And then, at some point during the pandemic, I stopped liking clothes. It was not simply the ennui of an overworn wardrobe or the simultaneously excruciating and pleasurable withdrawal of the appraising gaze of others. No, it was an involuntary reaction, an oppressive disinterest, as though they had suddenly and irrevocably ceased to cast their spell. I had begun to dress in a way that felt alien to me – like the antithesis of what I thought to be my true self. A stint in New York had darkened my wardrobe, stripping it of colour and simplifying its form. A disastrous house move, days before the first lockdown, had left me hundreds of miles from most of my clothes; family illness had required me to shed decorative layers until my remaining wardrobe felt stark and bare. It took a while to dawn on me, and then it was a startling loss. I write about and photograph garments for a living. I had spent my 20s trying and largely failing to work in the fashion industry. Clothes were my currency. My wardrobe had always been both who I was and who I wanted to be.

During this time, I tried to shop. I browsed online, made desultory purchases I felt nothing for and could not bring myself to wear; things that made no sense because I seemed to have forgotten how to both dress and shop. Slowly, it became apparent that the lockdown renunciation had somehow detached me from my own body. I kept buying things that were the wrong size, wide-leg trousers two sizes too big, a drapey dress that on my body is skintight, as though my love of clothes had previously shored up my body schema, keeping a latent dysmorphia at bay. The diffuseness of my body image was slightly terrifying: an unpleasant hall of mirrors giddiness, Alice in Wonderland vertigo each time I tried something on.

App

It was the clutter that first drew me to it. The way that things appeared to be almost arbitrarily plonked en masse, loose categories heaped together like donations at the church bring and buys. The search function that only made the very slightest effort to sort, and the fact that people seemed willing to sell almost anything – empty packaging stained t-shirts, Balenciaga handbags all jostling for space – gave it a slightly anarchic feel, like a flea market moved into the digital realm. It reminded me of nothing so much as the Waste, the Saturday market that ran along the Kingsland Road, where house clearance companies and rag-and-bone men would tip a week's worth of detritus they could sell by no other means onto the grimy pavements below. You, the potential buyer, were compelled to rummage: to get down on your knees and sift through the broken fuse boxes and limbless plastic dolls. Searching for something worth taking home. It was, of course, my idea of heaven. The initial sifting without a particular focus or aim, then the more focused appraisal of the potential treasures you had found. Turning each one over in your mind until you could tell if it would fit within your life, if it met an as-yet unspecified and unacknowledged desire. The app felt like that: curating piles of chaos and then mentally trying them on for size. The rummaging mediated by the screen.

Little by little, on long train journeys home, I make furtive attempts to identify what I like. These attempts are largely unsuccessful: ugly jumpers, an ill-fitting bikini, the long green dress I try and fail to resell. Yet in these failed attempts, I begin to feel again the piquancy of wanting. I am starting to rummage again to try out and play with desire. A long wool cape I do not need, and which makes precisely no sense in my life, catches my eye. Gold earrings that the seller has failed to identify as Eighties Givenchy glitter on the screen. Honed by years of charity shop shopping, my high tolerance for imperfection serves me well. So that, as packages arrived, as I become shame-inducingly recognisable to the man at the grocery store, I begin to find a language: a Paul Smith blazer, TOTEME boots, the ridiculous Calcaterra cape, the miraculous Givenchy earrings bought for a pound. Through these tiny, tentative, and then increasingly frequent forays, I am defining myself – perhaps for the first time clear in who and how I want to be. As though somehow, in the emptiness of successive lockdowns devoid of others' gaze, I have found a different kind of space; able to see/look at myself as a whole. This is not the crystalline precision of fashion editors or the confidently stylish: I still dress by rummaging, trying things on briefly, then discarding them in heaps and piles. I still err, at times longing for the comfort of bright things I will not wear, trying on muumuus and ball gowns, experiencing the sweaty panic of getting stuck in too-tight dresses under the clammy lights of charity shop changing rooms. But underneath there is a precision, a decisiveness I previously lacked. I am wide trousers, clothes by Shirin Guild, gold chains, a particular shade of navy and red lip.

As I unwrap parcels and slip their treasures on, I come to understand, perhaps for the first time, what isn't me as well as what might be. Running my fingers through my wardrobe, I realise that it is not simply that these garments do not fit my body or my life anymore but that I no longer want them to. Something has shifted; I have ceased to need them – they no longer have a hold. I begin to list things, at first carefully, with lengthy descriptions, and then as I begin to understand the immediacy of the app, quickly and casually, with the fervour I used to reserve for rummaging. There is a piquancy to these interactions and a few times, I have faltered. Finger hovering over the accept button, paralyzed with doubt, wondering if I am losing someone I have yet to become. There have been regrets – a beautiful gold skirt, the dress I wore the day of my best haircut, a boring but incredibly practical pair of shoes – but they have been fewer than expected. Mostly I have been rewarded in this letting go, have enjoyed shedding small aspects of myself that no longer serve me. As I sort, the things I love most – a minuscule green skirt, the wedding dress I never wore, my grandmother's brocade are folded and put away – held tightly in a clear plastic box. Layered, they lie there, the archeological strata of my life. Occasionally I visit them, taking them down and turning them, but our relationship is different now. I think of them less often; I am happy to return them to the box. I am holding myself together. I have (I think) finally found myself in clothes.

Material Ambiguities: Time, clothing and grief during terminal illness

Isabel Mundigo-Moore

'What are we to do with the clothes of the dead?' Karena de Perthuis asks about clothing, repair, and loss, after Peter Stallybrass, in her essay, 'Darning Mark's Jumper'.[1] De Perthuis positions wearing the clothing of the dead as an act of mourning and outlines how darning her partner Mark's jumper during his terminal illness was an 'act of love'.[2] In reflecting on clothing and grief, this paper builds on these writers' works to ask: what happens to the clothes of the dying? As the bodies that once wore them begin to die, garments enter a liminal state. What happens to clothes as they shift from being a person's valued possessions to their loved one's mementos? Not yet a responsibility for those left behind, not yet something to be 'done away with', clothing is a threshold of what is to come.

These questions emerged in the final months of losing my father to a rare form of cancer. His doctors diagnosed his illness ten years before he died, and it became critical when it spread to his brain. When my father started receiving palliative care in the final year of his life, his approaching death started to loom. Having moved to the UK from Canada in my early twenties, my experience of his decade-long illness was concentrated into video calls and visits home where he lived with my stepmother and nine-year-old sister. As his disease became terminal, there was little I could do to remedy it; what I could do was be with him, spend time by his side and soak up as much of him as I could. While he was dying, my father remained firmly hopeful his situation would change, that things would get better. Therefore, he and I did not often discuss the prospect of his untimely death at fifty-five years old. When I spent time with him in his room, we hovered around the topic, choosing instead to listen to music, heal old wounds, speak of my childhood and tell each other we loved the other.

During the time we were able to spend together in his final months of life, my father was often sleeping but enjoyed my company, so I sat with him reflecting privately on the past, the present and the strangeness of what was about to come. As it moved from imminent to all-consuming, my father's incurable cancer confronted me in how it remained mysterious even as we lived it. How could something so terribly silent be the agent of so much tragedy? To conceive what was happening to our family was slippery, I could never quite grasp it; I felt desperately helpless about something that never totally felt feasible. Silence spread, both amongst our family and socially, as is so often the case with long-term illness. I felt suspended in emotional limbo. Amidst my inability to comprehend and express how I felt, I had a growing awareness that my father's clothing could potentially reconcile this mounting ambiguity, and in some way lead to an emotional understanding even as we could not find the words to speak about what was happening.

In my doctoral work, I investigate the intersections of clothing and love, so the pull to theorise my emotional response to my father's clothes throughout his suffering came naturally. It was a small thread of clarity I could hold onto, and so I did. In the final two weeks-long visits home to be with him in his bedroom, I began to consider my relationship with the garments that belonged to my father, as well as how my love, our family's love and time itself intersected during the concluding months of his life.

This paper therefore uses autoethnographic observation to demonstrate the affective transformation garments undergo during terminal illness, as they assume the ability to materially represent these non-linear and emotionally conflicted periods of life and potentially supplement the paucity of language when it comes to articulating grief. This research draws on Carolyn Ellis and Art Bochner's evolving framework for autoethnography – including evocative autoethnography and narrative inquiry – which incorporates the researcher's own narratives and feelings into the research.[3] My position as both subject and researcher is significant, as I came to investigate clothing as emotional objects with a deep understanding of their potential. I therefore had expectations for them, which were not necessarily met, as I will discuss. As researcher, by employing this method I aim to 'sensitise' readers to 'experiences shrouded in silence' and articulate how our attachments to clothing and its affective qualities express socially difficult, or even taboo, emotions and experiences.[4] As a subject, conducting this autoethnographic work allows me to address the silence I felt during this experience as I found that my father's clothing surfaced what we could not say. This was my first experience of the premature death of a loved one. My unfamiliarity with this category of experience coupled with my secular upbringing led me to seek cultural systems to support me through this experience. Writing this paper during my father's illness and death empowered me to break the silence that enclosed us and enabled me to draw upon my specific experience to make available often-hidden feelings and observations around death, grief and illness. Drawing on myself as research enabled me to map what I felt during this experience: the research is catharsis.

To form the critical analysis of the primary data, this essay builds on material culture frameworks, particularly Ellen Sampson's work on the affective qualities of worn garments and the affective turn in fashion studies as outlined by the authors and editors of *Fashion and Feeling*.[5] Ilya Parkins and Roberto Filippello – picking up the threads of Deleuzian affect theory and queer affect theorists – look at the growing interest in 'feeling' in fashion studies to 'question ocularcentric epistemologies and offer nuanced reflections on the embodied reparative opportunities offered by clothing'.[6] I too draw together fashion and feeling to consider the multiple temporalities of my experience and introduce the concept of *human wear time*. I use Sara Ahmed's affect theory, particularly that of 'sticky' objects, to explore the ambivalence produced by worn garments.[7] To investigate the object-ness of my encounters with my father's clothing, I also draw on 'thing' design theory, as well as Julia Kristeva's concept of 'the abject' to outline a framework for understanding what I call *abjective clothing*.[8] Stacey Pitsillides defines 'thing' theory as 'a philosophical branch, grown from Martin Heidegger's (1971) mediations on the entomology and categorization of things as opposed to objects', which allows for 'an exploration of the agency of the dead through what is left behind or translated within the bereavement process'.[9] Using this framework, this article analyses the object agency of both my father's clothing and my own as he died. Bringing material culture, affect and 'thing' design theory together enables me to look closely at emotional possibilities of human-object attachment, while simultaneously identifying the object agency and limits within that relationship. To borrow a phrase from Parkins and Filippello's observations of Sampson's research, this work aims to demonstrate clothing's ability to 'index subjective complexity'.[10] By concurrently looking at the emotional possibilities and limits of clothes, this essay offers what Pitsillides calls 'a plurality of narratives' around death.[11]

In considering both my father's and my relationship to his clothes, I interrogate his wardrobe as a series of 'memory-objects' and how illness impacts the embodied experience of what I call the *mind-body-dress* network, changing my idea of who my father was at the end of his life.[12] This article examines how clothes can affect us, what happens when clothes-as-objects do not "work" and the complexities of emotional attachment and material comfort in death and mourning. I have been specifically influenced by de Perthuis's reflection that in writing her gravely ill partner into her paper, she 'was materialising his presence, a presence denied only by his illness'.[13] Writing this article not only felt like a way to comprehend the unexplainable tragedy that was unfolding as my father passed, but it became my route to acknowledging the love that persisted during our pending loss.

Dad, His Body, His Clothes

When I think of my dad, I remember many versions of him throughout my life. In recollecting our memories together, his personhood is woven together with the things he wore, as his physical changes were both embodied and sartorial. René König wrote that fashion 'substitutes for the real body an abstract, ideal body; body as idea rather than organism', which recalls my idea of my father in my memories.[14] Through forming an attachment to his clothes, the abstract and the physical iterations of my dad intersected – both my father dressed in his clothing and my attachment to the *idea* or *memory* of him wearing the clothes. Design theorist Donald Norman posits this process as:

> (1) the visceral, which is linked to perception and appearance; (2) the behavioural, which is the person's behaviour with the item in which pleasure and use are dominant factors; and (3) the reflective, where a person can reflect upon his/her experience, and this may be driven by emotions.[15]

My understanding of my father reflects this attachment process. He was who he was to himself, and he was who he was to me. And my father had many different selves, formed through the many social and cultural forces of his life as well as how he loved new hobbies, became obsessed and then would find another. It was part of what made him *him*, and his clothing reflected this. My dad immigrated to Canada from Chile in his early twenties, during Augusto Pinochet's dictatorship. There, he met and married my mother. They became young parents when I was born in the early 1990s. During this period, my dad dressed in baggy T-shirts, faded denim, printed loose shirts. Through my childhood, he earned degrees and started to dress more formally for his job as a children's aid worker, his dress a reflection of the urban, North American lifestyle he and my mother built together. Later, my parents began going to the gym more frequently and my dad became as strong as he was tall, filling his clothes differently. Very briefly, in the early noughties, he wore a goatee. Throughout my teens, he became a Buddhist and a vegetarian, so Earth Shoes and Birkenstocks began to feature more prominently on the shoe rack. His frame softened, he wore more colour, warm linens, frameless glasses and khaki trousers. When my parents separated, his change in style reflected his new life: he grew his grey hair long and bought vintage clothes, like a leather pilot jacket, in downtown Toronto. At 45, he became a new father again and wore relaxed pieces to reflect the life he, my stepmom and my new baby sister formed in the beachside part of town. He wore more stripes and shades of blue. I share this condensed personal history to summarise the social and cultural forces that impacted what my father wore as he aged. These elements shaped him into these various "selves" I knew throughout my life. These were the people I carried with me and could feel I was losing as I watched him die.

From a phenomenological perspective, my dad's dressed body constantly created these selves that I connected to, his mind, body and dress 'operat[ing] dialectically: dress works on the body, imbuing it with social meaning, while the body is a dynamic field that gives life and fullness to dress'.[16] Lucia Ruggerone theorises that through getting dressed daily, the body is in the active state of 'perpetual becomings'.[17] With each sartorial choice he made, my father became – to me – different versions of "dad": he was the sports dad, the eccentric dad, therapist dad, serious dad, relaxed dad, trendy dad. What he wore became him. As things, in the 'permeable state between subjects and object', my father's clothes worked to form who my father was to me.[18] I witnessed my dad through major life events and points of change, I saw him age and grow and I was accustomed to new iterations – or 'becomings' – of who he was through his dress. The most significant change, though, came in the later stages of his cancer.

Terminal illness amplifies the reciprocity of the *mind-body-dress network,* the simultaneous forces that shape a dressed self. In my father's case, his loss of certain functions changed the needs of his dressed body over time. Even for someone who always took pride in his appearance (whatever phase he was in), ultimately, he prioritised practicality and comfort alongside his self-expression. Multiple surgeries, rounds of radiation, side effects, drugs for the side effects, and the disease, and the pain it caused changed his physicality, both in terms of his strength and abilities. My father's cancer brought with it a deterioration of his bodily agency, which included his clothing choices. This wasn't something my father talked about with me, though. I wondered if he felt as Anne Boyer writes in *The Undying: A Meditation on Modern Illness* that it sometimes feels 'more painful to talk about having cancer than to have it. It is more difficult to recreate the experience and impressions of an illness than to endure them'.[19] He was at the 'centre of the scene' of his pain, language could not comprehend nor express all that his body was going through.[20] That he did not often articulate the extent of his physical pain to me reflects Elaine Scarry's idea that, 'physical pain does not simply resist language but actively destroys it, bringing about an immediate reversion to a state anterior to language'.[21] She explains that pain is not '*of* or *for* anything. It is precisely because it takes no object that it, more than any other phenomenon, resists objectification in language'.[22] Though he could not or did not articulate the full extent of his pain, I understood it. Inflicted with his sickness, my father became smaller, his smile shifted and the clothes he wore changed, too. Due to the intimate nature of the mind-body-dress relationship, his pain could not resist objectification through the clothes he wore.

In her work on 'happy objects', Ahmed acknowledges that 'bodily transformations might also transform what is experienced as delightful. If our bodies change over time, then the world around us will create different impressions'.[23] Where this occurs for pleasure, this also occurs for pain. Because my father's cancer depleted his body of warmth and comfort, clothes not only offered provision for these needs, but they were also the material accompaniment of the pain of which he did not speak. The radiation and surgery he had on his head left it bald and sensitive, so he became a hat person. In one of her many acts of love, my stepmother took care to buy him an array of hats to choose from and he wore them with panache. Buying these hats for him was an example of care becoming 'vivid and material'.[24] Seeing him wear the hats more often informed me of his increasingly sensitive skull. His woolly hats protected him, took care of him, reflected the love he received; they also embodied the pain of terminal illness. After an emergency surgery to his shoulder, my father could no longer lift his arm to get into certain shirts, so loose-fitting cotton T-shirts became his go-to, paired with pyjama bottoms and his favourite navy cardigan. I found myself grateful for items of ease: the garments that folded around his broken shoulder; the billowy fabric of flannel bottoms; the well-worn shirts that would become his second skin; the puffer gilet that kept him warm when he was cold, even during the summer months. If I recall him during the last phase of his life, I recall these garments, with his slippers, a silk hat, a beard, a cane. The clothes and accessories the body allowed, rather than linguistic communication, expressed the internal suffering and the changes the body endured through illness. With these sartorial shifts I witnessed how as cancer gradually altered my dad, his clothes ushered in a new, final version of him. With these changes, came an affective shift.

Clothing, Time and Pending Grief

As my dad wore more of the practical garments his illness necessitated, what was happening to the clothes that most reminded me of the father I wanted him to be, the one I missed? These changes were the first clues of the shifts that occur to the clothes of the dying. Did my father's regular clothes simply become lifeless, separated from the body that once animated them? Central to understanding this shift is time, which loosened and multiplied over the final months that my dad was sick. In watching someone we loved pass away from cancer, it felt like my family entered another realm, away from the ordinary passage of time. A series of serious matters became part of our everyday. What would be emergencies to others became commonplace; important decisions became habit. The constant stress inherent to this state altered my sense of time. Waiting for someone I loved to die over a period of months or years is a horrible feeling: the tragedy is that it is happening at all, but due to their prolonged suffering there are times when it feels like death will not come soon enough. My father was too young to die, it was happening too soon; while at the same time in watching him suffer, death took too long. In this, time becomes paradoxical, simultaneously moving too quickly and too slowly. As a result, I often felt inexplicably tired or anxious, other times I felt numb and despondent. I shared these feelings with a close friend who works for the bereavement charity, Marie Curie. She taught me the term 'anticipatory grief', which refers to a feeling of grief *before* an impending death. It is 'often not acknowledged, talked about or even understood'.[25] My sense of imminent loss was conflicted: pending, unresolved, expected and unwanted. The ongoing tragic feeling formed a private cloak of depression amongst our family, often left unspoken so we could get through it. As Ann Cvetkovich notes, 'what gets called depression in the domestic sphere is [. . .] what often keeps people silent, weary, and too numb to really notice the sources of their unhappiness (or in a state of low-level chronic grief – or depression of another kind – if they do)'.[26] This depression-as-ordinary feeling represents 'an effort to describe the present through attention to the felt experience of everyday life, including moments that might seem utterly banal in comparison with the moments of shock'.[27] Depression seeped, quietly and over time, into the everyday. Despite its gravity and complexity of emotions, because long-term illness takes time, it becomes mundane.

Here, in the ordinary, is where time and the clothing of the dying intersect. This is because clothing exists in time through both material and abstract forms, making it a useful tool to understand how time can transform when anticipating a loved one's death. Clothing exists before, during and after what we might call *human wear time*, a term I use to describe the duration of clothing worn on the body. For Sampson, 'time is present in all material things; they are both of "a" time (when they were made, altered, or used) and material manifestations of the passage of time itself'.[28] Everyday clothing – as things – therefore carry multiple meanings and representations of time. This duality between clothing and time enables several possibilities, linking to König's claim that 'fashion is really limitless, we only have to appreciate that it is not confined to concrete matter'.[29] If 'fashion' here can be interpreted as everyday clothing, then König suggests that clothes are not confined to the limits of the concrete matter of the human body; the body can be a site from which clothing transforms into an abstract image. Therefore, clothing is present and part of the flesh while also representing the memory of someone's personhood. Clothing was part of my father while he was healthy, it was present when my father was ill, and it continues to exist in the clothes that remain and will always be part of my father's memory. His clothes' ongoing nature signified what was to come – that their materiality would endure beyond my father's life and remain present (materially and immaterially) as long as we, his loved ones, remember him. Clothing is now and then; it is past, present, future. Like our ongoing, pending grief, my father's clothing exists in temporal multiplicities despite being part of the ordinary. As he lay dying, my father's clothes materialised these abstract forms of time.

Entering The Wardrobe of The Dying

When my father's cancer treatment was declared as palliative care – which in his case, thanks to the universal healthcare system in Canada, meant that nurses, physiotherapists and other clinicians would regularly visit him at home – he was almost completely confined to the house. Our sense of time '(memories of the past, tentative ideas about the present, hopes and anxieties regarding the future)' could not 'be separated from space'.[30] Our family's pending loss was related to my father, stepmother and sister's home and the surrounding nature of their chosen town. The timing of my father's death was unpredictable, which meant sharing our experience as it happened with anyone outside the immediate family was difficult. Our experience of watching him die was insular; it was private, intimate and relegated (both spatially and emotionally) to the rooms of his family home.

Anna-Mari Almila's observation of theorising everyday dress addresses the entanglement of self, space and clothing in that 'the garments themselves, the human bodies and the environments inhabited by those bodies must all be considered in relation to each other'.[31] In our situation, my father's garments were spatially situated both on his body in his bed and in his nearby wardrobe; there was the dressed man in his bed with a pile of pyjamas nearby to swap through when needed, and there was his wardrobe adjacent to the bedroom, filled with the clothing he rarely used anymore. In wardrobe studies, the 'wardrobe' can be viewed as a symbolic, physical and psychological space.[32] Understanding clothing as repositories or containers of lives lived in them, I could sense that the proximity of my father's wardrobe to his deathbed meant that he was always resting right beside his own material memories.[33] Therefore, during these visits to my father's bedside, versions of him were present simultaneously: the person who lay in front of me and the person I remember wearing the clothes in his wardrobe. Clothes, being both worn and unworn in the space of the dying body connected to them, became the nexus and site of multiple selves. Sitting where I was on the sofa beside his bed, the spatial design of his bedroom meant I was triangulated between the past and our present. The door was often left ajar: from where I would sit, while gazing at my father lying in front of me, I could easily glimpse a shirt's pattern, a colourful sleeve, or see stacks of jumpers I knew by heart. Between the garments of the past and his slow present, I could sit with our impending loss. The glimpses of my father's unworn garments were flickering signs of his life lived and lost. The clothes of the dying embody the mortality of the body to which they are connected.

During my last trip, as my father's days began to fill more with sleep than wakefulness, I secretly – though desperately – sought comfort by finally reaching into his wardrobe. This was not something I did often, it was always a private space he shared with my stepmother. Yet, I felt the pull of my father's wardrobe's potential. I sought the comfort I recognized in de Perthuis's writing on clothing and mourning:

> Unexpected garments—a ragged jumper, an old jacket—are not what you wear to mourn; rather, the wearing is the mourning itself, the materialisation of the absent body. To believe in the possibility of such haunting is to banish the notion that clothes are empty of the person who once wore them. Instead of inanimate, ghostly, and empty, they are poetic, vital, and alive; the dress, the jacket, the jumper, a body remembered. Maybe, even (why not?), its soul.[34]

I had a sudden, hopeful intention to be met with the life contained in the garments my father could no longer wear. Familiar with theoretical writing about worn clothing, I anticipated being greeted with varying emotions, through sight but also through other senses such as the smell and touch of the garments that hung there. I thought of Ellen Sampson's work on clothing and affect, specifically the dual capacity of garments to affect both symbolically and bodily/materially. I carried Sampson's understanding of clothes – that they are 'both the locus and the agents of affect, while at the same time being affected themselves' – with me.[35] I was aware of the humanness of clothes, their existence on the body and their ability to entangle with the people who wear them. I therefore felt prepared to sit in the potential evocation of feelings in my father's clothes in the hopes that consolation would be among them.

Feeling my father slip away, I sought out the 'soul' of him. I felt, in reaching for his clothes, I could hold someone who was disappearing from me. Stallybrass felt that his late friend Allon's jacket *was* Allon. He says, 'If I wore the jacket. Allon wore me.'[36] So too, in my way, I felt that maybe I could reconcile my anticipatory grief, wear my father's clothes and feel the father that could still hug me, when the one that lay sleeping could not. In wanting to enter his closet, I sought out the person he was when he could instinctually reach for an outfit, the person who could bring together the shades of turquoise he loved so much. Through my attachment, the clothes – as objects in the wardrobe – became a network of relational containers for my hope. I wanted to be comforted and reassured by my father's clothing as he was dying in the same way de Perthuis and Stallybrass were by the clothes of their loved ones after death.

The wardrobe itself was a walk-in closet, half filled with my father's clothes, half with those of his wife. It mostly housed his button-down shirts and trousers on hangers with his jumpers folded on wire shelves above. As I walked into it, I immediately recognized his scent (the hardest smell to describe, the unique scent of a person you love), but his side of the wardrobe also had that slightly dusty, stored-clothing smell, an indication of the clothes' disuse. In physically being in the space, I had an immediate, all-encompassing understanding of the person he had been slowly leaving behind. In briefly gliding my hand across my dad's hanging shirts, I was surrounded by the past versions of him, which felt even more present than they were in memory. This made the contrast to my actual dad even more painful as he slept in the bed a few feet away. I understood at this moment why Stallybrass referred to the clothes of our loved ones who die as both 'reassuring and terrifying'.[37] In materialising his past selves, his clothes evoked an eerie uncanniness: my father was concurrently with me and already gone. My hope transformed into grief. The smell, the signs of wear, made palpable the person I was losing. Holding and touching his clothes in these few minutes felt like holding the many people my dad was to me throughout my life. Through the clothes' materiality, my dad's life – time itself – condensed in my hands. I felt haunted by their 'ghostly' presence.[38] I particularly longed to wear a white sweatshirt with floral embroidery I had given him as a gift and that we had shared. But when I picked it up and held it, the fact that I would be the sole next wearer felt unbearable. Encountering his clothes like this enabled me to grasp the slippery situation that had eluded me: I finally felt how grave our situation was. In my disappointing attempt to find comfort in my father's unworn clothing, I treated his wardrobe as though he was, in a way, already gone. When I entered his wardrobe and confronted his clothing as he was dying rather than in death, I materialised the terror of the unknown sorrow to come.

This encounter prompted me to consider the affective transformation clothing undergoes during impending death. Why could these objects not bring me the same comfort in dying as they do for others in death? I had already felt the loss of my father and yet these objects were not working in the way I had hoped. Perhaps if the belongings of a lost loved one embody them, then their possessions, their clothes, also embody the potentially unresolved pain they leave in their absence. For Joan Didion, the belongings of her late husband and daughter were not welcome reminders of them. She wrote in *Blue Nights*, 'in fact I no longer value this kind of memento. I no longer want reminders of what was, what got broken, what got lost, what got wasted'.[39] With death, Didion's loved ones' possessions became objects 'for which there [was] no satisfactory conclusion' and 'serve only to make clear' how inadequately she appreciated the moments that they evoked.[40] Didion's experience reflects what Stacey Pitsillides summarises as becoming 'confronted with the thingness of an object, in particular, when an object stops working for us'.[41] When I encountered the garments in my father's wardrobe before he had passed away, their thing-ness not only prompted a deep sense of grief. Because he was still alive, the grief was still anticipated, not actualised, so his garments could not yet bring me comfort: they represented a different time, part of the accumulation of his life story and reminders of the life he no longer would be able to live. I felt frustrated that his past selves were already gone. The clothes were already traces of prior eras, which worsened the inexorability and strangeness of this new and final one. My hopeful attachment to his clothes became agonising because they articulated so much of what was not being said, that which felt impossible to acknowledge. The memories they once evoked soured. The clothing my father no longer wore symbolised the person he was leaving behind, while the clothing he could wear embodied the illness that took him away. By choosing to encounter these objects at this point in his palliative journey, before he died, their meanings shifted without resolution.

In Limbo: Abjective Clothing

In dying, one's garments and personal items lose their purpose while remaining present in the lives of those who care for the terminally ill; clothes' needs and functions as objects convert through disuse. That my father's clothes could not yet provide me with comfort as he was dying incited my curiosity about their object-ness. Why did I feel alienated by objects I had hoped would bring me comfort? This became clear when I found myself saddened to discover my father's belongings in other parts of the house. In the weeks before my father moved to a hospice, my stepmom offered my boyfriend a pair of my dad's winter boots to wear on a snowy walk in the Canadian wilderness. My boyfriend, A, visiting on his first trip from the UK, had packed only trainers. As we got ready for the walk by the front hall closet, my stepmom told A, *Arturo wouldn't mind, he probably won't wear them again*. Though it was a generous offer, and A likely would have preferred them, he declined. In the moments after my stepmom kindly offered A the boots, we three sensed a silent truth: it was too soon to pack my father's boots away as mementos, too late for him to ever use them again. As the (previous) wearer of the boots, my dad's lack of agency filled the space, unspoken. That they were well-worn, creased and salt-stained reflected the life he had lived in them. Sampson's description of the resonance of worn shoes accounts for the significance of this moment. Worn shoes 'do not represent a single trace, but a complex record of many gestures performed and lost'.[42] In my dad's case, his boots were part of his everyday winter life in Canada, part of the walks he loved in the nearby woods, there with him shovelling the snow before taking my sister on daily school runs. The boots accumulated the traces of his life. As cancer took away his opportunity to do these things, to live his life, then my father's boots were representative of the life both 'performed' and now 'lost' in them.

Sampson writes:

> The worn shoe does not bear the marks of a single performance but, rather, the traces of many: our clothing contains multiple imprints of our lives. Frequently, garments become more resonant, more affective, the more they are worn: the more entangled they become with the wearer and the world. However, the layering of the marks is cumulative but not linear. Marks are simultaneously partially erased and further embedded by the over-writing of the next. Erasure takes place through the performance of the next experience.[43]

If my boyfriend were to accept the boots as his own, then my father's 'erasure' would be complete: his inability to re-wear them prematurely actualised his death. As a family, we were not ready to face this finality, and not yet ready for his boots to become containers for our grief. So, they sat, as they always have, on the rack beside the rest of our shoes. Despite becoming purposeless, they remained in place. It was then that I understood that my father's unworn clothing and shoes had become akin to Julia Kristeva's description of the 'abject', which refers to that which has been separated from the norm due to a change in meaning. In this separation, the abject holds the power to disturb that which is conventional, caused by a lack of respect for 'borders, positions, rules. The in-between, the ambiguous, the composite'.[44] My father's boots – alongside the rest of his now unworn clothing in his wardrobe and around the house – became 'radically excluded'.[45] The clothes in his wardrobe felt like 'jettisoned objects' hiding in plain sight and while I could avoid my father's wardrobe, the belongings that had made their way into other rooms throughout the house caused a constant confrontation with the truth I did not want to face.[46] His coats in the front hall closet, his summer hats in the basket by the garden door.

In accruing these qualities, they became what we might call in my own coinage *abjective clothing*, clothes that both cause and represent an uneasy sense of ambiguity through their change in meaning. In this symbolic alienation, abjective clothing can be unsettling if encountered. My father's body being estranged from his clothing changed their meaning: due to illness, the shoes, shirts, jumpers, jeans and the rest of the unworn belongings he unwittingly abandoned. From my perspective, I could not yet wear his clothes as a form of mourning, as a means of remembering the many versions of himself that my dad was over my lifetime, because they were still his. But I could not fully reject them either: part of me still ached for the comfort I hoped they would bring once he was gone. Because his clothes had affected me, they were still 'sticky'.[47] In defining 'sticky' objects, Sara Ahmed notes that 'affect is what sticks, or what sustains or preserves the connection between ideas, values, and objects'.[48] For abjective clothing, the tension of what remains stuck and new feelings that attach cause the unease. We could not anticipate the encounter due to the shift in meaning. We did not have what Ahmed, drawing on Nietzsche, calls 'anticipatory logic' that my father's now abjective clothing was 'to be feared'; we only understood retrospectively that these objects were the 'the cause of feeling'.[49] In their new state of un-wornness while still "belonging" – in the sense that they remained his possessions – my father's clothes entered a state of limbo: they became material reminders of who a person was and who they would soon leave behind. While my father was still alive, hope remained, though the loss of him grew closer every day. In Ahmed's affective framework, abjective clothing is both anticipatory causality of affect (grief) and retrospectively the cause of feeling (unfulfilled hope). The abjective clothing of the dying embodies this duality, they contain both the persistent hope and the grief of those the dying will leave behind.

Love and 'The Clothes Of The Dying'

Sensing this ambivalence in myself and in my father's clothes, I began to comprehend how a lack of material comfort could allow me to acknowledge these conflicting feelings. I observed this further with the ambivalence of the clothes *I* wore while spending time with my dad in his final months. In this sense, the clothing of the dying extends to the clothing the dying's loved ones wear, too. Again, familiar with the emotional qualities clothing can possess, I felt myself wanting to evoke these feelings in every item of clothing I wore while with my dying father. I thought of the thing-ness of things with each thing-based interaction I had with my dad.[50] Through the things we wore, I wanted to capture the love and loss we shared too. In Ahmed's words, 'to give value to things is to shape what is near us.'[51] With each hug we shared, I tried to remember the shirt I was wearing hoping that my clothes would become containers of these loving moments. I was told that my trip home during the late summer of 2022 would likely be my final visit while he was alive. Living abroad, I had packed a small bag of comfortable clothes to wear. I did not care much about what they looked like; I was generally spending time indoors. Most days, I wore a long white linen dress and a navy cotton-knit cardigan. In one embrace, I felt myself wrap my arms around my dad, thinking of the cloth I wore as a means of accompaniment, a continuation of this hug, should it be one of the last ones. But as proven, time shifts meaning during long-term illness, and in this case, saying goodbye became long-term too. Time becomes an experience of endurance when watching someone die. My father lived for another six months, so we shared many more "final" hugs. This meant that now that my father is gone, I cannot remember what I was wearing the last time I held him. I can hold the moment in my head, but by this time I had given up trying to secure material significance to one outfit or garment. I learned that material significance could not be forced; it does not always 'stick', especially when trying to capture a drawn-out, ongoing process.[52] Once again, meaning collapsed. Time, space and connecting my memories to the clothes I wore melted away the closer we got to his death. The overbearing exhaustion of saying goodbye time and again governed my affective qualities. Instead of remembering exactly what I wore the last time I held my father, I hold a series of garments in my mind from the period that I spent with him as he was dying. Both the clothes he wore and mine, entwined.

Conclusion

I began this paper by asking, 'What happens to the clothes of the dying?' as a means of comprehending the loss of my father to cancer. In seeking to explore this topic, I have considered how time, grief and love intersect with clothing and death. Through this, I have demonstrated the value of autoethnographic methods to explore embodiment, affect and rationality. This article looked at the attachment I have to my father via and to his clothes through his life, and how, as his body and dress changed through cancer so did my understanding of him. By looking closely at our private world, filled with the ongoing anxieties that surround experiencing a loved one's pain, I have explored how my father's terminal cancer changed the meaning of his clothes to me and shifted my emotional attachment to them. In outlining the affective relationship of *mind-body-dress network* and my own understanding of *human wear time*, this essay deepened understandings between embodiment, temporalities and the material world. The clothing of the dying embodies the suffering of the body that once wore them, as well as the hope and grief of the loved ones the dying will leave behind. I specifically examined how being confronted by an object when it emotionally does not "work" made me consider clothing of the dying as *abjective clothing*. Our collective inability to find purpose for my father's old winter boots as he died indirectly forced my family to confront his soon-to-be death and his subsequent absence from our lives. The clothing of the dying both held our ambiguous feelings of hope and grief and reflected them back to us. Placing the boots back on the shelf allowed us, his loved ones, to acknowledge the pending loss we could not articulate.

As clothes become disused during terminal illness, they bear the potential to reproduce the ambiguity of anticipatory grief. By looking at how garments of the dying intertwine with the affective relationships of their loved ones, I uncovered how clothes can mirror the specific emotional intricacies of losing someone you love. Investigating my father's clothing allowed me to grieve in a way that secular social structures in my North American context do not encourage. In this context, where grief is so often experienced in private, in silence, investigating the clothing that endured the process with me allowed me to understand and articulate the complexities of my experience of my father's terminal illness. This paper emphasizes Ahmed's final suggestion in 'Happy Objects' that 'we might want to reread melancholic subjects, the ones who refuse to let go of suffering, who are even prepared to kill some forms of joy, as an alternative model of the social good'.[53] Sometimes, allowing ourselves to be stuck in uncertainty enables us to face the unimaginable. Looking closely at my father's clothing, my own in relation to him, and how we were woven together in love, allowed me to sit simultaneously in comfort and discomfort. Spending time acknowledging the life he lived in his clothes, the people he became through dress, allowed me to understand who he was as I lost him to illness. By confronting my father's clothes as he died, I found meaning within the ambiguity and I would encourage further investigation of this mode of looking. How can identifying *abjective clothing* in our everyday help to reflect other ambiguities in our emotional lives? How can the material world aid us in addressing unspoken aspects of human social life, within a Western context and beyond? What other socially hidden emotional topics can the material world help to better articulate, understand, reframe? The emotional boundaries I found within these material encounters became possibilities: I understood objects and the feelings I carried through this experience differently. The clothing of the dying exposed a new depth of understanding I gained through this loss.

Epilogue

I wrote this paper through my dad's final months, through his death, and now, the afterwards. Since he died, I have had time to consider certain garments of my own that evoke memories of holding his hand as we walked or watched a film, of spending time together as a family, before he lost his sight, before he left us. I can piece together now which of my clothes were with him the last few times I saw him. I have inherited a couple of his belongings and have finally been able to wear them. I recently wore my dad's white jumper with the embroidered floral details while eating lunch with my mum, and I spilled some soup on it. We noticed that my dad had already stained the jumper, symbolic of his "messy" self. The moment I too stained it, my mum and I both felt his ghostly presence and I felt I *was* him. At last, I found comfort in my father's clothes; we mourned him, cherished him, and even briefly, accepted he was gone.

I began this piece to understand my grief, to align myself with others who have grieved parental loss and perhaps offer a way of mediating sorrow through the material possessions that offer insight into our inner worlds. As I wrote, my grief took different shapes, it wove between my material and immaterial worlds. In this work, temporalities collided once more: his illness prompted this investigation, his death enabled this work to preserve his life, to exist. The existence of this research therefore became a cumulative grief process itself, reflecting shifts that occurred as and when my father died. The material world continues to guide and form my understanding of my father's death. In losing my father, which I will process for a long time to come, his worn (and then not worn) clothes inspired me to comprehend objects, feelings and love within limbo, and to find solace in the ambivalence and inexplicability of his loss.

Acknowledgements

I dedicate this article to my father, Arturo Mundigo. I would like to thank my family and friends for their love and support in my writing of this. I would also like to thank Dr Ellen Sampson and my peer reviewers for their encouragement, guidance and feedback. Thank you to the writers and theorists whose writing built the foundations of this piece. And thank you very much to Dr Rosie Findlay, who believed in this work from its early stages and guided it to the end as editor. I am so grateful for her care.

A Life in Clothes

Ruth Gershon

The children of ruling families are born in the purple. Those of Vaudevillians are born in a trunk. But families in the rag trade, what are we? Born in rags suggests merely poverty. Born in garments sounds clinically implausible. Growing up in north-west London, In Schmatters was the term I heard most often.

Most of my relatives were In Schmatters. Papa, my grandfather, owned a workshop, inherited by my father, his eldest son. By the time I was born, at the end of the war, it was in Charlotte Street; a few years later, it migrated to Soho. It provided employment for my father, an uncle, and an aunt, and was the substance of Papa's headship of a large immigrant cousinage in London. Most of my family's friends and neighbours were In Schmatters, too. Just one or two may have been In Furs (winter suits sometimes needed trimmings). My mother's sister married a bespoke men's tailor, my brother's father-in-law was In Coats, my best friends' fathers were respectively In Hats and In Zips.

These trades have a particularly important defining characteristic, which I want you to take seriously. There are many commodities in whose production and distribution a businessman can take satisfaction, but clothes are a special case. No matter how commonplace, how routine their presence in a working life becomes, they retain their capacity to evoke aesthetic pleasure and to inspire pride in workmanship. Despite their literal superficiality, they are fundamentals of our daily existence, our goings-out and our comings-in. And what might seem at first sight a feminized undertaking, unlikely to underpin the authority of the paterfamilias, turns out quite otherwise.

A man In Schmatters did not just provide for his family; he literally clothed them. He brought home garments from his own factory, and from those of his friends. He moved in, was indeed sovereign over, female as well as male worlds. He, rather than his wife, knew what was seemly and suitable, what was conventional and what was Selling Well; he knew what was run of the mill and what was a cut above. You did not wear run of the mill. Even when Business Was Terrible, even when things were *In dr'Erd* (buried), your clothes were at the model end of the trade. Daddy could always do that much for you.

Standards of dress were the common coin of conversation. It was not merely a question of compliments or (*sotto voce*) expressions of bewilderment, mockery, regret or surprise. As children In Schmatters, we could expect our appearance to be commented on in ways that might not be thought normal in other circles. We were advertisements for our parents in more ways than one.

'That's nice dear, very nice. Turn around and let me see the back. Is it one of Daddy's?'

Never shall I forget the disbelieving guffaws when, complimented at Oxford on my 'Mondrian' mini-dress, I guilelessly replied, 'Thank you. It's one of my uncle's.'

It was not Mummy, but Daddy who bought me my first lipstick and eyeshadow and nylon stockings. He brought them all back from a business trip to Paris when I was about thirteen. (I had begun to beg for stockings, but not the other things, as all my friends were coming out of socks at the weekends. 'Don't listen to her,' said my older brothers. 'We never had them, did we?') The stockings were nothing less than Christian Dior, thirteen denier, a beautiful shiny mushroom colour, and as much part of a fairy world as a bridesmaid's dress. The lipstick was a suitable and very fashionable pale pink. The eyeshadow was made up of interlocking sparkling pastel blocks in pink, green, blue, grey and mauve.

Did he choose my mother's make-up for her, too, and her perfume? Today, one or two friends express surprise that at the age of eighteen I still received my clothes from my father, shopped only for shoes and accessories on my own account. I explain that we were in the trade, we were short of money, I was sample size; but of course that is not the whole story. And perhaps the whole story is encapsulated in the memory of the only time I ever refused a garment, a pale blue jersey-knit (possibly made up in crimplene) two-piece. There was something visibly wrong with the revers of the jacket. You couldn't possibly have gone out in it. As I recall the anger, disappointment, indeed near-hysteria of my father's reaction, I realize that this was one of the many occasions on which I shortened his life.

Yes, of course he chose my mother's clothes. I turn to the collection of wedding photographs and there, in the set for Janet's wedding, is Mummy in a devastatingly glamorous cream brocade strapless ankle-length sheath. The photograph is in black and white, but I know that the long gloves are a soft emerald-green suede

(I've still got them) and that the drape across one shoulder is a strip of velvet in the same colour.

My mother's face is—well, it's not smiling. It is not that she looks wistful, or absent; her expression is more one of discontent. She looks imposed upon, and only half resigned; she is powered by a kind of passive resistance—to the camera? to the photographer (my father)? Surely not to the costume. We talked about that once, and she said, 'I wanted lamé, but your father insisted on brocade.'

Daddy was for a long time a keen photographer who developed his own film. If he had wanted a smiling model, he would surely have asked for one. Did he ask, and she refuse? No, he must have seen in my mother's bearing an approximation of the haughty disdain affected by mannequins at the very top of the trade: women who had to be, literally, models for the aristocracy, to impersonate them on catwalks, in showrooms and in glossy magazine images, without betraying the reality of changing in cramped back rooms in Great Titchfield Street, and submitting to the touch and scrutiny of designers, manufacturers, customers. With stern, abstracted faces, chins and noses in the air, they pretended to own themselves and the clothes they stood in.

My mother's wardrobe, even when the furs and the jewellery had had to be sold, was never less than elegant, and there were always flashes of gorgeousness— silk blouses, a patterned jacket lining—gleaming on hangers between the darker suits and skirts. But I cannot recall seeing her eyes sparkle at the sight of a particular colour, or her fingers reach out to squeeze a piece of fabric the way my aunts and uncles reached out to pinch our cheeks. When we asked her, she said her favourite colour was green, but she rarely wore it. She seemed to take little pleasure in her appearance beyond the satisfaction of not having got it wrong. She dressed with a frown, as if carrying out a duty, almost as if the accoutrements of womanhood were a form of punishment. All this changed dramatically after she was widowed.

As I entered young womanhood I became, allegedly, 'sample size'. I put away childish clothes and put on factory samples, often of considerable opulence. I remember swaggering around Hendon Central in a copy of a 1961 Cardin suit in a brilliant blue-and-black tweed with a fur collar; going to the sixth form dance at South Hampstead in an A-line dress in an olive-green plaid wool with a stiffened skirt; preening myself in draughty synagogue halls in a brown dress in a kind of mohair which softened and blurred the large checks of the pattern. Many of these clothes did not suit me and none of them fitted. Perhaps they would not have fitted anyone: the skirts were always a bit clumsy and long, the tops a bit too bloused. Did I realize this? Did I think that perhaps I had not stopped growing;

that one day I would, and indeed should be the same size as other people; my mother for example? I could see that these were Very Nice Clothes, Very Good Material, and I felt quite privileged to be wearing them. I must, at some level, have believed that it was me, and not the garment, that was in the wrong.

I was eighteen when Daddy had his heart attack. A few months later I packed my bags, and my samples, for Oxford. Stocks were subsequently replenished from my uncle's factory and there were cast-offs from my new sisters-in-law. In my loss and anger it is easy to forget that the sage-green winter coat was made up from a pattern of my own choosing, and that Daddy had sewn the lapels himself by hand; that he made the painting smock and the costume for the title role in the school play in next to no time when I needed them. There were clothes, made with love, just for me, that fitted perfectly.

Mazeltov

Everyone got married. It happened by magic, but it happened to everyone. First you got engaged, and an announcement was printed in the *Jewish Chronicle* and possibly in *The Times* as well. The girl was given a ring with a diamond on it. A person who had been one alone was now in a couple, and did the circuit of relatives in a different way. Eventually there was a wedding. The preparations, absorbing huge amounts of energy and demanding great powers of financial, social and aesthetic generalship, took months to complete. Afterwards, everything that happened at the wedding was talked about in the minutest detail, at home, in *shul*, and sometimes in the shops, too, for what seemed like years.

My mother knew all about it. She spoke about dressmakers' prices; into this sacred female space the factory did not intrude. Of course, nobody bought a wedding dress off a rail in a shop. I heard about headdresses, trains, bouquets, shoes, fabrics. I learned that velvet did not make up well, and that it was a waste of time trying to design something that could be worn later, with minor adaptations, as an ordinary evening dress. (A wedding dress is what it is, and not some other thing.) I heard about West End caterers, and about halls and hotels for receptions. Keeping my head down, I heard about misbehaviour, imagined slights, family feuds, people not speaking to each other.

My father was one of four siblings and my mother one of six; with nine cousins older than myself I had plenty of opportunities to rehearse these protocols. Even when no relatives were marrying there were other weddings offering lower levels of participation: going to the synagogue ceremony, if not actually to the reception; going to the house before the bride set off for the synagogue, if not to the ceremony itself; as if you had to keep touching the magic to keep it in existence, so that one day it would rub off on you.

There were also bar mitzvahs, and there were other occasions for which you dressed up: Masonic dos, and dances and banquets held to raise funds for charities. But there was nothing like a wedding. This was the pinnacle, the height of glory, the moment when every family made its mark upon the world. This is how we do things, this is our idea of good food, of fine clothes. This is how we enjoy ourselves. This is how we scatter largesse.

Everyone got married.

Of course, not everyone was *still* married. You knew some war widows, and life was tough for them, as they had to go out to work. Then there were the very old ladies whose husbands had died, like Nana, or Mrs Cornfeld in the house opposite who taught me Hebrew, or Mrs Simmons further down the road whom I accompanied to synagogue, making that obligatory sabbath walk, the mile up Station Road to the Burroughs and on to Raleigh Close, whatever the weather. And it was even possible for things to go wrong. You might marry too young, like Sharon Levy, who lived next door to Mrs Simmons. Sharon was only seventeen and headstrong, and ended up getting divorced. Or you might still be walking home from synagogue with your parents when you were nearer thirty than twenty, like Rosalind Meyer, the doctor's daughter, and that was not good either.

Rosalind's best friend Stephanie Leigh married out. Her parents sat *shiva* for her as if she had died. Rosalind did get married eventually. At another wedding, nearly thirty years later, she told me that when she was at college she joined the drama club and was cast as Juliet. Romeo was Indian, the handsomest man she had ever seen. She knew that she could not possibly play opposite him without falling in love. So she gave up the part, and left the club. Of such experiences I, a little girl, did not even dream.

Because so many of my cousins were so much older than me, when it was time for them to get married, it was time for me, too, to have a beautiful dress and shoes, to have my hair done specially, to carry a posy, to be given a present. I, too, went for dressmakers' fittings, heard debates about the relative merits of round and square necklines, saw colour schemes put together with meticulous care. I knew that the costuming of me and my fellow bridesmaids was as important as that of the bride.

I don't remember feeling particularly excited beforehand, nor any shyness or embarrassment during the day itself. The pageant was, literally, normal. Wearing wonderful clothes, posing in front of the congregation and the camera, was something you just did from time to time. This does not mean that I took the clothes for granted. They had all the respect and reverence they deserved.

The first frocks were pale blue, the skirts almost down to the ground. The material of the skirt—the top layers at least—was net. It was a different net from that used in curtains and ladies' hat veils; it was unlike any fabric I had ever seen or worn. It was stiff and strong as well as light as air; it floated around me; it was from another world. I was still at an age when I believed in fairies. My costume confirmed everything I had ever heard about dresses spun from gossamer, about transformation scenes; at the touch of a wand I was Cinderella going to the ball.

Like Cinderella's, the shoes were the most amazing of all, though not made of glass; the fabric a heavy, deep cream satin brocaded with silver. For Susanne's wedding, two years later, the net was white and covered by a long, wine-red velvet cape; for Leonie's we had white taffeta with velvet sashes in a deep moss green. For Valerie, it was back to pastels: a sugared-almond shade of lavender, with white satin ballet shoes dyed to match.

Everyone was wearing wonderful clothes. It didn't matter if in real life they were old or fat or ugly; here everyone was splendid. All the men had dinner jackets and cummerbunds. The band played, and whoever asked you to dance, whether it was the best man or Mr Posen next door, was Prince Charming. People laughed and told jokes and played games like children. They made a big fuss of you and you could do no wrong. You were a princess for a day, and some day you would be queen. One of these men in dinner jackets would make a move, trigger a switch that would turn you into a radiant cloud of whiteness, create a being of unassailable, supernatural beauty that everyone would want to be nice to for ever and ever.

I can remember no goodbyes, no going-away outfits. I suppose I must always have been taken home early. The bride and groom vanished from my sight as if in a puff of smoke at the midnight hour. Long, long afterwards they returned to earth. We would go to a house somewhere for tea and there would be Susanne or Leonie in ordinary clothes. Everything seemed beige. There would be nothing much to do, and you would look to see if they had the Eiffel Tower in a snowstorm on their mantelpiece. And ages and ages after that, Susanne or Leonie would come to us for tea, and you would see a baby at the end of a big white breast.

Still, there remained the consolation of the photographs, of which we always had our own copies. I was allowed to appear unbespectacled on wedding days, and would spend hours poring over the image of my flawless loveliness, all too briefly released from the bad spell cast upon it by eye tests. And then I would hunt for other photographs, of weddings which happened before I was born. Auntie Lily with four or five grown-up bridesmaids with huge picture hats. Markie and Sadie, Sadie a tiny bride with an enormous train, Markie smiling in his topper and tails, not a hint that within the hour he is going to be outside, minus both, in a punch-up over the Communist Party, or so the story goes . . . where are Mummy and Daddy?

I didn't actually ask for years; some Freudian repugnance to knowing too much about my own origins? And at the time it did not register that there were no wedding photographs for Mummy's sisters either; neither Miriam, who lived round the corner, nor Leah and Vera, who went to join Auntie Rosa in America in the 1920s, and got married there. When I finally got round to asking, Mummy said none were taken.

'It wasn't a white wedding. I wore a brown suit.'

It had never quite sunk in that if the wedding day was what all girls aspired to, it was also what all girls' parents put money aside for. That if everyone got married, it followed that everyone had money. Mummy did not speak about this; but she did speak about the fact that she didn't have an engagement ring. This, she told me quite early on, was because she didn't think Daddy could afford it, so she let him think she didn't really want one. She seems to have regretted this, and perhaps to have told me about it as a kind of warning.

Changes

At twelve, I had to fast the full twenty-four hours on Yom Kippur. And I had already started my periods. Progressive for her time and place, my mother invited and answered my questions. It was all very natural and wonderful and it meant that you could have babies.

But growing up into a woman didn't seem very natural and, as I looked in the mirror and then looked around me, it didn't even seem inevitable. It couldn't just happen: being a woman was obviously about being good-looking, which I no longer was. On top of that it required massive professional expertise and a perfect faith in the importance and efficacy of that expertise. There seemed to be a class of girls who did know all about it, who were allowed into nylons and high heels and lipsticks before anyone else, who dedicated hours and hours to setting their hair and applying mascara and nail polish, and who flirted convincingly and successfully with boys. They would leave school at fifteen and could expect a diamond ring by the time they reached twenty-one. Those of us who were staying on at school to take our O-levels and A-levels were the babies, the retarded ones. We weren't competition. We weren't even in the game.

Adolescence came with a set of instructions which did not really help. They were often subliminal, and largely negative. You should not be loud, or unladylike. Don't wave your hands about. Don't be common, flash, spivvy or cheap. (This applied to my brothers, too. They were forbidden suede shoes.) Not too much jewellery. Don't wear loads of makeup. Don't wear high heels with trousers.

If you thought the hidden message was, don't be—horrible word—a *shiksa*, a non-Jewish woman, you were not quite there; for it was just as important not to be a *klafta*, a gross, coarse, unrefined woman who was almost by definition Jewish. The old-fashioned English working-class expression, rough, was also used. Most confusing of all, despite our orthodoxy, our willingness to stand up and be counted over issues such as school dinners and school prayers, was the almost unspoken injunction not to look too Jewish.

This was partly concealed under the rubric of caution—don't draw attention to yourselves; partly under the pious reminder—what one Jew does reflects on all the other Jews. But the fact that my eldest brother was constantly mistaken (by other Jews) for an Englishman was the source of a certain satisfaction, as was the incident when my mother and I went to buy a scarf at Fenwick's, and the saleswoman, seeing my gold *Magen David* on a chain, whispered, 'Well, I would never have thought you were one of us.'

By the age of fifteen I was totally confused. You had to grow up, but you couldn't convince your mother you needed a bra until you'd been wearing a more 'developed' friend's cast-offs for months. Your purpose in life was to be beautiful, and the fact that you weren't was simply ignored. You had to be a nice Jewish girl, but not *too* Jewish. Everyone got engaged and married, but for you to go out with boys was a procedure so fraught with hazard that how you ever reached your ultimate destination was a mystery.

I had to find some escape routes. At fifteen I took the one marked religion. I became deeply committed to orthodoxy and joined a youth movement which excluded the possibility of mating games on the dance floor, restricted the scope of flirtation, banned lipstick on *shabbos*, and shorts and short sleeves at all times.

I also joined the Campaign for Nuclear Disarmament, understanding The Struggle largely as an extension of prayer, prayer made manifest in mighty, righteous demonstrations. And I did pray, every night, that the bomb would not drop, that there would be peace in the Middle East, peace in the Congo . . . but I also wanted to wear that black-and-white badge which I thought looked particularly sharp on the lapel of my school blazer (though I removed it as soon as the uniform regulations were invoked).

Most of my religious group joined the campaign, too, but I identified the real essence of the movement in a small crowd of girls at school who were infinitely more worldly and more knowing than the rest of us. They smoked cigarettes and had urgent grown-up tasks outside. They were in the Young Communist League as well as CND. They had important responsibilities for holding meetings, manning offices, selling newspapers, leafleting and stewarding demos; the school rather tried their patience. They were strikingly beautiful but didn't bother with make-up or nail varnish, as far as I could see. They wore dark duffel coats and black stockings.

I had my camel-coloured duffel coat dyed navy (I convinced my mother that it was a good move: I could now wear it to school). I got my dentist boyfriend to take me to a folk song night at the Partisan and could almost believe that his orthodox beard blended with the bohemian faces around us. Sometimes I went out with my school friends and met their comrades. I was too much in awe of their men (they really didn't seem like boys, even those who were still at school) to be able to speak to them. It wasn't just because they were broodingly, romantically dark and handsome with Russian first names, it was their godlike self-possession, the glowing youthful certainty with which they predicted the end of the world, which struck me dumb.

Very suddenly, without giving formal notice, or telling me privately beforehand, my friends left school and signed themselves up at a poly for their A-levels. I wrote a poem about standing on a seashore, abandoned by two birds soaring into the sky.

The world was in trouble; activism was the black and grey reality of staying out late and making your own rules. Out in the cheerfully lit and coloured suburbs, I kept *shabbos* and *yom tov*, and marched only on Easter Monday. I still loved smart clothes, and I didn't even want to smoke. But I did yearn for the trappings of the gods. Easter Monday 1960 was my sixteenth birthday. My father had let slip that he had friends In Leather; he was going to try and get me a black leather jacket. All day long I marched, and sang. The world was coming to an end. Polaris—*oh-no*. We march to save our children (this made all of us giggle, even the sophisticated immortals), *We* shall *not* be *moved*. The unheard song to which I marched was black-leather-*jack*-et, black-leather-*jack*-et, no one will be more terrific than me . . .

I got home to a drum of talcum powder. Of course I said nothing—1960 was obviously going to be another bad year at the factory—though in recent years I have begun to wonder how many of the loved ones of my adult life have been made to pay for that particular disappointment. I often tell this tale, apparently to show myself up as a desperately, comically shallow teenager; in reality, to proclaim that not only was I rather hard-done-by and quite a little saint, but also that I was always, always, fashionable, in the swim, and Of My Time.

Acts of praise

You wore your best clothes to *shul*. These included gloves and a hat. You needed a Good Coat, not the one you wore to school, naturally, and Good Suits, and dresses for the very hot summer days, when your gloves were white. You had new clothes for the festivals. The annual cycle of Passover, Shavuot, Succoth, New Year and the Day of Atonement was marked by a succession of different costumes, though you might pare the significant acquisitions down to a spring suit for Passover (when, to your intense disappointment, it was almost always too cold to go out in it) and a new coat for the autumnal High Holydays, adding hats, dresses or separates for the festivals in between. You might never go anywhere else; there might be no public outings, apart from going to school, in the rest of your year; but you still had to have and replenish your stock of formal costumes.

There were, of course, shoes and, if you were not too orthodox to carry one on a sabbath or holiday, handbags to be thought of, as well as hats and gloves. Absolutely nothing was allowed to clash. Though you might have one smash item, such as the hat, it was important for everything to look as if it belonged with everything else.

The layout of the synagogue afforded the best possible view of these ensembles. Women prayed in an upstairs gallery on three sides of a square; there was no lattice-work or veiling such as more orthodox congregations used to conceal male and female worshippers from each other. Week in, week out, it was possible to appraise, from a good distance, the success of each woman's efforts, to see what colours and materials complemented each other, what shape of hat suited what style of garment. I did these aesthetic exercises constantly, automatically, almost unthinkingly, and without reference to the relative cost of each outfit, for of course in the conventional sense the clothes did not cost anything; they all came from someone's factory.

(These exercises have stood me in very good stead. Since my mid-teens I have known what can and what cannot be worn with what. If you have mastered this trick, no one can tell that you are wearing your daughter's friends' cast-offs, and you can save your money for a proper haircut. The downside is that you cannot switch it off, that you are constantly judging people's appearance, silently adjusting their colour schemes and accessories, and wondering why they dress as they do. If you're going to wear that coat, you need a darker pair of tights. If you're going to wear that hat, you've got to put your hair up. Nice skirt, shame about the shoes. *Nul points. Dix points!* Wish I was tall.)

For men it may have been slightly easier, as there were fewer options. But the suit had to be well cut from good cloth, the shirt and tie had to match, the hat had to be chosen with care if the wearer was not to look like an idiot. Anything cheap or ill-judged threw into question the range of a man's professional and family connections; cast doubt, indeed, upon his ability to manage his own affairs. For men and women alike, to dress well was to show that you knew your business.

But there was a sense, also, that it was owed to God. You did not present yourself in his courts dressed like a sloven. You did not come together with others as a recognizable community of his Chosen without looking a credit to him. It was not so much that we thought of him as the great garment manufacturer in the sky; more that, since he feeds and clothes us, to dress badly would be as impious as to waste food or to make it unpalatable. If food was disgusting, in what spirit would we thank God for it?

On the day that we did not eat, three times the normal congregation crammed into the synagogue. As a child I felt stifled, penned in by all the adult bodies upstairs in the ladies' gallery, overpowered by the smell of powder and eau de Cologne, and the humid air that striped the walls with condensation. The mink stoles of old ladies stared at me with beady eyes and snouts while I acknowledged in my prayers that even the pre-eminence of man over beast was as nothing. Herded together, helpless before an unknown future, we were begging for clemency. People were animals; grown-ups were babies; we were all, in the end, naked.

Something still puzzles me. The general principle applied that we were not to draw attention to ourselves. And yet we made ourselves conspicuous every week of the year, as, obeying the injunction not to use transport on the Sabbath, we trudged along Vivian Avenue or Golders Green Road in our finery. Even if our clothes were decent rather than opulent, with no furs or jewels in evidence, in the late Fifties and early Sixties a good hat and matching pair of gloves stood out oddly among the throng of shoppers scurrying for their groceries. Odder still was the effect of white plimsolls with the rest of your ensemble, if these were the only non-leather shoes which you could find to wear on the Day of Atonement. (These were indeed, if truth be told, the worst of all the mortifications; lucky the Nike-proud Jewish teenagers of today.)

According to the *Drapers Record*, we were living in an era when 'Sunday best' clothes were disappearing from the majority of the population's wardrobes. So we were out of time, as well as out of place. Our clothes, supposedly our protective armour, could even expose us to injury. My brother David, after sitting for his Common Entrance exams, was interviewed in his bar mitzvah suit by a headmaster who rejected him with the pronouncement: you're too neat and tidy; you'll never get your hands dirty; your sort don't know how to work. In bewilderment and anguish my mother threatened to mess up his hair and put mud on his face the next time. It proved not to be necessary; but she could be forgiven for wondering if the reason so many people took my other brother, Alan, for an Englishman was that he could not wear a suit for five minutes without looking as if he had slept in it.

It all comes back to me when I glimpse a Muslim or a Hindu neighbour walking down the street in festival clothes; calm and unhurried, in a different atmosphere from the cars speeding past. Perhaps it is possible for what you wear to create an aura, for you to carry your holiness with you, untainted by indifferent or profane surroundings. But there is always a tension between what you and others are doing. On a boiling hot afternoon, when you are going back to the synagogue in your best dress to organize permitted sabbath games for the younger ones, you can hardly be unaware that everyone else is peeling off in the garden or at the swimming pool. And the longing can grow for the cars not to be there, for the non-believers not to be there; for everyone's looks to mirror your own; for everything around you to belong to the heavenly city. It never surprises me that people who wear strange costumes often throw stones; that theocracies are fashion dictatorships.

I can never walk out in a good hat and coat without thinking: I could be going to *shul*. But my way of dressing changed when I gave up orthodoxy, and the contents of my wardrobe are not restocked as they used to be. These days, if I buy a suit, it has to be in a colour that will see long service in the workplace; anything pastel will get too little wear to repay the investment.

That headmaster grasped the wrong end of the right stick. The clothes were about work, and not about work. They concealed the labour we had put into them; and they were that labour's reward. They were *shabbosdik*, that is, of and worthy of the sabbath. They were designed for celebration and for prayer. They set us apart from the rest of our own lives; and probably from the lives of other people. You could say, they took us to another world.

Mechullo: bankrupt

The Jewish master tailor, with his small workshop or factory, was often one of the pre-war immigrants who, in the early 1900s, were 'sweated' homeworkers but who gradually improved their position by taking contracts for the production of clothing in bulk instead of working on piece rates as homeworkers. Margaret Wray, *The Women's Outerwear Industry* (London, Duckworth 1957).

Up in a lift that wobbles to a vast hall of noise. In a tin cubicle high above Lexington Street is Daddy, with Beverley, his secretary (until she gets married), who used to be a Land Girl in the war—hard to imagine, a Jewish Land Girl; she's not even particularly tall. There is a giant's table for a huge layered slab of material. Joe the cutter moves a wire through it. Later Uncle Louis replaces him. Auntie Lily sits at one end checking buttons and buttonholes. There are also some men who are pressers, otherwise it is all ladies. The noise comes from their sewing machines. Each seam is a roar. Sometimes it looks and sounds as if the roars are synchronized.

. . . a smaller factory tended to have lower overhead costs per unit, resulting from economies in supervision and simpler record-keeping requirements. . . . [it] could . . . be equipped relatively cheaply, as most of the essential pre-war machinery and equipment was inexpensive, compared with the general run of industrial equipment. Machinery could be hired on easy terms, or bought on hire purchase, and small factories equipped with lockstitch machines could be rented for a small weekly sum.

Some of the ladies are black; a very pretty lady is Greek. The only machinist I ever really get to know is Mabel, who has been with Daddy even before her marriage to Pat. She has always been with Daddy. Even when the others have to be laid off, Mabel is kept on.

. . . the average factory employee [worked] for only forty weeks in the year. . . . the worst seasonal fluctuations were, however, in the London fashion trade. Outdoor factories in London seem to have been in production for only about thirty weeks in the year.

Outside, Berwick Street market where Mummy shops for vegetables on the days she visits. At one point she visits almost every day. She is not like some of the wives, Pat Harris or Stella Lewis for instance, who march in, demand to see the books, and decide that they might as well stay because they couldn't make a worse mess of things themselves. She must be there, literally, to hold his hand. And he must be close to mental breakdown. At Chanukkah, one of my brothers makes a joke of it, buying her 'Letts Businesswoman's Diary'.

... the initial orders for autumn and winter stock [were] placed about May each year and similar orders for spring and summer stock about October. The end of each buying season was marked by half-yearly sales, in January and July ... deliveries to the stores generally tapered off some weeks before the sales ... For a large part of their seasonal requirements they relied on repeat orders for deliveries from manufacturers at one or two weeks' notice.

I don't understand. We have been rich. I have memories, not all my own, of better days. We still have a television. We go to schools a long distance from home, and wear smart uniforms. How long since we have had a car? We still have paintings on the wall. One is a portrait of me, in a peach organdie frock, with thin blue velvet ribbons bunching my hair. (And that peach material, which did not and does not suit my skin, is still the colour of a lost paradise.) The piano stays on the parquet flooring in front of the French windows until I say I do not want to learn. Beyond the windows is the back garden, and a gardener. In the photograph drawer there are pictures of Mummy and Daddy in nightclubs in New York. Daddy takes me to Covent Garden to see the ballet, and a tray of tea is passed along to us in the interval.

In June 1941, the first Consumer Rationing Order introduced a scheme for rationing civilian clothing (which was retained until March 1949). ... New producers could only enter the industry by buying up the coupon capital of an existing business, or by securing an issue of coupons (known as a 'coupon float') from the Board of Trade, and applications for such 'floats' were generally refused. Between 1941 and 1949, therefore, the de-stabilizing effect of ease of entry, typical of the pre-war industry, was removed.

In 1949 we take a foreign holiday. My Hebrew teacher sniffs and says there are many lovely places to visit in this country.

...the reason for the manufacturer's prosperity lay in the certainty of his profit margin and the absence of the usual offsetting, end of season, losses. His normal pre-war trading risks were removed, because of the strength of wartime demand and because of the virtual elimination of fashion changes. The impact of the season on production was ended; he could deliver his garments to the distributor as soon as they were ready; he no longer had to hold stocks and the rate of turnover of his working capital (and so his yearly profits) was increased. . . . most of his uncertainties about cloth supplies and prices were removed and, at the same time, he had a strong demand for his products and could make his own conditions about delivery dates with the distributor.

We go to France and Italy. The images come mainly from Daddy's photographs. A little girl in plaits and a smocked frock, holding balloons in a gloved hand, with the Eiffel Tower in the background. I know I remember the gloves for myself. Cousin Golda bought them in Galeries Lafayette. They are crochet, a pattern of flowers and fishnet, ecru; they have no weight, and yet I can feel them encasing my fingers and palms and wrists, so crisp, so dry . . . And at Diana Marino I am kitted out with shorts, a skirt, a bolero, and a little ruched top that can be worn on or off the shoulders, all in the same strong pattern of dark blue and red that stands out in the sunshine but is an unusual selection for a five-year-old . . . I nag them for a straw hat like a Chinaman's, and they give me one to keep me quiet. I am spoiled rotten.

In 1949 and 1950, the end of rationing and the rush to buy clothing . . . resulted in an increase in sales which brought consumers' expenditure above the 1938 figure for the first time. This was soon followed in 1951 by a fall in clothing sales, as increased prices and well-stocked wardrobes combined to reduce demand.

The ten plagues of Egypt are recited at Passover. For each one a drop of wine must be spilt from your cup. We chant as we spill it.

DOM: blood.

1950–51 marked the end of the post-war boom for the clothing industry. Re-armament and the Korean War caused a large increase in raw wool and cotton prices, which affected utility as well as 'general' clothing production, because subsidies for utility cloth had been withdrawn in 1948.

SFARDEYA: frogs.

High cloth prices necessitated considerable increases in clothing prices at a time when the end of shortages and restrictions in other industries was leading to a growing supply of other goods that competed with clothing for the consumer's growing power.

KINIM: lice.

Moreover, with the end of rationing, in 1949, new clothing producers could once more enter the industry and fashion became an important determinant of demand. Manufacturers had to adapt production to trading conditions that they had not experienced for ten years or more.

OROV: wild beasts.

. . .the smaller producer, particularly the outdoor contractor, was exposed to the full force of seasonal changes in demand. Most contractors made new contracts each season; the volume of work available tended to fluctuate considerably, so that they could not estimate with any certainty the demand for their services.

My father sits with his head in his hands. But I can see the colour of his face and neck. It is bright beetroot red.

DEVER: pestilence.

. . . they had to cover extra payments for over-time working during the season and for the retention of at least a nucleus of skilled workers in the slack periods . . .

It is the middle of the night, and there is shouting in the bedroom next to mine.

SHECHIN: boils.

. . . the seasonal orders soon diminished and they were often left with unsold stocks . . .

It is early morning and Daddy is being sick in the bathroom.

BOROD: hail.

. . . they frequently found themselves short of money to meet even weekly wage payments and had hastily to sell their stocks at cut prices.

It is the middle of the afternoon and I come home from school bringing a friend back for tea. Daddy and Uncle Louis are there, sitting on the couch in the lounge.

ARBEH: locusts.

. . . retail sales were seriously affected by unseasonable weather, as in the summer of 1954.

They are there day after day through the summer, watching the racing on television.

CHOSHECH: darkness.

The result of over-production was considerable instability, which showed itself in seasonal unemployment, in a high rate of bankruptcy . . .

MACAS BECHOROS: the death of the first-born.

A presser left his machine on all night. The factory has burned out.

In 1960, I think, we had another bad summer. It is not true, Daddy writes in a letter which is printed in the *Drapers Record* and which I pin on my bedroom wall, that the industry's troubles come from the plethora of radical new styles on the market. It is the unseasonal weather which has restrained sales and produced the current slump. The public have taken the Empire line and the A-line to their hearts.

I get a beautiful sample of each. The 'Empire' is in navy-blue velvet, the 'A' is a pink and green cotton print. I wear them to friends' birthday parties and to youth club socials, though the Empire is good enough for weddings. I perch gilt or plastic headbands over my urchin cut and leave my glasses off. By now I have two pairs of shoes with 'potato' heels, one in white leather and one in pinky red, each with a lattice front recalling cross-tied ballet ribbons.

At home I am often blamed in general terms for 'being unconscious'. But I am not really supposed to know what is going on. No one sits me down and tells me. If we do not have a car, I do not question the fact. If things disappear to be sold, I do not notice. It registers with me that we do not go on holidays, but I do not feel hard-done-by. Thanks to Noel Streatfeild, Frances Hodgson Burnett, Edith Nesbit and numberless fairy tales, I know that being poor is almost the precondition for being the hero in a story. I feel that a romantic cachet has descended upon us, and that I am quite as good as the girls I go to school with in Hampstead.

But as I get older, I do become conscious. I go to *shul* with my elderly neighbour, or with school friends. Daddy has not kept up his membership fees, has quarrelled with them all and stormed out when the bills fell due. Mummy is not involved with the Ladies' Association, or with the League of Jewish Women. I get involved: I help to run the Children's Service (I buy a pair of very light brown, chisel-toed lace-ups with my wages, and am going to be able to finance a trip to the Edinburgh Festival), and I am *madricha* in a youth club that organizes *shabbos* activities for younger children.

I am on my own out there. From somewhere the words come into my head: we have no standing.

I sense that other families may not be lurching from one crisis to the next, that other parents are not necessarily anxious about the exposure of their circumstances. Sometimes we are told not to answer the door, or the phone. At school, I am startled to be called to the headmistress's study to be asked when my music tuition will be paid, but I do not miss a beat; my mouth opens and I hear myself saying that the cheque is in the post.

A school friend is shocked about the *shul* membership business. I make the narrative one of bloody-minded independence (having joined CND, I am beginning to fancy myself as a social critic), but she is aware of the practical implications. You have to be buried some day, and if you are not a member of a *shul*, she says, there is no one to take care of it.

That year, we attend High Holyday services somewhere else: a synagogue founded locally in the 1930s by very Orthodox German refugees. Within this community, we ourselves are almost foreigners. Yet Daddy does have an acquaintance there, Mr Rosenblum, someone for whom Daddy found work when he arrived here with nothing.

Was it only the next spring that Mr Rosenblum came to our door, to tell my mother that she need not worry, that he would take care of all the arrangements?

Apparently things were looking up. He was driving round the provinces, picking up orders. On his way home, not a mile away, he felt very ill. He stopped the car outside the cottage hospital. He had had a heart attack, they said, and kept him in.

He did not look too bad when we went to see him. As the days went by and he rested he began to feel, he told a nurse, better than he had done for ages. He became his old self again at visiting times, sending us all on errands around the ward.

Numbers were restricted for visiting hours. On Tuesday night, Mummy and David went. Alan had to be out of London. I stayed in and washed my hair. It was very long in those days. It took time to dry. They came back and we had a late supper. Then the telephone rang and it was the hospital.

Nobody had expected it. He was fifty-five. He had one son who was a solicitor, one who was qualifying as an accountant, and a daughter who had won a scholarship to Oxford. And he thought business was going to get better. Mummy says that he was even hoping to make enough money to set aside for my wedding.

We covered the mirrors.

A cousin gave me a black jumper to wear for the week, although it wasn't strictly necessary. An old woman came on the day of the funeral to make ritual tears in our garments. A shriek came from my mother's throat as the razor went through the lapel of David's new suit. He had worked so hard and saved so long for the material. And we had, to be honest, been left with nothing but what we stood up in.

I never said goodbye and I still can't. I see him in every well-dressed, middle-aged Jewish businessman. I've seen him in a film sequence of Al Jolson dancing, and I've seen him in a Karsh photograph of Humphrey Bogart. I see him in a tweed jacket, with a pipe and a walking stick, clothes and props that were more solid than he was. I've seen him in every slightly built, dark-haired, childish and unreasonable man that I've ever fallen for.

I see him in the clothes he made for me, and I buy new ones that resemble them even if they don't suit me any more. I own and keep dresses that he made or chose for my mother. I've still got the satin sash to the black velvet dress with the boat neck, three-quarter sleeves, tight bodice and full ballerina skirt that he made for me just after I won the scholarship. I wore it to a Masonic uncle's Ladies' Night; we danced together in the Charleston competition (he had taught me how to years before) and we were astounded not to be given the prize. We had been so confident that we walked up to receive it.

I don't know what would have happened. Schmatters boomed again in the 1960s, but anyone could get into it then. My brothers had their professional qualifications, but he might have felt humiliated at being advised by them. Oxford would for a time have made me a stranger. If I had had a brilliant career, he might have shrivelled; but my not being a star would have robbed him of his dream life. I don't know. This part of me has come away and cannot be stitched back.

I didn't play with dolls. I can't even recall having any, although friends did: great plastic babies with 'Rosebud' or 'Pat. Pending' embossed on their backs. But I do remember seeing something at a friend's house that I instantly craved. It was a cardboard figure of a girl which came in a box containing dozens of stiff paper cut-out costumes—coats, skirts, jackets, dresses and hats. The girl could be dressed for country or town, for school, shopping, holidays or parties. One day I came home from school and was told 'close your eyes and put out your hands'. There was the box. Same girl, different occasions, different outfits. Life in miniature. Heaven.

It still astonishes me to contemplate this child, so early and so completely adapted to a multiple-persona'd self. I seemed always to have known that one man in his time might play many parts, but one woman had to play many parts at a time.

This may explain both the contradictions of my teenage years and the gusto with which I embraced them. For, even as I gave up (for a time) mixed dancing, polished up my Hebrew and attended theological seminars, I pored over *Paris-Match* and studied pictures of Brigitte Bardot. Even as I contemplated an orthodox marriage which would have required me to cover my head with a wig and make monthly visits to a ritual bath, I was seeking out long men's sweaters to wear over a straight skirt and black stockings, and imagining myself in a Paris club with Juliette Greco.

But there were times when I didn't know what to wear or who to be. Could I actually be myself without looking too Jewish? Could you be the type that passed exams and still be glamorous? At that Masonic evening I had my hair up in a French pleat, and though I say it myself I looked a million dollars. Somewhere behind me I heard my father say: 'And that's what they give a scholarship to Oxford!' as if to suggest that I was nothing but a pretty face. What he meant, of course, was that his daughter had cracked it, got the double. I hadn't; only he would ever think so.

I still haven't found the answers. Is there something within which revolts against being pinned down, which yearns for yet another metamorphosis? There is a disease associated with clothes which is like the gambler's neurosis: the belief that out there, there is just one more purchase to make and you will finally find the one, true, right outfit, the one by which you will be both transformed and restored to yourself; you will be undisputably the fairest one of all and, at last, the real, essential you. Crooked shall be made straight, bumps shall be smoothed. Fastened into that belief, the Wandering Dresser is condemned to the torments of an eternal adolescence.

Am I still where I was when his heart stopped? I think so, yes. No one else has thought me the cleverest and the prettiest girl in the world. No one else has seen me as the embodiment of so many ambitions and fantasies. No one else could legitimize quite so many costume changes. He was the only Other in whose heart it could all be held together.

I wish I'd known it sooner; I wouldn't have tried to pin the job on anyone else. This is the only conclusion I can come to. It fits, and I'll wear it.

Notes

Introduction

Rosie Findlay

1 Lucia Ruggerone, 'The feeling of being dressed: Affect studies and the clothed body', *Fashion Theory* 21, no. 5 (2017), 578.
2 Mary-Ellen Roach-Higgins and Joanne B. Eicher, 'Dress and identity', *Clothing and Textiles Research* 10, no. 4 (1992), 1.
3 Roach-Higgins and Eicher, 'Dress and identity', 1.
4 Carol Tulloch, 'Style–fashion–dress: From black to post-black', *Fashion Theory* 14, no. 3 (2010), 276.
5 Tulloch, 'Style–fashion–dress', 276.
6 Roberto Filippello and Ilya Parkins, *Fashion and Feeling: The Affective Politics of Dress* (London: Palgrave MacMillan, 2023), n.p.
7 Gavin Van Horn citing Thomas Berry, 'Kinning: Introducing the Kinship Series' in Gavin Van Horn, Robin Wall Kimmerer, and John Hausdoerffer (eds.), *Kinship: Belonging in a World of Relations, Vol. 1: Planet* (Libertyville: Center for Humans and Nature Press, 2021), 3.

Darning Mark's Jumper: Wearing Love and Sorrow

Karena de Perthuis

1 Roland Barthes, *The Fashion System*, trans. M. Ward and R. Howard, University of California Press, Berkeley and Los Angeles, 1983, 298.
2 Akiko Fukai, 'A New Design Aesthetic', in L. Mitchell (ed.), *The Cutting Edge: Fashion from Japan*, Powerhouse Publishing, Sydney, 2005, 20.
3 Barbara Vinken, *Fashion Zeitgeist: Trends and Cycles in the Fashion System*, trans. M. Hewson, Berg, Oxford and New York, 2005, 69.
4 Georg Simmel, 'Fashion, Adornment and Style', in D. Frisby and M. Featherstone (eds.), *Simmel on Culture*, Sage, London, 1997, 204.
5 'Susannah' in Zoe Edwards, 'Make Do and Mend: Darning', http://www.coletterie.com/tutorials-tips-tricks/make-do-and-mend-darning.
6 Giselle Walker and Elizabeth Leedham-Green, 'Introduction', in G. Walker and E. Leedham-Green (eds.), *Identity*, Cambridge University Press, Cambridge, 2010, 4.

7 Lesley Chamberlain, *A Shoe Story: Van Gogh, the Philosophers and the West*, Harbour, Chelmsford, 2014, 85.

8 Ibid., 86.

9 Ibid., 88. Through Heidegger's letters and writings, Chamberlain traces his influences back to the medieval philosopher and theologian, Duns Scotus, as well as to the poets Rainer Maria Rilke and Gerard Manley Hopkins and artists Paul Cézanne and Vincent van Gogh.

10 See, for example, Daniel Miller (ed.), *Materiality*, Duke University Press, Durham and London, 2005.

11 Peter Stallybrass, 'Worn Worlds: Clothes, Mourning and the Life of Things', in D. Ben-Amos and L. Weissberg (eds.), *Cultural Memory and the Construction of Identity*, Wayne State University Press, Detroit, 1999, 39.

12 Philip Roth, *Patrimony*, in Stallybrass, 'Worn Worlds', 33.

13 Colm Tóibín, *The Master*, Picador, London, 2004, 266.

14 Elizabeth Wilson, *Adorned in Dreams*, University of California Press, Berkeley and Los Angeles, 1985, 1.

15 Jean Cocteau, *Beauty and the Beast: Diary of a Film*, Dover, Mineola, 1972, 7.

16 Stallybrass, 'Worn Worlds', 31.

17 A more sinister ghostly inhabitance of clothing by the dead appears in James's early short story, *The Romance of Certain Old Clothes*, in which a dead wife gets her revenge when a promise is broken. My thanks to the anonymous reviewer who brought this text, as well as others, to my attention.

18 Stallybrass, 'Worn Worlds', 28.

19 Ibid., 29.

20 Elizabeth Wilson, 'Magic Fashion', *Fashion Theory*, vol. 8, no. 4, 2004, 379.

21 Elizabeth Wilson, 'Notes on Fashion as Fetish', *Vestoj*, no. 2, 2011, 190.

22 Ibid., 189.

23 Wilson, 'Magic Fashion', 379.

24 Wilson, 'Notes on Fashion as Fetish', 189.

25 The authoritative 'text' (used by both Wilson and Stallybrass) on the history of theories of fetishism is a series of essays by William Pietz called 'The Problem of the Fetish', published in the journal, *Res: Anthropology and Aesthetics*, 1985, 1987, 1988.

26 William Pietz, 'The Problem of the Fetish, IIIa: Bosman's Guinea and the Enlightenment Theory of Fetishism', *Res: Anthropology and Aesthetics*, vol. 16, 1988, 107.

27 John Atkins quoted in Pietz, 'The Problem of the Fetish', p. 110. Atkins was an English slaver and the author of *A Voyage to Guinea, Brasil, and the West Indies, in His Majesty's Ships the Swallow and Weymouth*, London, 1737.

28 Stallybrass, 'Marx's Coat', 186.

29 Ann Rosalind Jones and Peter Stallybrass, *Renaissance Clothing and the Materials of Memory*, Cambridge University Press, Cambridge, 2000, 2.

30 Ibid., 11.

31 Stallybrass, 'Marx's Coat', 183.

32 Igor Kopytoff, 'The Cultural Biography of Things: Commoditization as Process', in A. Appadurai (ed.), *The Social Life of Things: Commodities in Cultural Perspective*, Cambridge University Press, Cambridge, 1986, 64.

33 Mauss quoted in Stallybrass, 'Marx's Coat', 185.

34 Jones and Stallybrass, *Renaissance Clothing*, 4.

35 Kopytoff, 'The Cultural Biography of Things', 64.

36 Ibid. The terms 'commodification' and 'commoditisation' are commonly listed as synonyms (see, for example, OED). Douglas Rushkoff helpfully distinguishes between the two: '"Commodification" is a somewhat Marxist idea, referring to the way that market values can replace other social values . . . "Commoditization" [refers] specifically to the way that goods that used to be distinguishable in terms of attributes end up becoming mere commodities in the eyes of the market or consumers. Commodification is more of a crime of the market against humanity, while commoditization is more of a market problem for the manufacturers of branded goods.' (Douglas Rushkoff, 'Commodified vs. Commoditized', http://www.rushkoff.com/commodified-vs-commoditized/.) In anthropology, however, the two terms are used interchangeably with 'commoditisation' the more common. Although Appadurai uses the latter term, in the interests of clarity, here I have mostly retained the terminology of commodification.

37 Stallybrass, 'Marx's Coat', 196.

38 Ibid., 193.

39 Kopytoff, 69.

40 Ibid.

41 Ibid., 80.

42 Ibid., 80, 75.

43 Wilson, 'Magic Fashion', 379.

The Same Yellow Dress

Amy Key

1 Sheila Heti, *How Should a Person Be?* (London: Harvill Secker, 2013), 115–116.

2 Quoted in Lauren Milligan, 'Fashion Flashback: McQueen's Asylum Show', *British Vogue*, August 7, 2014, https://www.vogue.co.uk/gallery/erin-oconnor-on-walking-in-alexander-mcqueen-asylum-show.

3 Brenda Shaughnessy, 'McQueen is Dead, Long Live McQueen', *Poetry* 207, No. 2 (November 2015), 160.

The Work of Human Hands

Fiona Wright

1 Sofi Thanhauser, *Worn: A People's History of Clothing* (London: Allen Lane, 2022), xi.
2 Ibid.
3 Ramij Howlader, Monirul Islam (Rajib), Tanjibul Hasan Sajib and Ripon Kumar Prasad, 'Standard Minute Value for a T-Shirt', in Caroline Evans and Alessandra Vaccari (eds.), *Time in Fashion: Industrial, Antilinear and Uchronic Temporalities* (London: Bloomsbury, 2020) 69.

Things to Think About When You Are Buying Clothes

Meena Kandasamy

1 India's Union Agricultural Minister Radha Mohan Singh submitted the figure of 11,400 farmer suicides in the year 2016. The figures have been higher in previous years: 12,602 in the year 2015. See Indian Asian News Service, '11,400 farmers committed suicide in 2016: Govt tells Lok Sabha.' *Firstpost*, July 20, 2017.
2 This is a widely used statistic, as reported by Reuters. See Mayank Bhardwaj and Rajendra Jadhav, 'Indian farmers cotton on to new seed, in blow to Monsanto'. *Reuters*, August 3, 2016.
3 As reported by Vandana Shiva for *Seed Freedom* (2015), 'most of the 300,000 farmer suicides in India since 1995 (when the WTO came into force) are concentrated in the cotton belt. And 95% of the cotton in India is controlled by Monsanto'. Also, here's some background: Monsanto was only able to enter the market in 1988 when the World Bank gave India a $150 million loan to privatize its seed industry and deregulate it. While this helped bring better technology to India, it also disrupted the traditional ways farmers would save seeds and develop their own hybrids. Close to 90 per cent of the cotton grown in India today uses Monsanto's technology, which is licensed to forty-nine Indian seed companies. Indian patent laws prevent life forms from being patented, but Monsanto's seeds are genetically engineered and qualify for an exception. According to *Reuters*, 41 million GM cotton seed packets were sold last year, earning royalties of 6.5 billion Indian rupees ($97 million) for Monsanto.
4 A study by the University of California at Berkeley has found a correlation between a 1 degree Celsius rise in average temperature on any day in the growing season corresponding to sixty-seven more suicides. They argue that climate change could have contributed to the death of more than 60,000 farmers and farm workers in the last three decades in India. See Michael Safi (2017).
5 For an engaging portrayal of the farmer suicides in Vidarbha, please watch the documentary 'The Dying Fields', on PBS's *Wide Angle* (directed by Fred de Sam

Lazaro, 2008). The 'a farmer commits suicide every eight hours' statistic is from the documentary but is also quoted in Neil Genzlinger's review of the programme for *The New York Times* (2007).

6 Projected estimate by the Cotton Association of India for the year 2016-17, see Vimukt Dave, 'CAI projects 33.60 million bales cotton production for 2017-2017', *Business Standard*, August 30, 2016.

7 In my home state of Tamil Nadu, I remember vividly that in the last decade weavers have been pushed to the brink of poverty and starvation. Beginning in 2002, both major parties in the state (the DMK and the AIADMK) have competed with each other to open *kanchi thotti* 'gruel centers' (soup kitchens) where these starving weavers could have a meal – and charity organizations, welfare organizations, churches, religious establishments have also followed suit to try and mitigate their difficulty. For more information, see Asha Krishnakumar's report for *Frontline* 'Weavers in Distress' (2002). For a recent story on the cotton weavers of the state, where you encounter a picture of people leaving the weaving profession to sell newspapers because of acute poverty, refer to Divya Chandrandrababu, 'Tamil Nadu cotton weaves on wane get a boost', *The Times of India*, April 25, 2016.

8 Karl Marx, *The Poverty of Philosophy*. Marx/Engels Internet Archive (Marxists.org), 1999 [1955].

9 As Morris David Morris writes, 'by 1921, 12 per cent of the workforce of the Bombay mills was Untouchable. As in the railways, Untouchables were concentrated in the least preferred sectors of the mills. Over 72 percent of Untouchable men were in the ring-spinning department, where they comprised 40 per cent of total male workers and were almost comprehensively shut out of the higher-status and better-paid weaving department.' Quoted in Oliver Mendelsohn and Marika Vicziany, *The Untouchables: Subordination. Poverty and the State in Modern India* (Cambridge University Press, 1998), 89.

10 Original quote: 'In those days many accidents used to occur in the throstle departments of mills and workers considered them very unsafe to work there. Since workers from upper castes usually did not agree to working in them, they were spared for the untouchable worker.' Paresh Majmundar, quoted by Jan Breman, *The Making and Unmaking of an Industrial Working Class: Sliding Down the Labour Hierarchy in Ahmedabad, India* (Amsterdam: Amsterdam University Press, 2004), 18.

11 Salim Lakha, quoted by Breman, *The Making and Unmaking of an Industrial Working Class*, 17.

12 Breman, *The Making and Unmaking of an Industrial Working Class*, 131.

13 Dr Ambedkar's evidence before the Southborough Committee (1919) which was one of his first political engagements. What we have is a transcript of his deposition from the records which reads as follows: 'In the mills in the Bombay Presidency the untouchables were not yet allowed to work in the weaving department: in one case an untouchable

did work in the weaving department of a mill saying that he was a Mohammedan, and when found out, he was severely beaten.' See Babasaheb Ambedkar, *Writings and Speeches*, Vol. 1 (Dr Ambedkar Foundation, 2014 [1979]), 274.

14 Babasaheb Ambedkar, 'Evidence Before the Simon Commission', retrieved from: https://archive.org/stream/Ambedkar_CompleteWorks/14D.% 20Dr.%20 Ambedkar%20with%20the%20Simon%20Commission% 20D_djvu.txt. (Accessed: August 1, 2017).

15 For an in-depth and meaningful account of early trade unionism in Madras, as well as the issues of caste/untouchability, the role of the political movements and parties of that time, do read D.Veeraraghavan's *The Making of the Madras Working Class* (New Delhi: LeftWord Books, 2013).

16 Dr Ambedkar writing in the *Bahishkrut Bharat* (3 February 1928), quoted in Shailaja Paik, *Dalit Women's Education in Modern India: Double Discrimination* (London and New York: Routledge, 2014).

17 Paik, *Dalit Women's Education in Modern India.*

18 For more information on this revolt (also known as the *Maru Marakkal Samaram*), see Eliza Kent, *Converting Women: Gender and Protestant Christianity in Colonial South India* (Oxford: Oxford University Press, 2004) and Robert L. Hardgrave, *The Nadars of Tamilnad: The Political Culture of a Community in Change* (Berkeley: University of California Press, 1969). More particularly, the chapter 'Cloth, Clothes and Colonialism' in Bernard S. Cohn's *Colonialism and its Forms of Knowledge: The British in India* (New Jersey: Princeton University Press, 1996) provides valuable background and knowledge.

19 Divya Arya, 'The woman who cut off her breasts to protest a tax', *BBC News*, July 28, 2016.

20 B. Kolappan, 'Ramadoss consolidates intermediate caste groups against Dalits', *The Hindu*, Chennai, December 2, 2012.

Under the Weather

Jane Tynan

1 Samuel Beckett, *The Unnamable* (New York: Grove Press, 1958). Original French *L'Innommable* published in 1953.

2 Fred Miller Robinson, '"An Art of Superior Tramps": Beckett and Giacometti', *The Centennial Review* 25, no. 4 (1981): 331–344.

3 Henri Cartier-Bresson, *Alberto Giacometti 1961*, 1961, photograph, Victoria & Albert Museum collection.

4 Janet Martin-Nielson, 'Scientific forecasting? Performing objectivity at the UK's Meteorological Office, 1960s–1970s,' *History of Meteorology* 8 (2017): 202–221.

5 Mary Douglas, *Purity and Danger: An analysis of the concepts of pollution and taboo* (London: Routledge, 1966).

6 'The Flu is caused by Changeable Weather' [advertisement for Tuck & Co. Hull, UK], *The Daily Mail*, April 19, 1920, 2.

7 Tim Ingold, 'Weather-World,' *International Lexicon of Aesthetics*, Spring Edition (2023), 4.

8 Ingold, 'Weather-World', 3.

9 William Somerset Maugham, *Rain and Other Stories* (New York: Grosset & Dunlap, 1921).

10 Maugham, *Rain and Other Stories*, 1921.

11 Jacqueline Allen-Collinson, George Jennings, Anu Vaittinen and Helen Owton, 'Weather-wise? Sporting embodiment, weather work and weather learning in running and triathlon,' *International Review for the Sociology of Sport* 54, no. 7 (2019): 777–792.

12 Sunny Xiang, 'Militarized Comfort: How to Feel Naked While Wearing Clothes', in Roberto Filippello and Ilya Parkins (eds.), *Fashion and Feeling: The Affective Politics of Dress* (Cham: Palgrave Macmillan, 2023), 41–62.

13 'Burberry's Equipment for the Services' [advertisement for Burberry], *British Warships*, 1940. Photo by: Hilary Jane Morgan/Design Pics/Universal Images Group via Getty Images.

14 Arne Naess, *Ecology, Community and Lifestyle: Outline of an Ecosophy* (Cambridge: Cambridge University Press, 1991).

Paradise Engraved

Krys Osei

1 For further discussion of 'Black is Beautiful', see Tanisha C. Ford, *Liberated Threads: Black Women, Style, and the Global Politics of Soul* (Chapel Hill: University of North Carolina Press, 2015).

2 For further discussion on African women's photographic and fashion history and their wider negotiation of power relations through the camera and the sewing machine, see Catherine E. McKinley, Edwidge Danticat, and Jacqueline Woodson, *The African Lookbook: A Visual History of 100 Years of African Women* (New York: Bloomsbury Publishing, 2021).

3 For more on the emotional transmission of family photographs within the context of African diaspora, migration and visuality, see Esther O. Ohito, 'What Can We Not Leave Behind? Storying Family Photographs, Unlocking Emotional Memories, and Welcoming Complex Conversations on Being Human', *Occasional Paper Series* vol. 45, 2021.

4 See Tanisha C. Ford, *Liberated Threads: Black Women, Style, and the Global Politics of Soul* (Chapel Hill: University of North Carolina Press, 2015) and Simidele Dosekun, *Fashioning Postfeminism: Spectacular Femininity and Transnational Culture* (Urbana: University of Illinois Press, 2020) for more discussion of African women's dressed place-making.

The Men Who Dressed Me: Buscemi, Cash and Dad

Honor Wilson

1 *Fargo*, directed by Joel Coen and Ethan Coen (1996), London, UK: Amazon UK.

2 Lilah Ramzi (2019) 'An Ode to the Campiest Film You've Probably Never Seen', *Vogue*, 19 April. Available at: https://www.vogue.com/article/what-a-way-to-go-shirley-maclaine-camp-film (Accessed 13/04/2024).

3 *Fargo*, directed by Joel Coen and Ethan Coen (1996).

4 Jeffrey Adams, *The Cinema of the Coen Brothers: Hard-Boiled Entertainments* (New York: Columbia University Press, 2015), 133.

5 See Dan Poush (1968) *Before the First Performance: Blowing Smoke Rings* [Photograph]. John R. Cash Revocable Trust.

6 Liza Corsillo (2016) 'TBT: When Johnny Cash Suited-Up for His Legendary Folsom Prison Concert', *GQ*, 14 January. Available at: https://www.gq.com/story/tbt-johnny-cash-suit-folsom-prison (Accessed 12/04/2024).

7 Phineas Harper (2024) 'So you'd never wear a skirt in public? Men, you don't know what you're missing', *The Guardian*, 3 January. Available at: https://www.theguardian.com/commentisfree/2024/jan/03/skirts-men-fashion-feminism (Accessed: 10/04/2024).

8 Elizabeth Wilson, *Adorned in Dreams: Fashion and Modernity* (London: I.B. Tauris, 1987), 122.

9 Queen Official (2008). *Queen – I Want To Break Free (Official Video)*. 1st September. YouTube [Online Video]. Available at: https://youtu.be/f4Mc-NYPHaQ?si=SxHPC2rzlUTxMaMR (Accessed 25/062024).

10 *What Am I?* (1980), Hay-on-Wye/Y Gelli Gandrylland Mansfield: BFI Player.

'The Cool'

Yomi Ṣode

1 Robin Hobb, *Fool's Errand* (London: Voyager, 2001), 65.

2 Deji Akomolafe, 'Frank Lucas: How a $100,000 Chinchilla Coat Exposed Harlem's Kingpin', *Criminal*, July, 2024. https://vocal.media/criminal/frank-lucas-how-a-100-000-chinchilla-coat-exposed-harlem-s-kingpin.

3 Yomi Ṣode, *Manorism* (London: Penguin, 2023).

A Leg to Stand On: Prosthetics, Metaphor, and Materiality

Vivian Sobchack

Although part of vernacular expression, "A Leg to Stand On" is also the title of a book by phenomenological neurologist Oliver Sacks that deals with a topic somewhat related to the present one: Sacks's experience with a neurologically damaged leg. See Oliver Sacks, *A Leg to Stand On* (New York: Simon and Schuster, 1984).

1   Roland Barthes, "The Jet-man," in *Mythologies*, trans. Annette Lavers (New York: Hill and Wang, 1957), 72–73. The Bruno Schulz epigraph that begins this essay can be found in Bruno Schulz, *The Street of Crocodiles*, trans. Celina Wieniewska (London: Penguin, 1963), 59.

2   It is worth noting here that *trope* has a philosophical definition as well as a rhetorical one: a "trope" is a figural use of language, but it is also an argument advanced by a skeptic. In this regard a "tropological phenomenology" would take into account both senses of the word and would proceed in its "thick description" both fully aware and productively suspicious that lived-body experience is always also being imaginatively "figured" as it is literally being "figured out."

3   Paul Ricoeur, *The Rule of Metaphor: Multi-disciplinary Studies of the Creation of Meaning in Language*, trans. Robert Czerny, Kathleen McLaughlin, and John Costello (Toronto: University of Toronto Press, 1977), 309. Subsequent references will be cited in the text.

4   Helen Deutsch and Felicity Nussbaum, introduction to *Defects: Engineering the Modern Body*, ed. Helen Deutsch and Felicity Nussbaum (Ann Arbor: University of Michigan Press, 2000), 1–2.

5   Sarah S. Jain, "The Prosthetic Imagination: Enabling and Disabling the Prosthetic Trope," *Science, Technology, & Human Values* 24, no. 1 (winter 1999): 32.

6   Robert Rawdon Wilson, "Cyber(body)parts: Prosthetic Consciousness", *Body & Society* 1, nos. 3–4 (1995): 242.

7   Alison Landsberg, "Prosthetic Memory: *Total Recall* and *Blade Runner*," *Body & Society* 1, nos. 3–4 (1995): 175–89.

8   Joanne Morra and Marquard Smith, eds. "The Prosthetic Aesthetic", introduction to "The Prosthetic Aesthetic," special issue, *New Formations* 46 (spring 2002): 5.

9   See the blurb on the back cover of Gabriel Brahm Jr. and Mark Driscoll, eds., *Prosthetic Territories: Politics and Hypertechnologies* (Boulder, CO: Westview Press, 1995).

10   Jennifer A. Gonzalez, "Autotopographies," in *Prosthetic Territories: Politics and Hypertechnologies*, ed. Gabriel Brahm Jr. and Mark Driscoll (Boulder, CO: Westview Press, 1995), 134.

11   Chris Hablas and Steven Mentor, "The Cyborg Body Politic and the New World Order," in *Prosthetic Territories: Politics and Hypertechnologies*, ed. Gabriel Brahm Jr. and Mark Driscoll (Boulder, CO: Westview Press, 1995), 244–45.

12 Diane M. Nelson, "Stumped Identities: Body Image, Bodies Politic, and the *Mujer Maya* as Prosthetic," *Cultural Anthropology* 16, no. 3 (Aug. 2001): 314–53; and Melissa W. Wright, "Desire and the Prosthetics of Supervision: A Case of Maquiladora Flexibility," *Cultural Anthropology* 16, no. 3 (Aug. 2001): 354–73.

13 Diane M. Nelson, "Phantom Limbs and Invisible Hands: Bodies, Prosthetics, and Late Capitalist Identifications," *Cultural Anthropology* 16, no. 3 (Aug. 2001): 303–13.

14 Jain, "Prosthetic Imagination," 33, 39.

15 For a moving and specific discussion of mass amputation in Sierra Leone as a political counter to the slogan 'The future is in your hands!' see George Packer, "The Children of Freetown," *New Yorker*, Jan. 13, 2003, 50–61.

16 Steven L. Kurzman, "Presence and Prosthesis: A Response to Nelson and Wright," *Cultural Anthropology* 16, no. 3 (Aug. 2001): 374–87. Subsequent references will be cited in the text.

17 Ricoeur is quoting from Pierre Fontanier, *Les Figures du discours* (1830; reprint, Paris: Flammarion, 1968), 99.

18 Interior quotation is from Fontanier, *Les Figures du discours*, 41.

19 Donna Haraway, "Manifesto for Cyborgs: Science, Technology, and Socialist Feminism in the 1980s," *Socialist Review* 80 (1985): 65–107.

20 Drew Leder, *The Absent Body* (Chicago: University of Chicago Press, 1990).

21 Landsberg, "Prosthetic Memory," 175.

22 Freud, himself possessed of an oral prosthetic, writes in "The Uncanny" of phantasies of "dismembered limbs, a severed head, a hand cut off at the wrist . . . feet which dance by themselves," these chilling and "unheimlich" because "they prove capable of independent activity." See Sigmund Freud, "The Uncanny," in *The Pelican Freud Library, Volume 14: Art and Literature*, trans. James Strachey (Harmondsworth: Penguin, 1985), 366.

23 In this regard I would note that I have a small etching on my wall at home called "Break a Leg," which was given to me by a close friend. Referring to a theatrical phrase perversely meaning "Good luck," the etching shows an onstage chorus line of disembodied legs and is, for me, a delightful figuration of my own early preoccupation with my prosthetic and the general fantasy of the transference of agency—through metonymy—from subjects to objects.

24 Ricoeur, *Rule of Metaphor*, 56 (interior quotation is from Fontanier, *Les Figures du discours*, 79; emphasis added).

25 Ibid. (interior quotation is from Fontanier, *Les Figures du discours*, 87).

26 Ibid.

27 Wilson, "Cyber(body)parts," 242.

28 Rebecca Mead, "Opening Night: An Art-House Epic," *New Yorker*, May 13, 2002, 35.

29 Kurzman, in "Presence and Prosthesis," also discusses these issues—considering, in particular, how the materials and design of his leg are "based on the same military

technology which has blown the limbs off so many other young men"; how he has benefited from "the post–Cold War explosion of increasingly engineered sports equipment and prostheses"; and how the man who built his leg "struggles to hold onto his small business in a field rapidly becoming vertically integrated and corporatized" (382).

30 Ian Austen, "A Leg with a Mind of Its Own," *New York Times*, Jan. 3, 2002, D1.

31 Richard A. Sherman, appendix to *Phantom Pain* (New York: Plenum, 1996), 231.

32 Amy Goldwasser, "Wonder Woman," *I. D.: The International Design Magazine*, May 1998, 48.

33 It is worth noting that, as a model, Mullins does not always use her "Barbie legs" or opt for "passing." See, e.g., a fashion advertisement for *haute couture* clothing, photographed by Nick Knight, that appeared in *The Guardian*, Aug. 29, 1998; Mullins, purposefully doll-like in her seated pose, is revealed with two distinctly "mannequin-like" lower legs, the knee joints apparent, their condition rather worn, adding to Mullins's abandoned doll–like appearance.

34 Mead, "Opening Night," 35.

35 Ibid.

36 Nancy Spector, "Aimee Mullins," in *Matthew Barney: The Cremaster Cycle* (New York: Guggenheim Museum, 2003), n.p.

37 Harold Bloom, *A Map of Misreading* (Oxford: Oxford University Press, 1975), 74. Unfortunately, although I think it well worth doing, there is not room enough here to take "the prosthetic" as figure through all the tropes and attendant psychic defenses that Bloom lays out in a resonant—and relevant—argument and diagram (69–74, 84).

Rummaging: Losing and finding myself in clothes

Ellen Sampson

1 'Body schema' is a term that philosopher Maurice Merleau-Ponty (1962) used to describe the ways that objects could become incorporated into our bodily and sensory experience through use.

2 Didier Anzieu, *The Skin-Ego*, trans. Naomi Segal (London: Karnac, 2016 [1985]).

3 Esther Bick, 'The Experience of Skin in Early Object Relations', *International Journal of Psychoanalysis* 49 (1968): 484–486.

4 Michael Rustin, 'Narcissism and Melancholia from the Psychoanalytical Perspective of Object Relations', in Barry Sheils and Julie Walsh (eds.), *Narcissism, Melancholia and the Subject of Community* (Cham, Switzerland: Palgrave Macmillan, 2017), 44.

5 Magdalena Petersson McIntyre, 'Shame, Blame, and Passion: Affects of (Un) Sustainable Wardrobes', *Fashion Theory* 25, no. 6 (2019): 745.

6 Christina H. Moon, 'Closet Feelings', in Roberto Filippello and Ilya Parkins (eds.), *Fashion and Feeling* (Cham, Switzerland: Palgrave Macmillan 2023), 34.

7 Christopher Bollas, *The Shadow of the Object: Psychoanalysis of the Unthought Known* (New York: Columbia University Press, 1987), 4.

8 Anzieu, *The Skin-Ego*, 105.

9 Ibid., 106 (quoting Winnicott 1962: 59–60).

10 D.W. Winnicott, *Playing and Reality* (London: Tavistock Publications, 1971), 138.

Material Ambiguities: Time, clothing and grief during terminal illness

Isabel Mundigo-Moore

1 Karena de Perthuis, 'Darning Mark's Jumper: Wearing Love and Sorrow', *Cultural Studies Review* 22, no. 1 (2016), 66.

2 Ibid., 60.

3 See Carolyn Ellis and Art Bochner, 'Autoethnography, Personal Narrative, Reflexivity: Researcher as Subject' in *The SAGE Handbook of Qualitative Research*, Norman K. Denzin and Yvonna. S. Lincoln (eds.), 2nd ed. (London and New York: Sage Publications, 2000), 733–768; and Arthur Bochner and Carolyn Ellis, *Evocative Autoethnography: Writing Lives and Telling Stories* (New York: Routledge, 2016).

4 Carolyn Ellis, Tony E. Adams and Arthur P. Bochner, 'Autoethnography: An Overview', *Historical Social Research / Historische Sozialforschung* 36, no. 4 (138) (2011), 274.

5 See Ellen Sampson, *Worn: Footwear, Attachment and the Affects of Wear* (London: Bloomsbury Visual Arts, 2020); and Roberto Filippello and Ilya Parkins (eds.), *Fashion and Feeling: The Affective Politics of Dress* (Springer International Publishing AG: Palgrave Macmillan Cham, 2023).

6 Filippello and Parkins, 'Introduction', in *Fashion and Feeling*, 2.

7 Sara Ahmed, 'Happy Objects', in *The Affect Theory Reader*, Melissa Gregg and Gregory J. Seigworth (eds.) (Durham: Duke University Press, 2010), 29.

8 See Bill Brown (ed.), *Things* (Chicago: University of Chicago Press, 2004); Stacey Pitsillides, 'Digital legacy: Designing with things', *Death Studies* 43 (2019), 1–9, and Julia Kristeva, *Powers of Horror: An Essay on Abjection* (New York: Columbia University Press, 1984).

9 Pitsillides, 'Digital legacy', 427.

10 Filippello and Parkins, *Fashion and Feeling*, 18.

11 Pitsillides, 'Digital legacy', 426.

12 Sampson, *Worn*, 168.

13 de Perthuis, 'Darning Mark's Jumper', 60.

14 Rene König, *The Restless Image* (London: George Allen & Unwin Ltd, 1973), 58.

15 Donald Norman, quoted in Rebecka Fleetwood-Smith, Kate Hefferon and Carolyn Mair, '"It's like . . . it's me": Exploring the lived experience of clothing attachment during wear', *International Journal of Fashion Studies* 6, no. 1 (2019), 43.

16 Joanne Entwistle, 'Fashion and the Fleshy Body: Dress as Embodied Practice, *Fashion Theory* 4, no. 3 (2000), 327.

17 Lucia Ruggerone, 'The Feeling of Being Dressed: Affect Studies and the Clothed Body', *Fashion Theory* 21, no. 5 (2017), 580.

18 Pitsillides 'Digital legacy', 427.

19 Anne Boyer, *The Undying: A Meditation on Modern Illness* (London: Allen Lane, 2019), 133.

20 Ibid., 133.

21 Elaine Scarry, *The Body in Pain: The Making and Unmaking of the World* (Oxford: Oxford University Press, 1985), 3.

22 Ibid., 5.

23 Ahmed, 'Happy Objects', 31.

24 Boyer, *The Undying*, 54.

25 Katrina Taee, 'What is anticipatory grief?', Marie Curie. Accessed February 3, 2023. https://www.mariecurie.org.uk/talkabout/articles/what-is-anticipatory-grief/27127.

26 Ann Cvetkovich, *Depression: A Public Feeling* (Durham: Duke University Press, 2012), 11.

27 Cvetkovich, *Depression*, 12.

28 Sampson, *Worn*, 139.

29 König, *The Restless Image*, 51.

30 Susan Kaiser, *Fashion and Cultural Studies* (London: Bloomsbury Academic, 2013), 305.

31 Anna-Mari Almila 'The dressed body, material and technology: Rethinking the hijab through sartorial sociology', *International Journal of Fashion Studies* 5, no. 2 (2018), 310.

32 See Maura Banim and Ali Guy, 'Dis/continued selves: Why do women keep clothes they no longer wear?', in *Through the Wardrobe: Women's Relationship with their Clothes*, Ali Guy, Eileen Green and Maura Banim (eds.) (Oxford: Berg, 2001), 203–20; Saulo B. Cwerner, 'Clothes at rest: Elements for a sociology of the wardrobe', *Fashion Theory* 5, no. 1 (2001), 79–92; Sophie Woodward, *Why Women Wear What They Wear* (New York: Berg Publishers, 2007); Anna-Mari Almila 'What is "space" for dress? Theoretical considerations of a spatial turn for fashion studies', *International Journal of Fashion Studies* 8, no. 1 (2021), 7–23.

33 See Louise Crewe, *The Geographies of Fashion: Consumption, Space and Value* (London: Bloomsbury Publishing, 2017).

34 de Perthuis, 'Darning Mark's Jumper', 68.

35 Ellen Sampson, 'Entanglement, affect and experience: Walking and wearing (shoes) as experimental research methodology', *International Journal of Fashion Studies* 5, no. 1 (2018), 66.

36 Peter Stallybrass, 'Worn Worlds', in *The Textile Reader*, Jessica Hemmings (ed.) (New York: Berg Publishers, 2012), 36.

37 Ibid.

38 de Perthuis, 'Darning Mark's Jumper', 68.

39 Joan Didion, *Blue Nights* (New York: Alfred A. Knopf, 2011), 44.

40 Ibid., 45 and 46.

41 Pitsillides 'Digital legacy', 428.

42 Sampson, *Worn*, 159.

43 Ibid., 159.

44 Julia Kristeva, *Powers of Horror: An Essay on Abjection* (New York: Columbia University Press, 1982), 4.

45 Ibid.

46 Ibid.

47 Ahmed, 'Happy Objects', 29.

48 Ibid.

49 Ibid., 40.

50 Brown, *Things*, 427.

51 Ahmed, 'Happy Objects', 31.

52 Ibid.

53 Ibid., 50.

References

Adams, Jeffrey Todd. *The Cinema of the Coen Brothers: Hard-Boiled Entertainments*. New York: Columbia University Press, 2015.

Ahmed, Sara. 'Happy objects'. In *The Affect Theory Reader*, edited by Melissa Gregg and Gregory J. Seigworth, 30–51. Durham: Duke University Press, 2010.

Akomolafe, Deji. 'Frank Lucas: How a $100,000 chinchilla coat exposed Harlem's kingpin'. *Criminal*, July 2024. https://shorturl.at/ndQ2X.

Allen-Collinson, Jacqueline, George Jennings, Anu Vaittinen, and Helen Owton. 'Weather-wise? Sporting embodiment, weather work and weather learning in running and triathlon'. *International Review for the Sociology of Sport* 54, no. 7 (2019): 777–792.

Almila, Anna-Mari. 'The dressed body, material and technology: Rethinking the hijab through sartorial sociology'. *International Journal of Fashion Studies* 5, no. 2 (2018): 309–328. doi.org/10.1386/infs.5.2.309_1.

Almila, Anna-Mari. 'What is "space" for dress? Theoretical considerations of a spatial turn for fashion studies'. *International Journal of Fashion Studies* 8, no. 1 (2021): 7–23. doi.org/10.1386/infs_00035_1.

Ambedkar, Babasaheb. *Writings and Speeches*, Vol. 1, 2014 [1979]. Dr Ambedkar Foundation, January 2014. www.mea.gov.in/Images/attach/amb/Volume_01.pdf.

Anzieu, Didier. *The Skin-Ego*. 1985. Reprinted in translation by Naomi Segal. London: Karnac, 2016.

Arya, Divya. 'The woman who cut off her breasts to protest a tax'. *BBC News*, 28 July 2016. www.bbc.co.uk/news/world-asia-india-36891356.

Austen, Ian. 'A leg with a mind of its own'. *New York Times*, 3 January 2002, D1.

Bacharach, Burt F. and Hal David. 'Raindrops Keep Fallin' on My Head'. Single, 45 rpm. Scepter Records, 1969.

Banim, Maura and Alison Guy. 'Dis/continued selves: Why do women keep clothes they no longer wear?' In *Through the Wardrobe: Women's Relationship with Their Clothes*, edited by Ali Guy, Eileen Green, and Maura Banim, 203–220. Oxford: Berg, 2001.

Barney, Matthew, dir. *Cremaster 3*. 2002.

Barthes, Roland. 'The Jet-man'. In *Mythologies*, translated by Annette Lavers, 71–73. New York: Hill and Wang, 1957.

Barthes, Roland. *The Fashion System*, translated by Matthew Ward and Richard Howard. Berkeley and Los Angeles: University of California Press, 1983.

Beckett, Samuel. *The Unnamable*. New York: Grove Press, 1958.

Bhardwaj, Mayank and Rajendra Jadhav. 'Indian farmers cotton on to new seed, in blow to Monsanto'. *Reuters*, 3 August 2016. www.reuters.com/article/us-india-monsanto-idUSKCN10E05C.

Bick, Esther. 'The experience of skin in early object relations'. *International Journal of Psychoanalysis* 49 (1968): 484–486.

Bloom, Harold. *A Map of Misreading*. Oxford: Oxford University Press, 1975.

Bochner, Arthur and Carolyn Ellis. *Evocative Autoethnography: Writing Lives and Telling Stories*. New York: Routledge, 2016. doi.org/10.4324/9781315545417.

Bollas, Christopher. *The Shadow of the Object: Psychoanalysis of the Unthought Known*. New York: Columbia University Press, 1987.

Boyer, Anne. *The Undying: A Meditation on Modern Illness*. London: Allen Lane, 2019.

Brahm, Gabriel and Mark Driscoll, eds. *Prosthetic Territories: Politics and Hypertechnologies*. Boulder: Westview Press, 1995.

Breman, Jan. *The Making and Unmaking of an Industrial Working Class: Sliding Down the Labour Hierarchy in Ahmedabad, India*. Amsterdam: Amsterdam University Press, 2004.

Brown, Bill. *Things*. Chicago: University of Chicago Press, 2004.

Carlyle, Thomas. *Sartor Resartus*. Cambridge: Proquest LLC, 2008 [1841].

Cartier-Bresson, Henri. *Alberto Giacometti 1961*, 1961. Photograph. Victoria & Albert Museum, London. PH.826-1978.

Chamberlain, Lesley. *A Shoe Story: Van Gogh, the Philosophers and the West*. Chelmsford: Harbour Books, 2014.

Chandrandrababu, Divya. 'Tamil Nadu cotton weaves on wane get a boost'. *The Times of India*, 25 April 2016. https://shorturl.at/1o0ky.

Cocteau, Jean. *Beauty and the Beast: Diary of a Film*. Dover: Mineola, 1972.

Coen, Joel and Ethan Coen, dir. *Fargo*. 1996. Amazon Prime Video.

Coen, Joel and Ethan Coen, dir. *The Big Lebowski*. 1998. Amazon Prime Video.

Cohn, Bernard S. *Colonialism and its Forms of Knowledge: The British in India*. Princeton: Princeton University Press, 1996.

Corsillo, Liza. 'TBT: When Johnny Cash suited-up for his legendary Folsom Prison Concert'. *GQ*, 14 January 2016. www.gq.com/story/tbt-johnny-cash-suit-folsom-prison.

Crewe, Louise. 'Life itemised: Lists, loss, unexpected significance, and the enduring geographies of discard'. *Environment and Planning D: Society and Space* 29, no. 1 (2011): 27–46. doi.org/10.1068/d16709.

Crewe, Louise. *The Geographies of Fashion: Consumption, Space and Value*. London: Bloomsbury Publishing, 2017.

Cvetkovich, Ann. *Depression: A Public Feeling*. Durham: Duke University Press, 2012.

Cwerner, Saulo B. 'Clothes at rest: Elements for a sociology of the wardrobe'. *Fashion Theory* 5, no. 1 (2001): 79–92.

Dave, Vimukt. 'CAI projects 33.60 million bales cotton production for 2016–17'. *Business Standard*, 30 August 2016. https://shorturl.at/DvAQy.

de Perthuis, Karena. 'Darning Mark's jumper: Wearing love and sorrow'. *Cultural Studies Review* 22, no. 1 (2016): 59–77. doi.org/10.5130/csr.v22i1.4909.

de Sam Lazaro, Fred, dir. *Wide Angle*. 'The Dying Fields'. PBS. 28 August 2007.

Deutsch, Helen and Felicity Nussbaum. 'Introduction'. In *Defects: Engineering the Modern Body*, edited by Helen Deutsch and Felicity Nussbaum, 1–28. Ann Arbor: University of Michigan Press, 2000.

Didion, Joan. *Blue Nights*. New York: Alfred A. Knopf, 2011.

Dosekun, Simidele. *Fashioning Postfeminism: Spectacular Femininity and Transnational Culture*. Urbana: University of Illinois Press, 2020.

Douglas, Mary. *Purity and Danger: An Analysis of the Concepts of Pollution and Taboo*. London: Routledge, 1966.

Edwards, Zoe. 'Make do and mend: Darning', *So, Zo, What Do You Know?* Blog 3 February 2010. www.coletterie.com/tutorials-tips-tricks/make-do- and-mend-darning.

Ellis, Carolyn and Art Bochner. 'Autoethnography, personal narrative, reflexivity: Researcher as subject'. In *The SAGE Handbook of Qualitative Research*, edited by Norman K. Denzin and Yvonna S. Lincoln, 733–768. 2nd edn. London and New York: Sage Publications, 2000.

Ellis, Carolyn, Tony E. Adams, and Arthur P. Bochner. 'Autoethnography: An overview'. *Historical Social Research / Historische Sozialforschung* 36, no. 4 (138) (2011): 273–290.

Entwistle, Joanne. 'Fashion and the fleshy body: Dress as embodied practice'. *Fashion Theory* 4, no. 3 (2000): 323–347. doi.org/10.2752/136270400778995471.

Filippello, Roberto and Ilya Parkins, eds. *Fashion and Feeling: The Affective Politics of Dress*. Cham: Palgrave Macmillan, 2023.

Fleetwood-Smith, Rebecka, Kate Hefferon, and Carolyn Mair. '"It's like … it's me": Exploring the lived experience of clothing attachment during wear'. *International Journal of Fashion Studies* 6, no. 1 (2019): 41–62. doi.org/10.1386/infs.6.1.41_1.

Fontanier, Pierre. 1830. *Les Figures du discours*. Repr. Paris: Flammarion, 1968

Ford, Tanisha C. *Liberated Threads: Black Women, Style, and the Global Politics of Soul*. Chapel Hill: University of North Carolina Press, 2015.

Freud, Sigmund. 'The Uncanny'. In *The Pelican Freud Library, Volume 14: Art and Literature*, translated by James Strachey, 335–376. Harmondsworth: Penguin, 1985.

Fukai, Akiko. 'A new design aesthetic'. In *The Cutting Edge: Fashion from Japan*, edited by Louise Mitchell, 18–27. Sydney: Powerhouse Publishing, 2005.

Genzlinger, Neil. 'In India, debting farmers who reach despair's depths'. *New York Times*, 28 August 2007. www.nytimes.com/2007/08/28/arts/television/28fiel.html.

Golden, Eve. 'Clothes, inside out'. In *I Shop Therefore I Am: Compulsive Buying and the Search for Self*, edited by April Lane Benson, 133–153. Northvale and London: Jason Aronson Inc., 2000.

Goldwasser, Amy. 'Wonder Woman'. *I.D.: The International Design Magazine*, May 1998, 48.

Gonzalez, Jennifer A. 'Autotopographies'. In *Prosthetic Territories: Politics and Hypertechnologies*, edited by Gabriel Brahm Jr. and Mark Driscoll, 133–150. Boulder: Westview Press, 1995.

Gray, Chris Hables and Steven Mentor. 'The cyborg body politic and the new world order'. In *Prosthetic Territories: Politics and Hypertechnologies*, edited by Gabriel Brahm Jr. and Mark Driscoll, 219–247. Boulder: Westview Press, 1995.

Haraway, Donna. 'Manifesto for cyborgs: Science, technology, and socialist feminism in the 1980s'. *Socialist Review* 80 (1985): 65–107.

Hardgrave, Robert L. *The Nadars of Tamilnad: The Political Culture of a Community in Change*. Berkeley: University of California Press, 1969.

Harper, Phineas. 'So you'd never wear a skirt in public? Men, you don't know what you're missing'. *The Guardian*, 3 January 2024. www.theguardian.com/commentisfree/2024/jan/03/skirts-men-fashion-feminism.

Heti, Sheila. *How Should a Person Be?* London: Harvill Secker, 2013.

Hobb, Robin. *Fool's Errand*. London: Voyager, 2001.

Hollander, Anne. *Seeing through Clothes*. New York: Viking Press, 1978.

Howlader, Ramij, Monirul (Rajib) Islam, Tanjibul Hasan Sajib, and Ripon Kumar Prasad. 'Standard minute value for a T-shirt'. In *Time in Fashion: Industrial, Antilinear and Uchronic Temporalities*, edited by Caroline Evans and Alessandra Vaccari, 67–69. London: Bloomsbury, 2020.

Indian Asian News Service. '11,400 farmers committed suicide in 2016: Govt tells Lok Sabha'. *Firstpost*, 20 July 2017. https://shorturl.at/O5oyw.

Ingold, Tim. 'Weather-World'. *International Lexicon of Aesthetics*, Spring Edition (2023): 1–5. doi.org/10.7413/18258630136.

Jain, Sarah S. 'The prosthetic imagination: Enabling and disabling the prosthetic trope'. *Science, Technology, & Human Values* 24, no. 1 (1999): 31–54.

James, Henry. *The Romance of Certain Old Clothes*. 1885. Repr. Whitefish: Kessenger Publishing, 2004.

Jones, Ann R. and Peter Stallybrass. *Renaissance Clothing and the Materials of Memory*. Cambridge: Cambridge University Press, 2000.

Kaiser, Susan. 'Minding appearances: Style, truth and subjectivity'. In *Body Dressing*, edited by Joanne Entwistle and Elizabeth Wilson, 79–102. Oxford: Berg, 2001.

Kent, Eliza. *Converting Women: Gender and Protestant Christianity in Colonial South India*. Oxford: Oxford University Press, 2004.

Kolappan, B. 'Ramadoss consolidates intermediate caste groups against Dalits'. *The Hindu*, 2 December 2012. https://shorturl.at/5XdzO.

König, Rene. *The Restless Image*. London: George Allen & Unwin Ltd, 1973.

Kopytoff, Igor. 'The cultural biography of things: Commoditization as process'. In *The Social Life of Things: Commodities in Cultural Perspective*, edited by Arjun Appadurai, 64–92. Cambridge: Cambridge University Press, 1986.

Krishnakumar, Asha. 'Weavers in distress'. *Frontline*, 17 August 2002. https://shorturl.at/DFmzm.

Kristeva, Julia. *Powers of Horror: An Essay on Abjection*. New York: Columbia University Press, 1982.

Kristeva, Julia. *Powers of Horror: An Essay on Abjection*. New York: Columbia University Press, 1984.

Kurzman, Steven L. 'Presence and prosthesis: A response to Nelson and Wright'. *Cultural Anthropology* 16, no. 3 (2001): 374–387.

Landsberg, Alison. 'Prosthetic memory: *Total Recall* and *Blade Runner*'. *Body & Society* 1, nos. 3–4 (1995): 175–189.

Leder, Drew. *The Absent Body*. Chicago: University of Chicago Press, 1990.

Lee, Ang, dir. *Brokeback Mountain*. 2005.

Martin-Nielson, Janet. 'Scientific forecasting? Performing objectivity at the UK's Meteorological Office, 1960s–1970s'. *History of Meteorology* 8 (2017): 202–221.

Marx, Karl. *The Poverty of Philosophy*. Marx/Engels Internet Archive. Marxists.org, 1999 [1955]. www.marxists.org/archive/marx/works/1847/poverty-philosophy/.

Maugham, William Somerset. *Rain and Other Stories*. New York: Grosset & Dunlap, 1921.

McKinley, Catherine E., Edwidge Danticat, and Jacqueline Woodson. *The African Lookbook: A Visual History of 100 Years of African Women*. New York: Bloomsbury Publishing, 2021.

Mead, Rebecca. 'Opening Night: An Art-House epic'. *The New Yorker*, 13 May 2002, 35.

Mendelsohn, Oliver and Marika Vicziany. *The Untouchables: Subordination, Poverty and the State in Modern India*. Cambridge: Cambridge University Press, 1998.

Merleau-Ponty, Maurice. *Phenomenology of Perception*. Translated by Donald A. Landes. London: Routledge, 1962.

Miller, Daniel, ed. *Materiality*. Durham and London: Duke University Press, 2005.

Milligan, Lauren. 'Fashion flashback: McQueen's Asylum Show'. *British Vogue*, 7 August 2014. www.vogue.co.uk/gallery/erin-oconnor-on-walking-in-alexander-mcqueen-asylum-show.

Moon, Christina H. 'Closet feelings'. In *Fashion and Feeling: The Affective Politics of Dress*, edited by Roberto Filippello and Ilya Parkins, 27–40. Cham: Palgrave Macmillan, 2023.

Morra, Joanne and Marquard Smith, eds. 'Introduction: The prosthetic aesthetic'. *New Formations* 46 (2002): 5.

Naess, Arne. *Ecology, Community and Lifestyle: Outline of an Ecosophy*. Cambridge: Cambridge University Press, 1991.

Nelson, Diane M. 'Phantom limbs and invisible hands: Bodies, prosthetics, and late capitalist identifications'. *Cultural Anthropology* 16, no. 3 (2001): 303–313.

Nelson, Diane M. 'Stumped identities: Body image, bodies politic, and the Mujer Maya as prosthetic'. *Cultural Anthropology* 16, no. 3 (2001): 314–353.

Ohito, Esther. 'What can we not leave behind? Storying family photographs, unlocking emotional memories, and welcoming complex conversations on being human'. *Occasional Paper Series* 45 (2021): 1–10. doi.org/10.58295/2375-3668.1385.

Packer, George. 'The children of Freetown'. *The New Yorker*, 13 January 2003, 50–61.

Paik, Shailaja. *Dalit Women's Education in Modern India: Double Discrimination*. London and New York: Routledge, 2014.

Petersson McIntyre, Magdalena. 'Shame, blame, and passion: Affects of (un)sustainable wardrobes'. *Fashion Theory* 25, no. 6, (2021): 735–755. doi.org/10.1080/136270 4X.2019.167650.

Pietz, William. 'The Problem of the Fetish, IIIa: Bosman's Guinea and the Enlightenment theory of fetishism'. *Res: Anthropology and Aesthetics* 16 (1988): 105–124.

Pitsillides, Stacey. 'Digital legacy: Designing with things'. *Death Studies* 43 (2019): 1–9. doi.org/10.1080/07481187.2018.1541939.

Poush, Dan. *Before the First Performance; Blowing Smoke Rings*. 1968. Photograph. John R. Cash Revocable Trust.

Queen. *Queen – I Want To Break Free (Official Video)*. Music video. Posted 1 September 2008 by Queen Official. YouTube, 4:31. https://youtu.be/f4Mc-NYPHaQ?si=SxHPC2rzlUTxMaMR.

Ramsay, Lynne, dir. *We Need to Talk about Kevin*. 2011.

Ramzi, Lilah. 'An ode to the campiest film you've probably never seen'. *Vogue*, 19 April 2019. www.vogue.com/article/what-a-way-to-go-shirley-maclaine-camp-film.

Ricoeur, Paul. *The Rule of Metaphor: Multi-disciplinary Studies of the Creation of Meaning in Language*, translated by Robert Czerny, Kathleen McLaughlin, and John Costello. Toronto: University of Toronto Press, 1977.

Roach-Higgins, Mary-Ellen and Joanne B. Eicher. 'Dress and identity'. *Clothing and Textiles Research Journal* 10, no. 4 June (1992): 1–8. doi.org/10.1177/0887302X9201000401.

Robinson, Fred Miller. '"An art of superior tramps": Beckett and Giacometti'. *Centennial Review* 25, no. 4 (1981): 331–344.

Ruggerone, Lucia. 'The feeling of being dressed: Affect studies and the clothed body'. *Fashion Theory* 21, no. 5 (2017): 573–593. doi.org/10.1080/1362704X.2016.1253302.

Rushkoff, Douglas. 'Commodified vs. commoditized'. *Rushkoff*. www.rushkoff.com/commodified-vs- commoditized/. Cited in de Perthuis. 'Darning Mark's jumper'.

Rustin, Michael. 'Narcissism and melancholia from the psychoanalytical perspective of object relations'. In *Narcissism, Melancholia and the Subject of Community*, edited by Barry Sheils and Julie Walsh, 41–64. Cham: Palgrave Macmillan, 2017.

Sacks, Oliver. *A Leg to Stand On*. New York: Simon and Schuster, 1984.

Safi, Michael. 'Suicides of nearly 60,000 Indian farmers linked to climate change, study claims'. *The Guardian*, 31 July 2017. https://shorturl.at/8LIoz.

Sakado Takeda, Sharon, Kaye Durland Spilker, and Clarissa M. Esguerra. *Reigning Men: Fashion in Menswear, 1715–2015*. London: Prestel, 2016.

Sampson, Ellen. 'Entanglement, affect and experience: Walking and wearing (shoes) as experimental research methodology'. *International Journal of Fashion Studies* 5, no. 1 (2018): 55–76. doi.org/10.1386/infs.5.1.55_1.

Sampson, Ellen. *Worn: Footwear, Attachment and the Affects of Wear*. London: Bloomsbury Visual Arts, 2020.

Scarry, Elaine. *The Body in Pain: The Making and Unmaking of the World*. Oxford: Oxford University Press, 1987.

Schulz, Bruno. *The Street of Crocodiles*, translated by Celina Wieniewska. London: Penguin, 1963.

Shaughnessy, Brenda. 'McQueen is dead, long live McQueen'. *Poetry* 207, no. 2 (November 2015): 157–163.

Sherman, Richard A. *Phantom Pain*. New York: Plenum, 1996.

Shiva, Vandana. "How Monsanto wrote and broke laws to enter India." *Seed Freedom*. 27 July 2015. http://seedfreedom.info/how-monsanto-wrote-and-broke-laws-to-enter-india/.

Simmel, Georg, 'Fashion, adornment and style'. In *Simmel on Culture*, edited by David Frisby and Mike Featherstone. London: Sage, 1997.

Şode, Yomi. *Manorism*. London: Penguin, 2023.

Spector, Nancy. 'Aimee Mullins'. In *Matthew Barney: The Cremaster Cycle*. New York Guggenheim Museum Publications, 2003.

Stallybrass, Peter. 'Marx's coat'. In *Border Fetishisms: Material Objects in Unstable Space*, edited by Patricia Spyer. New York and London: Routledge, 1998.

Stallybrass, Peter. 'Worn worlds: Clothes, mourning and the life of things'. In *Cultural Memory and the Construction of Identity*, edited by Dan Ben-Amos and Liliane Weissberg, 27–44. Detroit: Wayne State University Press, 1999.

Stallybrass, Peter. 'Worn worlds: Clothes, mourning and the life of things'. In *The Textile Reader*, edited by Jessica Hemmings, 68–77. New York: Berg Publishers, 2012.

Taee, Katrina. 'What is anticipatory grief?' *Marie Curie*, 2020. www.mariecurie.org.uk/talkabout/articles/what-is-anticipatory-grief/27127.

Tennov, Dorothy. *Love and Limerence: The Experience of Being in Love*. Lanham and New York: Scarborough House, 1979.

Thanhauser, Sofi. *Worn: A People's History of Clothing*. London: Allen Lane, 2022.

Tóibín, Colm. *The Master*. London: Picador, 2004.

Tulloch, Carol. 'Style–Fashion–Dress: From Black to Post-Black'. *Fashion Theory* 14, no. 3 (2015): 273–303. doi.org/10.2752/175174110X12712411520179.

Van Horn, Gavin. 'Kinning: Introducing the Kinship Series'. In *Kinship: Belonging in a World of Relations, Vol. 1: Planet*, edited by Gavin Van Horn, Robin Wall Kimmerer, and John Hausdoerffer, 1–11. Libertyville: Center for Humans and Nature Press, 2021.

Veeraraghavan, D. *The Making of the Madras Working Class*. New Delhi: LeftWord Books, 2013.

Vinken, Barbara. *Fashion Zeitgeist: Trends and Cycles in the Fashion System*, translated by Mark Hewson. Oxford and New York: Berg, 2005.

Walker, Giselle and Elizabeth Leedham-Green. 'Introduction'. In *Identity*, edited by Giselle Walker and Elizabeth Leedham-Green, 1–8. Cambridge: Cambridge University Press, 2010.

Wenders, Wim, dir. *Notebook on Cities and Clothes*. Paris: Centre Pompidou, Centre de Création Industrielle and Road Movies Filmproduktion, 1989.

What Am I? 1980. *BFI Player.* https://player.bfi.org.uk/free/film/watch-what-am-i-1980-online.

Wilson, Elizabeth. *Adorned in Dreams.* Berkeley and Los Angeles: University of California Press, 1985.

Wilson, Elizabeth. *Adorned in Dreams.* Berkeley: University of California Press, 1987.

Wilson, Elizabeth. *Adorned in Dreams.* London: I.B. Tauris & Co. Ltd, 2003.

Wilson, Elizabeth. 'Magic Fashion'. *Fashion Theory* 8, no. 4 (2004): 375–385. doi.org/10.2752/136270404778051609.

Wilson, Elizabeth. 'Notes on fashion as fetish', *Vestoj*, no. 2 (2011): 190.

Wilson, Robert Rawdon. 'Cyber(body)parts: Prosthetic consciousness'. *Body & Society* 1, nos. 3–4 (1995): 239–259.

Winnicott, D. W. *Playing and Reality.* London: Tavistock Publications, 1971.

Woodward, Sophie. *Why Women Wear What They Wear.* New York: Berg Publishers, 2007.

Wright, Melissa W. 'Desire and the prosthetics of supervision: A case of maquiladora flexibility', *Cultural Anthropology* 16, no. 3 (2001): 354–373.

Xiang, Sunny. 'Militarized comfort: How to feel naked while wearing clothes'. In *Fashion and Feeling: The Affective Politics of Dress*, edited by Roberto Filippello and Ilya Parkins, 41–62. Cham: Palgrave Macmillan, 2023.

Notes on Contributors

Anne Anlin Cheng is Professor of English at Princeton University, specializing in modernism and the intersection of politics and aesthetics, drawing from the diverse fields of literature, psychoanalysis, law, and visual culture. She is author of three books of scholarship, *Ornamentalism* (2018), *The Melancholy of Race: Assimilation, Psychoanalysis, and Hidden Grief* (2000), and *Second Skin: Josephine Baker and the Modern Surface* (2000); and a book of personal essays entitled *Ordinary Disasters: How I Stopped Being a Model Minority* (2024). Her writings can also be found in *Hyperallergic*, *The Atlantic*, *The Huffington Post*, *The Los Angeles Review of Books*, *The Nation*, and *The New York Times*.

Desiree Cooper is a 2015 Kresge Artist Fellow, former attorney, and Pulitzer Prize-nominated journalist. Her debut collection of flash fiction, *Know the Mother* (2016), has won numerous awards, including the 2017 Next Generation Indie Book Award. Cooper's flash fiction and essays have appeared in *The New York Times*, *Flash Fiction America 2023*, *The Best Small Fictions 2018*, *Forward: 21st Century Flash Fiction*, *Electric Literature*, *The Rumpus*, *Oprah Daily*, and *Michigan Quarterly Review*. Her essay, 'We Have Lost Too Many Wigs', was listed as a notable essay in *The Best American Essays 2019*. Her first children's book, *Nothing Special*, was selected by the New York Public Library as one of the 10 Best Children's Books of 2022.

Stephanie Danler is a novelist, memoirist, and screenwriter. She is the author of *Stray* (2020) and the international bestseller *Sweetbitter* (2016). She is the creator and executive producer of the *Sweetbitter* (2018–2019) television series on Starz. Her work has appeared in the *Sewanee Review*, *The New York Times Book Review*, *Vogue*, *Airmail*, *T: The New York Times Style Magazine*, *The Paris Review Daily*, *Time*, *Travel & Leisure*, *Condé Nast Traveler*, and *New York Magazine*. Her non-fiction received an Honourable Mention in Best American Essays 2018 and 2019, and her criticism won the 2019 Robert B. Heilman Award from the *Sewanee Review*.

Karena de Perthuis is Senior Lecturer in the School of Humanities and Communication Arts at Western Sydney University. Her widely published research explores the intersection of fashion, the image, and the body, with a recurring interest in the fashionable ideal and our material/immaterial relationship with clothes. Karena is also co-editor-in-chief of the *International Journal of Fashion Studies*. She is currently writing a monograph, *The Fashionable Ideal: Undoing Bodies and Images in Fashion*, which interrogates the hegemonic aesthetic authority of the fashionable ideal and conceptualizes its counterpoint, an ethical fashion ideal embodying longevity, diversity, collectivity, community, and sustainability.

Rosie Findlay is Senior Lecturer in Media at City St George's, University of London. In her research and writing, she explores how politics surface in contemporary fashion media and communications, and the ways clothing interfaces with experience, memory, and imagination. Rosie is author of *Personal Style Blogs: Appearances that Fascinate* (2017) and co-edited two books, *Insights on Fashion Journalism* (2021) and *Remaking Fashion Media: Sustainable Narratives and Visions of Change* (2026). Her research and writing have been published in journals such as *Fashion Theory, Journal of Cultural Economy, Communication, Culture & Critique, Feminist Theory,* and *Granta*.

Ruth Gershon is a historian living in North-West London.

Meena Kandasamy is a poet, writer, translator, anti-caste activist, and academic based in India. Described by the *Independent* as a 'one-woman, agit-prop literary-political movement', her extensive corpus includes two poetry collections, *Touch* (2006) and *Ms Militancy* (2010), as well as three novels, *The Gypsy Goddess* (2014), the Women's Prize short-listed *When I Hit You* (2017), and *Exquisite Cadavers* (2019). In 2022, she was elected Fellow of the Royal Society of Literature and was also awarded the PEN Hermann Kesten Prize for her writing and work as a 'fearless fighter for democracy, human rights and the free word'. Her latest published work is *Tomorrow Someone Will Arrest You* (2023), a collection of her political poetry written in the last decade.

Amy Key is the author of *Arrangements in Blue* (2023), chosen as a Book of the Year by *The Sunday Times, Independent, Irish Times,* and *Granta* and shortlisted by Foyles for their Non-Fiction Book of the Year 2023. She is also the author of two collections of poetry, *Luxe* (2013) and *Isn't Forever* (2018). Her essays have appeared in the collections *At the Pond* (2019) and *By the River* (2024), as well as *Granta, Vogue, The Observer, The Poetry, Independent,* and elsewhere. Her Substack is So Glad I'm Me.

Robin Wall Kimmerer is a mother, scientist, decorated professor, and enrolled member of the Citizen Potawatomi Nation. She is the author of the #1 *New York Times* bestseller *Braiding Sweetgrass: Indigenous Wisdom, Scientific Knowledge and the Teachings of Plants* (2013) as well as *Gathering Moss: A Natural and Cultural History of Mosses* (2003) and *The Serviceberry: Abundance and Reciprocity in the Natural World* (2024). Kimmerer is a 2022 MacArthur Fellow. She lives in Syracuse, New York, where she is SUNY Distinguished Teaching Professor of Environmental Biology, and the founder of the Center for Native Peoples and the Environment.

Isabel Mundigo-Moore is a scholar, writer, and filmmaker in the field of clothing studies. Her work looks at people's emotional relationships to clothing, particularly the connections between clothing and love in experiences of dress. She is Associate Lecturer in Cultural and Historical Studies at London College of Fashion, University of the Arts London. Isabel holds an MA from London College of Fashion and a PhD from Northumbria School of Design. Her work has been published in *International Journal of Fashion Studies* and *Warehouse Review*, and she runs the Instagram account, *The Loving Archive*. Originally from Toronto, she now lives in Sussex with her partner, along with their dog and cat.

Krys Osei is Lecturer in Cultural Studies for Fashion, Jewellery and Textiles at Central Saint Martins, and Lecturer in Contextual Studies for the School of Media and Communication at London College of Fashion, University of the Arts London. Her experimental research maps Black cultural geographies of decorative repair in Accra, London, and Washington, D.C., through autoethnography, DJ scholarship, pleasure activism, and the multisensory adaptation of her mother's gardens. Her work has been published in *Fashion Theory: The Journal of Dress, Body & Culture, Communication, Culture & Critique, Feminist Media Studies*, and *Fashion Education: The Systemic Revolution*.

Ellen Sampson is an artist and material culture researcher, whose work draws upon phenomenology and psychoanalytic theory to explore the relationships between bodies and clothes, in museums and archives, and in everyday life. Her work uses film, photography, object-making, and writing to explore the materiality of garments, our tactile entanglements with them, and the power of bodily trace. Ellen is Assistant Professor in Design at Northumbria School of Design. She is the author of *Worn: Footwear Attachment and the Affects of Wear* (2020) and an editor of *Wearable Objects and Curative Things: Materialist Approaches to the Intersections of Fashion, Art, Health and Medicine* (2023). Her work has been exhibited at institutions including Somerset House, Z33, and Bard Graduate Center.

Vivian Sobchack is Professor Emerita in the Department of Film, Television and Digital Media at UCLA, and former Associate Dean of the UCLA School of Theater, Film and Television. Her books include *Screening Space: The American Science Fiction Film* (1987), *The Address of the Eye: A Phenomenology of Film Experience* (1992), *Carnal Thoughts: Embodiment and Moving Image Culture* (2004), and two edited volumes, *The Persistence of History: Cinema, Television, and the Modern Event* (1996) and *Meta-Morphing: Visual Transformation in the Culture of Quick Change* (2000). Her essays have appeared in *Screen, Film Quarterly, Camera Obscura, Quarterly Review of Film and Video, Art Forum International, Film Comment, History and Theory, Representations*, and *Body and Society*. In 2012, she was honoured with the Society for Cinema and Media Studies' Distinguished Career Achievement Award for the impact her wide-ranging body of work has had not only on film and media studies but also on the humanities, arts, and social sciences.

Yomi Ṣode is an award-winning Nigerian-British writer. He is a recipient of the 2019 Jerwood Compton Poetry Fellowship, shortlisted for the Brunel International African Poetry Prize 2021, and Arts Foundation Awards 2024. His debut collection, *Manorism* (2022), was shortlisted for the Rathbones Folio Prize 2023 and the T. S. Eliot Prize 2022. In 2021, his play, *and breathe …* premiered at the Almeida Theatre, London, to sold-out audiences and garnered four Black British Theatre Awards. He founded BoxedIn, First Five, The Daddy Diaries, and mentorship programme, 12 in 12. Yomi's debut novel, *The Interpreter*, has been acquired and will be published by Viking.

Thao Thai is the author of *Banyan Moon*, the July 2023 Read with Jenna title, Barnes & Noble Discover Pick, and Book of the Month selection. *Banyan Moon* was also selected by booksellers as an IndieNext pick and longlisted for the Center for Fiction's First Novel Prize. A recipient of the 2024 Ohio Arts Council's Individual Excellence Award, Thao's work has been published in the *Los Angeles Review of Books, WIRED, Elle, Lit Hub*, and other publications.

Jane Tynan is Assistant Professor of Design History and Theory in the Faculty of Humanities and leads MA Design Cultures at Vrije Universiteit Amsterdam. Her research concerns material cultures of clothing, with a focus on aesthetic and micro-political practices that shape modes of citizenship and governance. The politics and history of waterproofing is the topic of her current research project, which highlights the role of textiles and clothing in shaping perceptions and experiences of weather in the late twentieth century. Recent publications include *Uniform: Clothing and Discipline in the Modern World* (2019) and *Trench Coat* (2022). She is editorial board member of the *Journal of Design History* and co-editor of the book series Palgrave Studies in Fashion and the Body.

Esmé Weijun Wang is a novelist and essayist, the author of the *New York Times* bestselling essay collection *The Collected Schizophrenias* (2019), and the novel *The Border of Paradise* (2016), which was named one of NPR's Best Books of 2016 and one of Electric Literature's Top 25 Novels of 2016. Esmé was named by *Granta* as one of their Best of Young American Novelists. She is also the founder of The Unexpected Shape, providing online education and personal development resources for creative writers and ambitious people living with limitations.

Honor Wilson is a researcher and writer. He has a first class BA (Hons) in English Literature from the University of Liverpool and an MA with Distinction in English from City St George's, University of London in 2025, where he graduated with the highest dissertation and overall final award grades. His research interests include gender studies and the conventions of genre, which he explored in his Master's dissertation on the literary and anthropological conventions of genre, masculinity, and rites of passage rituals in two Cormac McCarthy novels. Honor lives in London, where he currently works as a teaching assistant for SEND secondary school pupils.

Fiona Wright is a writer and critic based in Sydney. Her book of essays *Small Acts of Disappearance* won the 2016 Kibble Award and Queensland Literary Award and was shortlisted for the 2016 Stella Prize. Her poetry collections are *Knuckled* (2011) and *Domestic Interior* (2017), and her most recent essay collection is *The World Was Whole* (2018). She is currently the Judy Harris Writer-in-Residence at Sydney University's Charles Perkins Centre. Her first novel, *Kill Your Boomers*, will be published by Ultimo Press in 2026.

Credits

Index